Nightingale's Nuns and the Crimean War

Nightingale's Nuns and the Crimean War

Terry Tastard

BLOOMSBURY ACADEMIC
LONDON • NEW YORK • OXFORD • NEW DELHI • SYDNEY

BLOOMSBURY ACADEMIC
Bloomsbury Publishing Plc
50 Bedford Square, London, WC1B 3DP, UK
1385 Broadway, New York, NY 10018, USA
29 Earlsfort Terrace, Dublin 2, Ireland

BLOOMSBURY, BLOOMSBURY ACADEMIC and the Diana logo are trademarks of Bloomsbury Publishing Plc

First published in Great Britain 2023
Paperback edition first published 2024

Copyright © Terry Tastard, 2023

Terry Tastard has asserted their right under the Copyright, Designs and Patents Act, 1988, to be identified as Author of this work.

Cover image: "The Mission of Mercy: Florence Nightingale receiving the Wounded at Scutari" by Jerry Barrett, oil on canvas, 1857.
(© IanDagnall Computing / Alamy Stock Photo)

All rights reserved. No part of this publication may be reproduced or transmitted in any form or by any means, electronic or mechanical, including photocopying, recording, or any information storage or retrieval system, without prior permission in writing from the publishers.

Bloomsbury Publishing Plc does not have any control over, or responsibility for, any third-party websites referred to or in this book. All internet addresses given in this book were correct at the time of going to press. The author and publisher regret any inconvenience caused if addresses have changed or sites have ceased to exist, but can accept no responsibility for any such changes.

Every effort has been made to trace copyright holders and to obtain their permissions for the use of copyright material. The publisher apologizes for any errors or omissions and would be grateful if notified of any corrections that should be incorporated in future reprints or editions of this book.

A catalogue record for this book is available from the British Library.

A catalog record for this book is available from the Library of Congress.

ISBN: HB: 978-1-3502-5158-8
PB: 978-1-3502-5159-5
ePDF: 978-1-3502-5160-1
eBook: 978-1-3502-5161-8

Typeset by Deanta Global Publishing Services, Chennai, India

To find out more about our authors and books visit www.bloomsbury.com and sign up for our newsletters.

Contents

List of Figures		vi
Acknowledgements		vii
Citations and abbreviations		viii
A note on names and terminology		ix
Introduction		1
1	'No use for angels without hands'	5
2	The road to the east	21
3	Winter ordeal	39
4	Vocation and resistance	57
5	Irish nuns at Koulali	71
6	Balaclava battleground	93
7	Ireland: Return and aftermath	111
8	England: Return and aftermath	129
9	'It was no time to save oneself'	145
10	Conclusion	149
Notes		163
Bibliography		189
Index		198

Figures

1	Convent of Sisters of Mercy, Bermondsey	81
2	A Sister of Mercy makes her vows at the Bermondsey Convent, November 1839	82
3	St Saviour's Anglican Convent, Osnaburgh St, London NW1	82
4	Aftermath of the Battle of Inkerman, 5 November 1854	83
5	Barrack Hospital, Scutari as it is today (now Selimiye Barracks)	83
6	One of the wards at Barrack Hospital, Scutari	84
7	Corridors at Barrack Hospital, Scutari, temporarily turned into wards	84
8	A ward in Koulali Hospital, 1856, sketched by a patient, showing a Sister of Mercy	85
9	Amputees at Chatham Military Hospital, photographed by Joseph Cundall, 1856	85

Acknowledgements

Every book of this kind depends upon hard-working archivists and librarians. Accordingly, I would like to express my thanks to:

Sr Catherine Heron RSM, Vida Milanovic and Sr Barbara Jeffery RSM of the Archives and Heritage Centre at the Convent of Our Lady of Mercy, Bermondsey, London;

Marianne Cosgrave, Mercy Congregational Archives, Dublin;

Jenny Smith, Sisters of Mercy of the Union of Great Britain Archives, Handsworth, Birmingham;

Jenny Delves, Archives of the Archdiocese of Southwark;

Fr Nicholas Schofield, Archives of the Archdiocese of Westminster; and

Jessica Woodward, Pusey House, Oxford.

I thank the archivists and institutions named above for permission to quote from material in their archives; also:

Lisa Quinn and Wilfrid Laurier University Press for permission to quote from the Collected Works of Florence Nightingale;

Marianne Cosgrave for the Sisters of Mercy, Ireland, and Professor Maria Luddy for permission to quote from the Crimean War Journals of the Sisters of Mercy; and

the Principal and Chapter of Pusey House for permission to quote from Ascot Priory Archives, Pusey House.

The staff of the London Library were indefatigable, performing wonders of book dispatch by mail during periods of lockdown.

Professor Lynn McDonald, the editor of the Collected Works of Florence Nightingale, patiently answered many queries and suggested further reading.

Professors Cormac Begadon, James Kelly and Mary Sullivan RSM, and Dr Noel Gill kindly read and commented on portions of the typescript, and Frances Topp researched the pictures.

For advice or help in different ways, I thank Vincent Clarke, Professor Saul David, Stewart Emmens, Carmel Fitzsimons, Fr Clive Lee, Fr David Evans, Prof Gerard Fealy, Dr Noel Gill, Mgr Martin Hayes, Dr Michael Hinton, Sr Bernadette Hunston SCJA, Dr Larry Kreitzer, Dr Maria Luddy, Dr Natasha McEnroe and Jonathan Scherer. And special thanks to Laura Reeves at Bloomsbury for shepherding me through the publication process.

Citations and abbreviations

Three important first-person accounts of Crimean War nursing are published in Maria Luddy, ed., *The Crimean Journals of the Sisters of Mercy 1854–56* (Dublin: Four Courts Press, 2004). These three are 'Memories of the Crimea' by Sister Aloysius Doyle; the Diary of Sister Joseph Croke; and the lengthier 'Account of the Mission of the Sisters of Mercy in the Military Hospitals of the East' by Mother Francis Bridgeman. These will be cited in the notes as Doyle/Luddy, Croke/Luddy, and Bridgeman/Luddy, respectively.

Some frequent sources are rendered as follows:

AAS	Archives of the Archdiocese of Southwark
AAW	Archives of the Archdiocese of Westminster
APA	Ascot Priory Archives, Pusey House, Oxford
Annals	The hand-written Annals of the Bermondsey convent.
BA	Sisters of Mercy Archives (Archives of the Institute of Our Lady of Mercy) at the Convent of Our Lady of Mercy, Bermondsey, London
CW	The *Collected Works* of Florence Nightingale, followed by volume number
LEAVES	*Leaves from the Annals of the Sisters of Mercy* Volume 2 by 'A Member of the Order of Mercy' [Mary Austin Carroll] (New York: Catholic Publication Society, 1885)
MCA	Mercy Congregational Archives, Dublin
HMA	Sisters of Mercy Archives (Archives of the Union of the Sisters of Mercy of Great Britain) at St Mary's Convent, Handsworth, Birmingham
NA	England and Wales National Archives, Kew, London

A note on names and terminology

The story of nursing during the Crimean War poses particular problems with names and terms.

The names of the Sisters of Mercy were traditionally prefixed with Mary, as in Sister Mary Aloysius Doyle, for example. I have usually chosen to omit Mary to avoid repetition.

Then there is the word *nun* itself. Strictly speaking in Catholic religious life there is a distinction between *nun* and *sister*. Nuns lead a more enclosed life with greater emphasis on the life of prayer. They take solemn vows. Religious sisters are traditionally more devoted to works of mercy and education, often referred to as the apostolic life. They take simple vows. In this interpretation, all the vowed women in this book would be religious sisters. However, in practice *nun* is often used to refer to both types of sisters, and I could not resist the alliteration in the title. Caitriona Clear reports that in nineteenth-century Ireland 'sisters were almost universally referred to as nuns, even by priests'.[1] It remains in popular usage both within the Catholic Church and in society. Also, there were several instances where sisters named in this book referred to themselves or others as nuns. The terms 'nun', 'sister' and 'religious sister' are used interchangeably to indicate consecrated women under vows, living in community and undertaking works of mercy.

The Anglican sisters came from two communities. The first to be founded was called the Park Village Sisterhood, or the Sisterhood of the Holy Cross, but at the time of the Crimean War, it was in the process of being absorbed by the Devonport Sisters of Mercy, founded and led by Priscilla Lydia Sellon. Their contemporaries sometimes referred to them as Sellonites, which I regard as pejorative. I shall refer simply to the Anglican sisters or Anglican nuns. To avoid confusion, I never refer to the Devonport Sisters as Sisters of Mercy. When I refer to Sisters of Mercy it is always solely in reference to the Catholic order founded by Catherine McCauley.

At the time of the Crimean War, the city we now call Istanbul was still often called Constantinople. Occasionally the new name was abbreviated to Stamboul. I have retained the old name. Place names such as Koulali, Balaclava and

Inkerman had variant spellings at the time, but here have been standardized in the form just quoted.

Finally, a word of warning is necessary about the duplication of hospital names in the theatre of war. There was a General Hospital at both Scutari and Balaclava, so the reader must excuse occasional longer appellations of 'General Hospital Scutari' or 'General Hospital Balaclava'.

Introduction

This is the story of the nuns who served with Florence Nightingale during the Crimean War. Much has been written about her, but the voices of the nuns have been heard mostly in specialist publications, if at all. These sisters accompanied Nightingale when she sailed in 1854. They were responding to a national outcry over the negligent care of sick and wounded soldiers, who were more likely to die of disease or neglect in hospital than on the battlefield. The war lasted from March 1854 to March 1856 and pitted Britain and France (and later Piedmont-Sardinia) against Russia. This was the first war in Europe since 1815. The allies were supporting the Ottoman Empire but also acting to contain Russian expansion. The ensuing conflict has been ill-served by being described as the *Crimean* War as if it were some localized conflict. In fact, British and French fleets blockaded Russian ports for the summers of 1854 and 1855, tying down powerful Russian land forces in Finland and south of St Petersburg.[1] In the South Caucasus, the Russians wrested the fortress city of Kars from a Turkish army and its allied advisers, a victory that could have opened the way for a thrust into Anatolia along the South coast of the Black Sea.[2] There were other actions off the North coast of Russia in the White Sea, and in Siberia where there was an attack on the port of Petropavlovsk. For the land war with Russia, the French sent out 310,000 men, and the British 98,000.[3] The effects of this war continued to be felt in the participating nations long after the conflict.

The nuns who went out as nurses showed resilience, courage and initiative, and won the respect of the soldiers among whom they served. Yet their contribution was frequently misunderstood. David Fitzgerald, a purveyor of supplies for the army and friend of the Irish sisters, described their work as 'delicate services, which a woman of feeling and propriety can bestow, and the calm soothing of a mild commiseration for the sufferers' pangs'.[4] It was reported in *The Times* that the doctors at Scutari preferred nurses who had been trained in hospitals to work methodically, because 'the Catholic nuns, from their habits of simple submission, possess this power remarkably'.[5] Immediately after the war a surgeon praised the Sisters of Mercy for being 'submissive to learn' and 'prompt to act'. In his opinion, the presence of these 'pious, gentle, confiding females' had been 'an unmixed good'.[6] But to describe their work in terms of submission and ladylike serenity diminishes the work of the sisters and the other nurses. The nuns were sought by Nightingale for their experience, skills and discipline which made them the most reliable cohort within her nursing team.

The task the nuns undertook required courage and initiative. They knew that the care of sick men exposed them to deadly infections. Like the other nurses in the party, they had to endure the discomforts, shortages and emergencies of army life at a time when the British army was particularly badly managed. Critics had said that women were not strong enough to take on such a nursing role. The nuns proved the critics wrong, challenging the perception that ladies had to be protected and did not belong in the army with its strongly masculine atmosphere. Along with the other nurses, they also helped Nightingale to establish nursing as a proper outlet for women's talents and abilities.

The Catholic nuns from England knew that if they acquitted themselves well, it could win a wider acceptance for them in English society, where centuries of post-Reformation hostility towards Catholicism still lingered, with doubts about their patriotism. Catholicism to some of its critics signified the fires of the Inquisition and loyalty to a foreign sovereign, the pope. Lurid stories circulated about convents, which were regarded with suspicion. In a public lecture in 1851, John Henry Newman had asked why Catholics were so despised by their fellow citizens. Much of the public was, he said, 'prompt to believe any story, however extravagant, that is told to our disadvantage'.[7]

The Anglican nuns faced a different challenge. They were the first of their kind since Henry VIII had robbed and destroyed the abbeys and monasteries of England. These Anglican sisters were pioneers of a new movement to create religious orders in the Church of England. From these communities, as with the Catholic nuns, whole new spheres of action would open up in teaching, social work and nursing. Some Anglican leaders felt there was no need for nuns in the Church of England, or feared them as the vanguard of a Romanizing movement. The Anglican nuns knew that if they performed honourably in the East then it would help establish a place for religious sisters in the Church of England.

Consciously or unconsciously, there was another challenge the nuns shared with Florence Nightingale herself: a struggle for women to be agents in their own lives, to be allowed to shape their own destiny. All this was wrapped in a sense of vocation, of being called by God to pattern themselves on Christ in their whole way of life.

Even with the strongest sense of vocation, personal feelings can emerge to complicate a shared vision. The Catholic sisters from England were led by Mother

Clare Moore, who would become Nightingale's lifelong friend, confidante and spiritual adviser. The Irish party was headed by Mother Francis Bridgeman, who almost from the beginning was locked in an adversarial relationship with Nightingale. Their ability to work together was seriously impaired, although Bridgeman's organizational flair and dynamism meant that she was able to outmanoeuvre Nightingale. After the war, the Irish nuns were almost written out of the story of Crimean War nursing, despite contesting the narrative that had developed around Nightingale. As one historian puts it, 'In the case of the Sisters of Mercy, remembrance of their deeds, especially in the public sphere, was (it would appear) non-existent until the 1960s.'[8] This changed with the pioneering work of Evelyn Bolster, herself a Sister of Mercy and the first nun to receive a PhD from the National University of Ireland.[9] Later, first-hand accounts of the war by Irish sisters, edited by Maria Luddy, put more information in the public domain.[10] Little has been written about the English Sisters of Mercy and their work in the Crimean War, apart from Mary Sullivan's account of the friendship between Nightingale and Clare Moore.[11] As for the Anglican nuns, the archives are scanty. Fortunately, two of the Anglican sisters left valuable memoirs of their experience in the war.[12]

Crimean War nursing was part of a wider movement in which consecrated women built hospitals, schools and orphanages. These women ameliorated the effects of Victorian poverty, and through their schools assisted the embourgeoisement of the working class. Their achievements were enormous. In many ways, apostolic sisters *were* the public face of the Catholic Church in Britain. If you were a Catholic in the first half of the twentieth century it was far more likely that a nun knew your name than a priest. Anglican sisterhoods also deserve to be given a better place in this movement. Today there is a network of historians writing about the history of women religious of Britain and Ireland.[13] Through their research and publications these historians are enlarging our understanding of the life and witness of vowed women.[14] Historiography has also benefited greatly from a recent panoptic study on nursing in the Crimean War.[15]

The nuns who went with Nightingale had their own small part to play as nurses in this vast conflict, but their modest role attracted criticism as well as admiration. There was curiosity about them too because female nursing in an army hospital was an innovation. The nuns and other nurses had to live in the occasional glare of publicity because the British public followed this war closely. Widespread newspaper circulation brought quicker and better-informed reports, and this was the first war between European powers to be photographed.[16] This reportage enabled the British public to enter into the war in their imagination. As Trudi Tate notes, representations of war 'entered British civilian culture more widely and deeply in the 1850s, and had a profound effect upon people's *imaginary* relationship with war'.[17] In addition to newspaper reports, the weekly *Illustrated London News* had a key role in this development. In 1855, the demand for news about the war saw its circulation rise to 200,000, assisted by the reproduction of Roger Fenton's photographs from the Crimea.[18] The *ILN* sent out two artist correspondents to the East, where they had free access to all parts of the allied lines and to the battlefields and were able to send back dramatic depictions of events.[19]

The nuns along with the other nurses had to overcome daunting challenges to care for sick, wounded and dying men. They brought humanity in a place of inhumanity. Their presence strengthened Nightingale herself as she tackled an obdurate bureaucracy and a sclerotic medical establishment. These religious sisters also took with them the usual human frailties. They tended to interpret the world around them in the social and national stereotypes of their day. Because they were human they could be proud, prejudiced or querulous. There were conflicts to be negotiated and disappointments to be overcome. There were even controversies that continued after the end of the war until they received belated recognition and honour.

1

'No use for angels without hands'

On 4 November 1854, a group of Englishwomen stood on the deck of the paddle-steamer *Vectis* to get their first look at Constantinople. It had been a stormy voyage from Marseilles and they were relieved to have arrived. Between the rough seas, the noise of the engine and cockroaches in the cabins in the cabins, they had lost a lot of sleep. Their leader was Florence Nightingale. Accompanying her were thirty-eight nurses, eighteen of whom were nuns. Ten of the nuns were Catholic and eight were Anglican. They had been chosen to help care for Britain's sick and wounded soldiers in the Crimean War.

The following afternoon they stepped into caiques to be rowed across the Bosphorus. As they skimmed across the water in the carved, flat-bottomed boats, storm clouds cleared and the sun shone briefly on the roofs of the city. From their cushioned seats they saw the Topkapi Palace, and beyond it, the gleaming dome of Hagia Sophia. But their attention soon focussed on the vast bulk of the hospital at Scutari on the other side. Here, wounded and dying soldiers awaited them. The women were determined, but apprehensive. Could they live up to the expectations of the crowds that had cheered them as they left England?

On approaching the dilapidated wharf at Scutari, they saw the corpse of a large grey horse being washed ashore, where a pack of dogs snarled and fought to get at the carcass. A curious crowd parted to allow the women to walk up a steep hill to Barrack Hospital. The vastness of it was intimidating but for now, there was no opportunity to explore. They were shown to their quarters in the north-west tower, where a section of rooms had been set aside for them. A large room was provided for the nurses, and next to it a small room for Nightingale herself. Another room accommodated five Catholic Sisters of Mercy who came from a convent in Bermondsey in south London. Up above a wide stone staircase were two more rooms, one of them set aside for the eight Anglican sisters. For the time being there were no beds. Mattresses were put on the floor by night and folded up by the day. (Iron bedsteads would arrive later.) Broken windows admitted piercing air and the roof leaked when it rained. No provision had been made for their supper, but soldiers took pity on the women and pooled their rations for them. As they lay down to sleep that night probably everybody in Nightingale's group wondered what they had let themselves in for. It was a bracing introduction to what lay ahead: shortages, improvisation, and a challenge to resilience as they found their place in the masculine environment of a military hospital.[1]

The mid-nineteenth century saw a wave of innovation by women in the Catholic Church responding to the needs of the times. Five sisters of the Sisters of Mercy from the convent in Bermondsey, south London, were part of that response. They took as their vocation Christ's command to feed the hungry, clothe the naked and care for the sick. The Bermondsey group was led by Mother Clare Moore. Her playful sense of humour was married to a strength of character that shrugged off a serious lung condition. It was later said that faced with a chaotic crowd of hospital orderlies, 'a glance from her dark grey eye, or, in graver cases, her uplifted finger' would be enough to bring order.[2] Over the next two years, she would become the friend, confidante and adviser of Florence Nightingale. Clare Moore's trusted lieutenant was Gonzaga Barrie. A woman of energy and good sense she would soon be placed in charge of a nearby hospital. Criticized by chaplains for giving the men novels to read, Gonzaga Barrie said that they would do the men more good than pious publications.[3]

The youthfulness of the Bermondsey sisters is striking. Clare Moore was forty. (At twenty-three she had helped to found a convent in Cork.) Gonzaga Barrie was twenty-nine. The others ranged in age from twenty-seven to thirty-two. They drew on the stamina of youth to shoulder their responsibilities in caring for traumatized and dying men. There were tensions and rivalries within the hospitals to be negotiated, as well as the authoritarian rule of Florence Nightingale. Each day they would be exposed to infection which eventually would strike their group too. They would need not only physical strength but also the centredness that came from their own sense of vocation.

The Anglican group was led by Mother Emma Langston, one of the founding members of the Park Village Sisterhood. Her strong desire to serve was sometimes inhibited by an element of self-doubt, so she relied heavily on Bertha Turnbull, who came from a long-established Scottish family. Bertha was later described as 'a woman of heroic mould, tall . . . self-disciplined, capable . . . endowed with a sense of humour and a loving heart'.[4] There was another Scot, Sarah Anne Terrot, daughter of a bishop and a keen observer of the world around her. She and another sister, Margaret Goodman, would later publish reminiscences of this time. The other Anglican nuns were Elizabeth Wheeler, who would soon feel the full weight of Nightingale's wrath, Clara Sharpe, who donated a small fortune to the community when she joined in 1850, Etheldreda Pillans and Harriet Erskine.

Florence Nightingale was disappointed, but not entirely surprised, to find that she and her nurses were not wanted. The medical staff feared that 'emotional' women might undermine the tight discipline necessary for an army hospital. The presence of women in a military hospital was for many doctors an unwelcome innovation. As the nursing historian Carol Helmstadter puts it, 'the government forced female nurses on an unwilling army medical department, placing Florence Nightingale in a complex and highly politicized position'.[5] There was also the undeniable fact that the women had come out in response to a public outcry over army failures in medical care which had been exposed in the press. They were resented by the doctors because their very presence seemed to imply criticism of the medical team. A few days after the nurses arrived Dr John Hall, Chief Medical Officer in the East had written to the head of the Army Medical Department to assure him that the Scutari hospitals were working well and that the army's medical difficulties had been exaggerated.[6] Hall was one of those who obstructed Nightingale. Clare Moore, the leader of the English group of Sisters of Mercy, recorded that when Nightingale arrived at Scutari, 'the nurses were discontented and troublesome, the medical officers opposed her having care of the sick, the purveyors were unwilling to place the hospital stores and clothing at her disposal'.[7] Some of the senior staff scornfully referred to Nightingale as 'the Bird'. At the same time, they feared her, because they knew she could communicate directly with Sidney Herbert, a Peelite politician and member of parliament who was currently the secretary at war. Herbert and Nightingale had been friends since 1847. She allowed neither his seniority (he was ten years older) nor his high offices of state to intimidate her. In correspondence, she would sometimes address him in forthright language. For his part, he enjoyed her company so much that he would even cancel dinner with the Duke of Newcastle in order to dine with her.[8]

Nightingale bided her time. She did not use her connections to insist on being given a role in the hospital. Instead, she made it clear that she would act only on the instructions of the medical officers. Her biographer Mark Bostridge describes her as maintaining a tactful balance between her sense of mission and her awareness of military procedure: 'As a woman, she had been granted a field of action that was unprecedented in the army's history, yet she behaved at all times with scrupulous attention to army regulations to ensure that neither she nor her staff could be accused of infringing them.[9] Nightingale quietly ordered her party to make flannel shirts, bandages, stump rests and slings. It was hard for them to see the troops suffer and not offer their help. Terrot wrote in her diary that she longed to go and comfort the wounded, but instead like the other nuns she had to exercise patience.[10]

It was a chance for the sisters to familiarize themselves with this vast hospital. Barrack Hospital, as its name implied, had previously accommodated troops in the Ottoman army. It was built as a quadrangle on the slope of a ridge, so there were two floors in the upper section and three floors in the lower one. It enclosed a courtyard which was muddy and rubbish-strewn. The larger rooms were turned into wards where a low wooden sleeping bench ran around the walls about 2 feet off the ground. This platform was often rotten and insect-infested. There was no operating theatre, which meant that any operations took place in the wards in full view of the other patients. One of Nightingale's first actions was to procure screens for this purpose. Smoke and steam permeated into the wards from the primitive wood-fired kitchens below.[11] Elsewhere in the building could be found a depot for troops, stables for horses and a canteen where spirits were sold.[12] Later, after the long, wide corridors had been turned into additional wards, Nightingale would estimate that the hospital contained the equivalent of 4 miles of beds.

While the waiting game went on, a Church of England chaplain seized the opportunity to utilize the Anglican sisters. He asked two of them to go down to the basement of Barrack Hospital to nurse a sergeant's wife who was dying of tuberculosis. Here they found around 200 wives of soldiers living in squalor. The dying woman was barely screened by rags hanging on a piece of string. One of the Anglicans recalled that she looked prematurely aged, 'ravages not the work of time, but of sorrow, want, and disease, her age being about twenty-six'.[13] As this woman lay dying, drinking and ribaldry went on in the room. The Anglican nuns sat with the sergeant's wife through the night until she died.

Florence Nightingale's group did not have long to wait for its call to action. On the day they stepped ashore at Scutari battle was being waged on the other side of the Black Sea. The British and French armies had landed an invasion force at the Kalamita Bay in Crimea on 14 September, with the ultimate aim of capturing Sevastopol, the main base of the Russian Black Sea navy. In the first glint of dawn on 5 November, the Russian army sent forward 35,000 men with the intention of pushing the allies off Mount Inkerman. The Russians took the British by surprise, helped by a dense fog. The result was a fierce, chaotic close-quarters engagement, all the more terrifying because the men could not be sure who was looming towards them through the eddying wisps of fog. In desperation, each side resorted to bayonets, rifle butts, rocks and even fists. A captain in the Coldstream Guards described the combat as 'hand-to-hand, foot to foot, muzzle to muzzle, butt-end to butt-end'.[14] The arrival of French troops tipped the balance in favour of the allies. The British lost around 600 killed and 1,900 wounded.

There was some medical treatment on the field. In triaging immediately after the battle, a surgeon of the Coldstream Guards carried out eighteen amputations on a table made from a door placed across two casks.[15] But the seriously injured faced a daunting journey across the Black Sea to the hospitals at Scutari. Some of them had to wait on the battlefield for two days before they were picked up. The wounded then endured a jolting journey down a muddy road to the harbour at Balaclava. Some went on mule-back, carried in panniers each side of a mule. Private Edward Cain of the 63rd Regiment remembered being loaded with others onto a bullock-drawn cart. 'There was one man with two legs and an arm off. He shouted very much all the way. He called out not to drive so hard, but the driver could not drive them easier, the place was so rough that the jolting could not be helped.'[16] At Balaclava, they were put on ships with minimal medical care. In a pattern that would repeat itself, in the journey from Crimea to Scutari the rough seas and the abrasion of the decks sometimes re-opened the wounds of the men.

From midday, on 9 November these wounded men from Inkerman began to pour into Scutari. Word had spread, and in anticipation, Nightingale ordered her group to make mattresses by sewing straw into sacking. An extra ward was then created by setting two lines of these primitive and scratchy mattresses on each side of a long corridor. The first patients limped in, followed by the others on stretchers. The pressing need for nursing care now overcame the reluctance of the doctors to allow women a role. Of the wounded, wrote Terrot:

> They seemed so thankful for any attention & of course anxious to get their wounds dressed yet so respectful & patient often saying no hurry should we attend to that poor fellow first pointing to someone more suffering but tho' in general most scrupulously attentive to decency of course they could not think of it in such suffering, the little nuns were busy dragging & cutting off coats and trousers and then such a display of bloody wounds.[17]

The men were usually careful about not exposing themselves in front of women, but their shared awareness of the urgency of the moment overrode their customary propriety. These wounds had not been dressed for four days. Sarah Terrot together with her fellow Anglicans, Mother Emma, Sister Harriet and Sister Margaret, cleaned out the wounds with warm water and lint, bound them in oilskin and sacking, and washed the men, before putting a clean shirt on each one. An Irish dragoon wounded in arm, thigh and leg at first refused to allow Terrot to treat his wounds, fearing that she would faint when she saw them. The men were pathetically grateful, with comments like, 'The very sight of a woman does us a power of good, it makes us fancy we've got home to our mothers.' The men also said that without the intervention of the French, they would have been overwhelmed by the Russians.[18]

After initially helping with the wounded, Clare Moore of the Catholic contingent was placed in charge of the linen store. Later she would be transferred to be a supervisor of Nightingale's store of extras, which plugged the gaps when official supplies of hospital goods ran out. These were jobs of unrelenting pressure, trying to bring order while a chaotic melee of orderlies and nurses all demanded urgent supplies for their patients. Meanwhile, in the wards and corridors, Moore's Sisters of Mercy were trying to adapt to a fast-changing situation which required new skills. Gonzaga Barrie wrote that after four days of tending the Inkerman wounded, she found herself

> quite hardened already to stumps, and large running wounds and gashes. Today I burnt and bandaged an amputated leg for the first time – the Doctor desired me . . . Plain gunshot wounds I can manage very well, but I don't much admire dressing shell-wounds . . . shell wounds seem to be most painful. I am quite surprised at myself. The men admire my services because my hands are soft, and I try very hard not to hurt the poor fellows.

One of them had been shot through the right lung, 'so that you could feel his breath through the hole'.[19]

'I am quite surprised at myself.' Gonzaga could never have anticipated on leaving Britain that she would have to burn the stump of an amputated leg, although precisely what this entailed is not clear. Cauterization by fiery heat had been long known, but it is more likely that Gonzaga was cauterizing stumps using a caustic preparation. The surgeon would have done his best to seal the soldier's stump by sewing a flap of skin over it, but any remaining flesh where the blood still seeped out would then be further sealed using an astringent preparation.[20] Sometimes the men were in such pain that they looked forward to the amputation, thinking it would relieve the pain of the shattered limb, but often they were disappointed. At the end of November, Gonzaga Barrie was dressing a gangrened wound in a man's leg, while he tried to draw a plan of Sevastopol for her and describe the fighting there.[21] This might have been an attempt to distract himself from the continuing pain.

It is unclear how much nurse training the Sisters of Mercy had acquired beforehand, but they had done their best to prepare. They had broken their journey to Scutari to spend a week in Paris, where they asked about the best nursing practice from the Sisters of Charity at St Roch. They also bought three cases of surgical instruments. Both the advice and the instruments proved invaluable.[22] Later, Gonzaga Barrie asked her sister in London to send out surgical spirit, steel probes, surgical scissors, forceps and caustic, her supplies of the latter being nearly all used up: 'You can guess how quickly it goes with hundreds of stumps.'[23] If the caustic was not used to seal stumps, then it would have been necessary to wash down the areas left soaked in blood after amputations. Normally the sisters left a ward when an amputation was about to take place, but Margaret Goodman witnessed a soldier's arm being amputated while attending to her own patient's urgent needs in an adjacent bed.[24]

A major part of the nursing was caring for men with stumps. The numerous amputations resulted from either artillery or small-arms fire. Russian artillery relied heavily on roundshot – literally just a solid iron ball – which, while not explosive, could have a deadly effect as it whizzed and bounced across the target area. Russian troops were armed with smooth-bore muskets. Although these were not as accurate as the rifles used by the British and French, the muskets could send a ball tearing into a man's body.[25] Henry Clifford, a captain in the Light Division, later recorded walking among the dead and noting 'the most frightful wounds – a cannon ball having torn away a limb, a musket ball shattered the head and distorted the face'.[26] Together, roundshot and muskets destroyed the limbs of many British soldiers. Nightingale wrote to a surgeon in England, 'In all our corridors I think we have not an average of three limbs per man.'[27]

It seems that the scale of the influx of casualties took the hospital authorities by surprise. Charles and Selina Bracebridge, family friends of Nightingale who had accompanied her to Scutari, wrote that in their opinion, many of the hospital officials 'lost their heads' as wave after wave of wounded arrived. By contrast, 'the women behaved with *perfect* fortitude'. Among the helpers they spotted Clare Moore, 'with her flowing veil, kneeling over a man, and mopping with a sponge his bleeding leg'.[28] One of the men had travelled with a ball lodged in the socket of his arm. His arm was amputated at Scutari and the ball was removed, but the damage had been done by infection. The smell of his suppurating arm nauseated him and a nurse, noticing this, placed a handkerchief soaked in eau-de-cologne over the wrappings. He thanked her and died twenty minutes later.[29] The smell in the corridor wards was overpowering, despite Nightingale's best efforts to improve ventilation and cleanliness. When she first arrived there were open tubs of excrement in the wards which she ordered removed and emptied immediately.

The wounded continued to come in, as the allied and Russian troops skirmished. Nine days after the first arrival the hospital was still barely coping. Nightingale said that 'this is the kingdom of hell no one can doubt', adding 'we are steeped up to our necks in blood'.[30] There was now a struggle to find enough beds, despite there being two hospitals. The other hospital at Scutari was the General Hospital, about half a mile downhill from the Barrack Hospital. It was about a quarter of the size of Barrack Hospital and it was relatively cleaner, although like Barrack Hospital its sewage system emitted overpowering odours. The initial intention had been that the Barrack Hospital would be for the sick and General Hospital for the wounded. This would have guarded against cross-contagion, but under the pressure of the situation, this policy was abandoned.

Nightingale assumed responsibility for the General Hospital also and placed Gonzaga Barrie in charge of her nursing team there. As at the Barrack Hospital, this team was a mixed group including both Anglican and Catholic nuns as well as paid nurses. But even with both hospitals in play, the number of patients began to increase until they began to run out of space. Bearers would carry an injured man from ward to ward, being turned away from each one. Sarah Terrot remembered the imploring look in the eyes of these men 'with death written on their discoloured faces', shunted around from ward to ward until at last, the orderlies 'could lay down their sad burden in some empty space from which a corpse had just been removed'.[31] In addition to the wounded of Inkerman, the nuns found themselves nursing the wounded from the earlier battles at Alma and Balaclava.

There were also soldier patients to be nursed who were not wounded but suffering from generic illnesses. Sarah Terrot and Elizabeth Wheeler were sent to a ward caring for those patients who were sick from infections or diseases. The reality, Terrot realized, was that the constitutions of these men had broken down under the hardship of army life. Their illnesses were 'the results of exposure to damp and cold, fatigue and bad and insufficient food – low fever, diarrhoea, dysentery and scurvy'.[32] It was an early lesson for her in how the inefficiency and indifference of the British army could be wasteful in human lives. In theory, many of these sick soldiers were curable, but in practice, whatever was tried did not seem to work and the mortality rate was high. She noticed that the men, who had been invalided out before the transfer to Crimea, had a sense of shame at not having taken part in the battles there. They felt that they were dying without the self-respect that would have come to battle-hardened veterans. With such lowered morale, it would have been harder for them to fight infection. It was painful for the nuns to witness this decline. 'Daily we missed some pale face that we had come to know and love, and who loved us.'[33] As the months passed, this problem of coming to terms with their feelings of sadness and grief would challenge the sisters.[34]

Terrot nursed with her fellow Anglicans Bertha Turnbull and Margaret Goodman at the General Hospital, walking there and back each day from the Barrack Hospital. Slowly the number of wounded in General Hospital decreased as they died or were discharged, and they were replaced by the sick. It was different up the hill at Barrack Hospital, where the other Anglican sisters were nursing, and the situation was far graver. Wounded or sick soldiers were still coming in large numbers throughout November and December. Without rapid transfer from the hospital to the cemetery, there would have been no room for the incoming patients. Sometimes ships with sick men on board sat outside the harbour for days, unable to find a berth, while the men who died daily were thrown overboard in weighted blankets to a watery grave. Terrot wondered why nurses were not allowed to accompany the transports and help save lives.[35] The debasement of the men did not end with their death in the hospital. Burial in the cemetery at Scutari was a perfunctory affair, with the dead man sewn into canvas or a blanket and taken to a grave as quickly as possible. An Anglican chaplain would read the funeral service from the Book of Common Prayer at the grave, where the soldiers would be buried in common graves in groups of ten. Once, as the Anglican nuns were having their breakfast, they heard a great commotion outside their window, and looking down found that an ox-wagon carrying a load of dead soldiers to the cemetery had become stuck in a hole. The Turkish drivers urged the oxen on, at which point the cart was freed with a great jolt that sent naked bodies of men tumbling to the ground, 'many of whose faces we might have recognized had we not at once turned away'.[36]

As November became December, the mental and physical pressure began to tell on the nuns. Rest and nourishment were in short supply. Out of a sense of propriety, nurses were forbidden to enter the wards after 8.00 pm, but the nuns were trusted women, so at the height of the Inkerman influx they would sometimes rise in the night to help men who were in great pain.[37] In theory, male orderlies were supposed to take over the night shift, but the nuns knew the orderlies would often be fast asleep. There was also cold weather to contend with because by December there was thick snow on the ground and no fire to heat their accommodation. Food was scant. The meat was stringy and hacked up roughly, and the bread was often mouldy. Sometimes the nuns felt faint with hunger. Sarah Terrot recorded 'tough meat & sour bread, no milk, rancid butter in small quantities, little tea & cold'.[38] For a time even fresh water was in short supply. The sisters were aware that they were there on the sufferance of the military medical officers. Clare Moore said that her group wanted to show endurance and stability, and so remained stoical despite the trials and exhaustion they experienced.[39] Not all the sisters were stoical. To Nightingale's irritation, the Anglicans made their discontent known. 'Let no lady come out here who is not used to fatigue and privation' Nightingale wrote in irritation, 'for the Devonport sisters, who ought to know what self-denial is, do nothing but complain. Occasionally the roof is torn off our quarters, or the windows blown in, and we are flooded and under water for the night.'[40] The stoicism of the sisters under these circumstances is the more remarkable because their room, which had previously contained five nuns, now had to squeeze in five more Sisters of Our Lady of Fidelity. These five came from the Convent of the Faithful Virgin at Norwood in south London and had travelled out on the *Vectis* with everyone else. After arrival they had immediately gone for two weeks to a convent at Galata, thus escaping the intense pressure of the Inkerman crisis. The reason for this respite is not clear. Their belated arrival at the hospital did not augur well for them, as they would soon find out.

Florence Nightingale could be implacable when she considered it necessary. The first to fall victim was one of the Anglican nuns, whose enthusiasm was her undoing. Elizabeth Wheeler was beloved by the men under her care. Sarah Terrot remembered that in Wheeler's ward eyes of the soldiers 'brightened with love and gratitude as they recognized Sister Elizabeth, and stretched out their wasted hands and arms to express the thanks they were too feeble to utter.'[41] Wheeler was a strong personality 'cheerful, frank, yet gentle'[42] and pushed hard to get the men the help she felt they needed. At this time the catering arrangements of the hospital were still haphazard. Nightingale could make up the shortfall from her store, but always sought medical authorization for this, and if it was not possible to obtain it the patients went short of what was required. Elizabeth Wheeler established a good working relationship with a Dr McLean from the Black Watch regiment, and together they pushed for much more food than was usually allotted for the fifty or sixty men in their care. In fact, said Terrot, 'Eld. [ress] Elizabeth & Dr McLean have both got into trouble by their zeal for their patients ... she & her doctor get more food than anyone else for their patients & yet are never satisfied.'[43] The results were evident. Terrot realized that the extra pudding, wine, milk and other food fed to the men in Wheeler's charge gave them a far greater chance of pulling through, compared with her own ward.[44] Wheeler's daily battle for extra food began to draw others into contention. Extra for her men meant less for others. A senior nurse scolded her, Wheeler became excited and anxious in her demands, and Nightingale had to appeal to her to be more reasonable. Wheeler's book was now marked.

Elizabeth Wheeler's concern for her patients eventually led her into calamity. She wrote a letter, probably to a member of her family, asking for supplies to be sent out to her in Scutari. It seems she did not intend the letter for publication, but it was passed on to the *Times* where it appeared on 8 December, presented as being from 'one of the Government nurses at Scutari'. Wheeler wrote about how, in four wards committed to her care, eleven men had died overnight 'simply from exhaustion, which, humanly speaking, might have been stopped could I have laid my hands at once on such nourishment as I know they ought to have had'. The food that was available was often poor quality: 'We have not seen a drop of milk, and the bread is extremely sour, the butter . . . in a state of decomposition, and the meat is more like moist leather than food.'[45] She appealed for wine, bottled chicken broth and preserved meats to be sent.

This letter in the *Times* angered the medical staff who had feared all along they were being blamed for shortages that were not their responsibility. The letter was a setback for Nightingale's attempts to overcome their suspicion and resentment. There was already an outcry in Britain over their soldiers dying needlessly in hospitals for want of basic provisions. The *Times* was not only publishing hard-hitting reports from its own correspondents, but it was also reprinting letters it had received from soldiers who were highly critical of the conduct of the war. On the same day as the Wheeler letter, the *Times* also published a letter from 'an officer of the 88th' who said that some regiments had suffered from medical neglect because their doctors 'held the old idea that the less their hospital expenditure the greater their chance of promotion'.[46] Elizabeth Wheeler's well-meant letter referred to Scutari hospitals, and as such, it fitted perfectly into a developing narrative that brave men were dying because of official complacency. The publicity ensuing from Wheeler's initiative weakened Nightingale's attempts to demonstrate the loyalty of her nurses. It undermined her authority as well. She knew that she had to be seen to act on this misstep by one of her team.

The author of the letter was soon identified as Elizabeth Wheeler. Nightingale was furious and sought to contain the damage. Coincidentally the Hospitals Commission was visiting Scutari at this time. It had been appointed on instructions of the House of Commons, where MPs were bringing pressure to bear on the government over the mismanagement of the war. Wheeler was questioned by the commission about the claims she had made in her letter, especially that shortages had contributed to the needless death of patients. Even in summary, her nervousness comes through, as she hesitates and occasionally backtracks. She was certain that the men's health had suffered from shortages of food and alcoholic 'restoratives', but crucially she conceded that she could not say that this had led to anyone's death. Nightingale gave evidence herself, insisting that no man had died or even suffered from want of food or drink.[47] Wheeler's fate was sealed. She was induced to resign. Nightingale also used the opportunity of Wheeler's dismissal to ask two more Anglican sisters to return to Britain: Etheldreda Pillans and Clara Sharpe. Etheldreda had difficulties coping with the coarse food provided. She was already weakened after suffering smallpox in 1848 and had suffered badly from seasickness on the journey.[48] Her constitution simply could not cope with the rigours of Scutari. Clara Sharpe, although adjudged good and gentle by Nightingale, was considered to be too clumsy.[49]

Just as Nightingale was dealing with Wheeler's impetuosity, a fresh crisis arose. To Nightingale's dismay, a wholly new party of nuns and other nurses arrived on 17 December. She had not been consulted about their recruitment and had a little prior warning from the British government. The new group was led by Mary Stanley, daughter of the bishop of Norwich and sister of the Dean of Westminster Abbey, a well-connected Church of England woman but already attracted to the Catholic Church. In her group were twenty-two nurses, fifteen nuns (Sisters of Mercy, like the Bermondsey group), and nine ladies. The Sisters of Mercy were from Ireland and were led by Mother Francis Bridgeman from Kinsale. Nightingale was taken aback. There was no space to accommodate them, she could not supervise an additional number of nurses, and she had always resisted well-meaning lady volunteers. Such ladies in Nightingale's experience often shrank from the actual tasks they were assigned. 'We have no use for angels without hands', she used to say.[50] Worst of all, the presence of more nuns would upset the delicate religious balance of the hospital. Both in Britain and in Scutari itself there was suspicion in some Protestant circles that the nuns were not only nurses but also recruiters for Rome and its alien creed.

This arrival of a new party of helpers would become the most serious human relations crisis of Florence Nightingale's Crimean War leadership. It would return to haunt her again and again because Bridgeman was soon locked in an adversarial relationship with Nightingale. Each would describe the other in terms of great bitterness. It was a contest in which Nightingale would be outmanoeuvred. Nightingale played for time. The Mary Stanley group was not immediately admitted to Scutari but found refuge with the Sisters of Charity across the Bosphorus at Galata.

Nightingale chose this moment to send the five Norwood nuns back to Britain. She did not want to take on the newly arrived Sisters of Mercy under Mother Francis Bridgeman. But if she was compelled to do so, then sending back the five from Norwood would do something to redress the religious balance. The Norwood nuns came from the Convent of the Faithful Virgin in south London where they ran an orphanage. It seems that they had neither nursing experience nor the ability to adapt to the hectic life of the wards. Curiously, their habit also seems to have given offence. They had set out from London wearing simple black dresses, but onboard the ship had changed into a white habit with a linen veil. When they first appeared on deck attired in white, Sarah Terrot initially failed to recognize them: 'On examining them more minutely, I thought I knew some of the faces.' Once she realized who they were, she felt that their new accoutrement 'seemed coarse and ill-shaped, and gave them altogether a ghastly and ungainly appearance'.[51] Even Clare Moore, normally the soul of charity, noted dryly that their habit was 'very remarkable'.[52] It seems to have become a symbol of their inability to cope with the demands of hospital life at Scutari. The Norwood leader, Sister Marie des Neiges, wrote to Manning describing their distress at this abrupt dismissal. She accused both Nightingale and Moore of coldness and of withholding work from them despite the Norwood sisters trying their hardest to fit in. The reasons for the dismissal are not clear, but the letter's focus on minor slights may indicate an inability to plunge into the demands of the urgent moment. On the other hand, these sisters' spirit of self-offering is clear from the letter, as is their pain at being sent away without being given a proper trial.[53]

Sending back both Anglican and Catholic nuns gave Nightingale some protection from accusations of bias. If criticized by the Anglicans she could point to the departure of the Catholic Norwood sisters, and plead the necessity of efficiency. If criticized by the Catholics, she could point to the departure of the Anglicans and plead that she had been even-handed. Either way, she could deny prejudice. She would have hoped that this would counter-balance any appearance of being anti-Catholic. If this was the hope, it was to no avail. In fact, as will be seen, Catholic criticism would be fierce and cause many complications.

Late on the evening of 23 December, the five Norwood nuns and the three Anglicans boarded the *Candia* for the journey home, along with two other nurses dismissed by Nightingale. The remaining Anglican sisters were hurt and angry. Nightingale reported to Sidney Herbert that the Anglican sisters were 'furious at the dismissal of their confederate, and charge me with tyranny'.[54] Terrot remembered this moment as 'a sudden and overwhelming sorrow to our party . . . a grief and an insult'.[55] Wheeler, generous-spirited to the end, refused to blame anyone. She regretted leaving her patients and having caused trouble for Nightingale. Terrot felt devastated by Wheeler's departure – 'that she, the noblest and best, should go in disgrace, was almost more than I could bear'. It seems that Elizabeth Wheeler's energy and vivaciousness had been buoying up the entire Anglican group. Terrot accompanied Wheeler to the embarkation, and when she turned back to her quarters she felt, 'alone, sick at heart and desolate, and from that time I never felt quite well'.[56] The dispatch of these three Anglicans was a demonstration that Nightingale was firmly in charge. But these dismissals left the Anglicans demoralized. As for the Catholics, she retained the loyalty of Clare Moore and her sisters, but the wider Catholic community at Scutari, especially the priests, was shocked at the abrupt dismissal of the Norwood nuns.

Nightingale believed that she was promoting a model of command and efficiency. In her eyes, this was crucial if nurses were to find a professional role in a modern, well-ordered hospital. Discipline was even more important in an army hospital. This emphasis is reflected in *Notes on the Health of the British Army*, which she wrote after her return to the UK. In the *Notes*, she made wide-ranging suggestions for improvements in the military medical system, backed up by extensive use of statistics, together with reference to her own experience. After describing how she recruited her corps of nurses, including nuns, for the Crimean War, she wrote: 'Discipline, founded on actual efficiency in the service, and without respect of persons, was immediately adopted, and this necessarily occasioned the sending home of those who proved incompetent. . . . A primary principle of discipline was that no interference with the regulations of the hospital, or with the legitimate orders of the medical officers, should take place.'[57]

Nightingale's venture was a pioneering one, conducted with high public visibility, and her brisk approach was no doubt necessary. But there was more at work here than a dispassionate efficiency. The astute Sarah Terrot noticed that deep down Nightingale was afraid that her nurses might be accused by men of being emotional and thus unfit for service. Terrot recorded that even before the incident of the *Times* letter, Elizabeth Wheeler's 'impatience, enthusiasm and want of caution', in fact, her zealousness and affection for her patients, had already attracted Nightingale's critical eye. Terrot concluded that this dismissal was intended as a warning to others not to make the same mistake.[58] Nightingale never wanted femininity to be associated with any kind of excess emotion, which could be construed as weakness. Her distrust of such emotion was on display a few weeks later, when some of the doctors at Scutari asked her to write privately to Sidney Herbert about the continued shortfall of basic supplies. In doing so she emphasized to the secretary at war that she wrote not from 'feminine compassion' but because she was speaking for 'men of experience' who were reluctant to voice their concerns, as this could prejudice their careers.[59] It was an old trope. Men were deemed rational, women emotional, and the testimony of women therefore less reliable.

On Christmas Day in 1854, the nuns had no time off from their duties. Moore and her sisters realized that although they were tired they had to resist feelings of dreariness for the sake of the men. After hurriedly attending a 6.30 am Mass, they worked hard all day and were able to reassemble only late that night. Kneeling before a picture of the infant Jesus, they sang *Adeste Fideles* with subdued voices, and a sense of peace and joy filled their sparsely furnished living quarters.[60] It was equally a working day for the Anglican nuns. As they passed from bed to bed, preparing wounds to be dressed, 'the pain-worn faces of the occupants brightened, and we were greeted with, "A merry Christmas to you". In one ward the men had each saved a small portion of flour and lard, an egg and some plums, which they took from beneath their pillow 'and began to concoct a Christmas pudding' which Goodman arranged to be steamed.[61] The Anglican sisters all received Holy Communion, but this could not remove the sadness they felt for the three of their company who had been sent back to Britain.[62]

Despite their tiredness or sadness, all the remaining nuns could have looked back with a feeling of achievement. The 'little nuns', as Terrot put it, had risen to the challenge, had adapted to the changing health care needs confronting them and blended into a hospital system. These nuns had given Nightingale the resilience and discipline she required, but at the same time, their discreet compassion also supplied humanity to the hospital system which it otherwise lacked.

There was one cheering note at the end of the year. Gonzaga Barrie had written a letter of consolation to the wife of a Presbyterian Scottish Fusilier who had died of his wounds. Barrie described how, at his request, she had brought him a large print New Testament and had visited him daily. 'Everything that could be done for his case was done. . . . He often spoke of you and the boys with great anxiety and affection, but he seemed quite willing to die, if such was God's holy will.' Barrie closed with a reminder of eternal life and assured the widow of her prayers. The letter was thoughtful, and one of many such letters she and the others would write to bereaved families, as did Nightingale. But this particular letter was passed to the minister at Crown Court, the Scottish church in Covent Garden, London. He read the letter from the pulpit and averred that despite the errors of the Catholic Church, this letter 'by a Romish Sister of Charity' showed that nonetheless 'there were not a few true Christians' in the Catholic Church. The letter, prefaced by his remarks, appeared in the *Times*.[63]

Dr Manning was delighted at the good publicity: 'A few such things will do more for us than all the books of controversy in the world.' Bishop Grant of Southwark, who had been the prime instigator in sending out the Bermondsey group and who had a close relationship with them, was more cautious. He worried that Gonzaga Barrie might have implied that 'those who died out of the [Catholic] Church can be saved, although we know that they cannot be saved unless they were invincibly ignorant, and who can tell, save our Dear Lord?'[64] He advised her in any future letters of this kind to avoid any intimations of salvation. These responses were of their times and a reminder of how carefully Nightingale and the nuns had to tread in matters of religion. The Presbyterian minister had allowed that sometimes Catholics could be Christians. The Catholic bishop had worried at the suggestion that a Presbyterian soldier could go to heaven. Even a simple gesture of kindness and concern could be controversial. Still, the publication of Gonzaga's letter in the *Times* was an unexpected testimony to the Sisters of Mercy. In today's terms, it was good public relations.

Meanwhile, disaster was once again unfolding 300 miles away in Crimea, where the bitter cold of winter was cutting a swathe through the British army. Nightingale had an inkling of this when 500 men arrived at Scutari on 19 December. She wrote to Sidney Herbert telling him that these new patients were 'frost-bitten, demi-nude, starved, ragged'. She added a warning: 'If the troops who work in the trenches are not supplied with warm clothing, Napoleon's Russian campaign will be repeated here.'[65] It was a prophetic word. The looming crisis about to hit the hospitals of Scutari would be more serious than the aftermath of Inkerman.

2

The road to the east

By the middle of the nineteenth century all the major European powers were watching the decaying Ottoman Empire with an eye to their own interests. They were anxious about the power vacuum that would open up if the Ottoman Empire collapsed. By 1850 the sprawling domains of the Porte, the Ottoman government, had contracted significantly as component parts sheared away. The Ottoman government was increasingly focussed on its Turkish heartland, but its empire still ran from the Danube to Mecca. Often referred to as 'Turkey', this empire was important commercially. An Anglo-Ottoman commercial treaty in 1838 enabled a large expansion of trade between Britain and the Ottoman Empire. Between 1840 and 1851 British exports to the Ottoman Empire increased nearly threefold in value. The Danubian principalities alone imported more goods from Britain than Russia. A Turkish historian concludes that 'it was very important, from the financial point of view, for Britain to prevent the Ottoman Empire from falling into other hands'.[1] In addition, Britain was always keen to protect the route to India. The narrow straits leading to the Black Sea were important channels not only for Danubian trade but also for Indian overland trade via the Black Sea port of Trabzon (the Suez Canal did not open until 1869)[2]. And both France and Austria were keen to retain their growing access to Ottoman markets.[3]

There was also a long-standing fear among the European powers that Russia might break out from the Black Sea by winning control of the Dardanelles. Russia also considered itself the protector of Orthodox Christians in the Ottoman Empire, which included Palestine. Since the mid-sixteenth century, the Patriarchs of Jerusalem had been resident in Constantinople and subject to the control of the Ecumenical Patriarchate, which was highly attuned to Ottoman concerns. In 1845, Russian pressure led to the election of a Patriarch of Jerusalem who returned to his see city.[4] It was a demonstration of Russian influence in the region. In addition, there was a steady stream of pilgrims from Russia to the Holy Places. Orlando Figes says that the Holy Land seemed almost a part of Russia itself: 'The idea of "Holy Russia" was not contained by any spiritual boundaries; it was an empire of the Orthodox with sacred shrines throughout the lands of Eastern Christianity.'[5]

Since the Ottoman-French treaty of 1740, France had carved a role in the Middle East analogous to that of Russia. In this case, France saw itself as the protector of Latin rite Christians (or 'Roman Catholics') in the region, including the Holy Places of Jerusalem and Bethlehem. This involvement of a Western power in the Holy Places marked a significant internationalization of the issue.[6] France was also heavily involved in Lebanon, where it befriended the eastern rite Maronite Christians, making Lebanon a sphere of French influence and investment. Since the exile and death of Napoleon, France had tried a Bourbon restoration, an Orleanist king, a republic and now a Bonaparte Emperor again. By projecting French power and appealing to Catholic sympathies, Napoleon III hoped to consolidate his rule. There was also a great deal of French sympathy for Catholic Poland which was seen as a martyred nation, controlled and stifled by Russian domination.

In response to French pressure in January 1852, the Ottoman government reluctantly conceded certain privileges for Catholics in Jerusalem and Bethlehem. Russia resented this concession which it felt affected its unique position in Palestine, and by implication throughout the Ottoman domains. A year later, Russia demanded a clarification of its right to protect and promote the interests of Orthodox Christians. The demand was rejected. Lord Clarendon, the British foreign secretary, said that what the Russians were asking for would have enabled them 'to exercise control over fourteen millions of the subjects of the Porte, and to render the Sultan a mere vassal of the [Russian] Emperor'.[7] The spiritual affinity that Russia felt with Orthodox Christians in Ottoman territories was real, but it is also true that the powers involved were using religious communities to advance their influence in the region. Even Britain claimed guardianship of the tiny number of Protestants in the empire and pushed for their formal recognition.[8] Religion was being used to advance the national and commercial interests of both Russia and the nations of Western Europe.

In July 1853, Russian troops moved into Moldavia and Wallachia, known as the Danubian principalities, to put pressure on the Porte, but the Ottomans resisted and on 4 October declared war on Russia. On 30 November, the Russian Black Sea fleet obliterated the Turkish fleet at Sinope. There was alarm across Europe at this demonstration of Russian power in the region, and indeed some of Tsar Nicholas I's advisers were urging a quick seizure of Constantinople. Britain and France felt impelled to support the Ottomans out of strategic and economic concerns. On 27 March 1854, Britain declared war on Russia, followed by France the next day. These diplomatic and political concerns had their own legitimacy and logic to the politicians, but such manoeuvrings were a long way from the ordinary concerns of the villages and towns that would supply the soldiers for the new war.

British and French armies headed towards their new theatre of war. At first, they were stationed at Varna, where cholera and other illnesses first revealed the army's unpreparedness. The Russians withdrew from Ottoman territory, but the allies decided to continue the war by crossing the Black Sea and attacking the Russian naval base at Sebastopol. In September 1854, the allied armies moved to the Crimea in a flotilla of hundreds of ships. On 20 September, they had their first taste of victory at the Battle of the Alma.

Articles in the *Times* alerted the British public to the unpreparedness of the British army's medical system. The *Times* was the most-read newspaper in Britain at the time of the war, with a daily print order averaging 61,000 copies. Its closest rival in terms of circulation was the *Morning Advertiser* with a print run of about 6,000.[9] During the war, the *Times* would become noted for the reports from the battlefield by its war correspondent, William Russell, but it was the newspaper's political and diplomatic correspondent at Constantinople, Thomas Chenery, who first raised the alarm in Britain. Chenery's report published on 9 October spoke of 'the unhappy wounded, who have returned to die or to linger out their period of suffering within the hospitals of the capital'. Many were victims of cholera, and 'everywhere the eye encounters pale faces, forms bending with weakness, fever-stricken spectres creeping along by the support of the walls'.[10] The serious defects of army medical care were unsparingly described in the reports that followed in the *Times* over the next ten days. Chenery reported on the fetid ships carrying the wounded from Balaclava to Scutari. Injured men on board were sometimes left without medical attention for a week, desperately clutching at passing surgeons for attention, before expiring in agony. At the hospital itself, there were insufficient numbers of surgeons, no nurses or even bandages. 'The commonest appliances of a workhouse sick ward are wanting', he wrote, 'and men must die through the medical staff of the British army having forgotten that old rags are necessary for the dressing of wounds.'[11]

On 12 October, the *Times* editorial drew a contrast between its readers sitting comfortably at home and the wounded 'going through innumerable hardships'. And then it pointed out that while there were no nurses for the British troops at Scutari, 'the French are attended by some Sisters of Mercy'.[12] The next day another report compared the British unfavourably with the French: 'Their medical arrangements are extremely good, their surgeons more numerous, and they also have the help of the "Sisters of Charity", who accompany the expedition in incredible numbers. These devoted women are excellent nurses . . . We have nothing.'[13] After these reports in the press, a cry went up for nuns to care for the wounded and sick of the army.

In some ways this call for religious sisters is surprising. A large proportion of British opinion regarded nuns with suspicion, and the Catholic Church as something alien, outside the mainstream of national life. Convents were sometimes portrayed as sinister places. Even while nuns were helping the war effort by their nursing at Scutari, a campaign was under way in parliament to expose the alleged horrors of convents, and there were calls for government inspection and regulation of convents. However, there was another side to popular opinion. During the French Revolution, many priests and nuns had taken refuge in England and had been met with sympathy. After a bitter struggle, many of the legal restrictions on Catholicism were removed through Catholic emancipation in 1829. Perhaps the most important element was unspoken, namely the ancient rivalry between France and Britain. It was unthinkable that the French, through the caring ministry of nuns, had something for its army that the British did not.

The British lacuna was immediately registered on the letters page of the *Times*. An anonymous correspondent wrote of the good work of sisters among the French, adding: 'It would be well if we could learn from the Roman Catholics the art of making the comforts of religion and the ministry of charity more accessible to all. Why have we no Sisters of Charity?'[14] In the *Guardian*, Earl Nelson urged the heads of Church of England sisterhoods 'to spare one or two sisters each for nursing in the Crimea'.[15] Lord Nelson's appeal was disingenuous. He knew that it could hardly be refused. After all, he was a sponsor of the Park Village Sisterhood, the first Anglican sisterhood, and supported it financially. On 18 October the *Times* editorial again reminded its readers that the wounded and sick French enjoyed the ministrations of Sisters of Charity, 'while we have nothing'.[16] Moves were already underway to recruit the nuns who would answer the call.

The phrase 'religious life' is sometimes used with a specific meaning, that is, life, in community under vows. In this sense, religious life had been followed by Catholic and Eastern Orthodox women and men for over 1,000 years. The traditional emphasis was on prayer and the interior life, usually accompanied by some degree of self-sufficiency in food production or other necessities. Catholic nuns in solemn vows lived within an enclosure and would rely on lay sisters to undertake the more menial chores and interact with the outside world. From the thirteenth century onwards there were attempts to create communities of women who could minister outside the enclosure. These moves were resisted by popes who declared that solemn vows and strict enclosure were essential to communities of religious women. Then in 1749, Pope Benedict XIV issued the decree *Quamvis Iusto*. This allowed women to live in community under simple vows with permission from the local bishop, who retained ultimate authority. Despite this recognition, they were still not officially religious sisters in the eyes of the Roman authorities, but in the nineteenth century more and more of these communities were founded. They looked like nuns, they lived like nuns and they took their work into the wider community. Ambiguity remained about their status until 1900 when Pope Leo XIII issued an apostolic constitution *Conditae a Christo*, which gave full recognition to religious sisters in simple vows.[17] The Vatican was recognizing what women had already made a reality.

After 1598, English Catholic religious life had continued in exile on the Continent, where a network of twenty-two convents continued to attract vocations from England, at a time when the public practice of Catholicism was proscribed.[18] These communities were often highly educated women who were well informed about the world outside. English Protestant travellers visiting these convents sometimes surprised themselves by coming away with a more positive attitude to life there. For instance, Tonya Moutray says that Hester Thrale Polizzi's travel narratives convey how 'the comfortable, social and even literary environment' within these communities impressed her, although like other travellers she was highly critical of the more strictly enclosed convents.[19] In the wake of the French Revolution, the majority of these communities returned to England and had a more sympathetic reception. They continued to attract vocations, but the main growth came from a new and very different development in religious life.

The nineteenth century was unique in religious life because of the number of new foundations made by women.[20] Many of the nuns of these new communities lived and worked among the urban poor. By 1900 there were approximately ninety different congregations of nuns at work in Britain, eleven of them founded in Britain itself to provide teaching, nursing and pastoral care.[21] These active religious women were recognized as sisters in simple vows, which distinguished them from nuns in enclosed convents who were in solemn vows. The Sisters of Mercy from the convent at Bermondsey who went out to Scutari were part of the rapid growth in religious life in the nineteenth century. Around their convent, the poverty must have seemed relentless. The adjacent docks provided hard and often dangerous work unloading the ships, but this work was irregular, making it difficult for the stevedores to earn a living. Bermondsey also housed many noxious industries, especially tanneries, and the air reeked with evil smells.[22] Housing was cramped and sometimes dark, as the crowded tenements were built ever higher. Often there was an average of five people in a room.[23] The Sisters of Mercy from the convent visited and encouraged, and helped alleviate the poverty where they could. The suffering they encountered at Scutari was not their first experience of human distress.

The eight Anglican sisters came from two communities, one originally from Park Village near Regents Park in London, the other from Devonport in Plymouth. The Park Village Sisterhood was established in 1845 and was the first post-Reformation community for religious sisters in the Church of England. Devonport opened three years later in 1848. These communities were a new and still fragile development in the Church of England. Given this newness, coming to the Crimean army hospitals was a venture of great courage. The Catholic sisters knew that they could draw on the institutional strength and solidarity of their church, but in the Church of England, nuns were regarded as an anomaly.

That there were any Anglican sisters at all at Scutari was extraordinary. The new communities of Anglican sisters were not universally welcomed in their own church. The destruction of England's religious orders in the Reformation not only removed monks and nuns from the Church of England, but also put their whole way of life under suspicion. There was opposition on the grounds that nuns and their promoters were a Romanizing influence and undermined the reformed nature of the Church of England. But there was also suspicion that religious life was inherently unhealthy for women, who were deemed prone to emotionalism or exploitation by controlling priests. Samuel Wilberforce, the bishop of Oxford, was one of the few bishops who were sympathetic to the restoration of religious communities. Even he, however, worried about what he called in 1854 'its development of self-consciousness and morbid religious affection . . . its un-English tone'.[24]

Wider cultural movements encouraged the development of Anglican religious life. In the first half of the nineteenth century the Romantic movement had opened what Isaiah Berlin called 'a new and restless spirit . . . a longing for the unbounded and indefinable . . . an effort to return to the forgotten sources of life'.[25] In religion it became respectable once more to have strong feelings allied to a sense of quest, searching for truth accessed in signs and mystery. One result was a renewed interest in England's medieval past which some regarded as a resource which could re-enchant a world robbed of beauty by the grim realities of commerce and industry. At the same time, from the 1830s onwards there was a movement in the Church of England to assert the church's innate authority, seen as deriving not from the state but from its own ancient roots. The High Church party looked to the first centuries of Christianity for authenticity. The more recent Tractarian movement stressed the continuity of the Church of England with the pre-Reformation church. Both could justify the establishment of religious communities for women by appealing to the past.

For women of faith, education and energy there was little they could do in the Church of England beyond visiting the poor. This combination of ability to seek an outlet, together with the mystical and ascetical impulse, brought increasing numbers of Anglican women into the fledgling convents of the mid-nineteenth century where they could carve out a new role for themselves. By 1900 more than 100 distinct communities had been created in the Church of England, and their sisters were a familiar sight in many parishes.[26]

As secretary of state at war, Sidney Herbert was aware of the rising clamour for nurses to help in the army hospitals at Scutari. On 15 October 1854, he wrote to Nightingale asking her to lead a party of nurses to the army hospitals there. He admitted that until then only men had been allowed to care for patients in military hospitals, but now it was time for female nurses:

> No military reason exists against the introduction, & I am confident they might be introduced with great benefit, for Hospital orderlies must be very rough hands, & most of them, on such an occasion as this, very inexperienced ones.... The difficulty of finding women equal to a task after all full of horror, requiring besides knowledge & goodwill, great energy, & great courage, will be great.[27]

Even then, he had to ask that she obtain the permission of her parents. Nightingale had already been wondering about leading out a small group privately and seized the hour.

Thomas Grant, the Catholic bishop of Southwark, had also noted the call for nuns to go to army hospitals in the eastern theatre of war and he acted quickly. Grant came from an army background: he had been born in France in 1816 where his father was serving as a sergeant in the 71st Highland Regiment. As the son of a military family, he had ready sympathy for soldiers. As a bishop, he was also alert to the need to protect and improve the public image of the Catholic Church. At a time of prejudice against Catholics, the witness of nursing sisters could be a good influence on public opinion. On Saturday, 14 October, after hearing the sisters' confessions at the Sisters of Mercy convent in Bermondsey, he surprised Clare Moore by asking for the sisters 'to go and nurse the sick and wounded soldiers'. When Moore told the sisters of his request she found no shortage of volunteers.[28] Grant had already proposed sending nuns to Sidney Herbert at the War Office and received a positive response. He was still negotiating the details when Clare Moore and four sisters departed for Paris on 17 October, ahead even of Nightingale. Bishop Grant's haste to seize the moment is striking. He may have anticipated an anti-Catholic backlash among the public that would force the government to change its mind. As one biographer of Nightingale notes, the public image of the French nursing sisters was a vague and idealized one. Few people in England had met a nun or knew much about their way of life. The reality of Catholic nuns having access to wounded soldiers 'came as a shock to many in England'.[29]

Luckily for Bishop Grant, his negotiations with Sidney Herbert concluded successfully. Grant wrote to Moore and the sisters, who were now waiting in Paris for Florence Nightingale's group to arrive. The agreement reached was that Nightingale would manage their duties as nurses. In matters of religion, they would be under their own superior. The sisters would be free to speak words of faith to Catholic patients but should not initiate religious conversations with others. In the same letter to the nuns, Grant spoke of how their witness could help overcome hostility towards Catholics. After commending the sisters to the Virgin Mary, he added:

> You must ask her to make you good nurses, that it may be seen how earnest and charitable Nuns are, and how much they excel all other Nurses. Tell the Sisters to take their will into their work and not to be afraid of wounds to death, and to help the sick in every way. You will disarm prejudice by your zeal and charity, and you will help many to die in peace.[30]

After Nightingale and her party of nurses caught up with the nuns in Paris they travelled together via Lyons to Marseilles, where they boarded the *Vectis* for the voyage to Constantinople.

The Anglican nuns were among those who set out with Nightingale. Mother Lydia Sellon, the superior of the Devonport sisters, had read Lord Nelson's appeal for Church of England sisters to nurse the soldiers. She went up from Plymouth to London to meet Nightingale who accepted an offer of eight Anglican sisters. Sellon then visited the Park Village Sisterhood and recruited three from there, to add to another five from her own group.[31] Sellon sent telegrams assembling her five from Plymouth and Bristol. Margaret Goodman remembered that on the evening of 19 October, she was startled 'by a violent ringing of the doorbell'. She found a carriage outside. Its driver handed her a telegram. It tersely instructed her, 'Let nothing prevent your reaching London by tomorrow morning.' The next day she and seven others assembled at St Saviour's Osnaburgh St, the home of the Park Village Sisterhood, where Mother Lydia asked them if they would go to Constantinople to nurse the Crimean War wounded. She was candid. It was a particularly dangerous assignment, and she would not be surprised if they declined.[32] They all agreed to go. Mother Emma Langston of the Park Village sisters was put in charge. It was a diplomatic balancing act by Sellon. The two communities had not formally merged, although it was generally accepted that Sellon would become the superior of both in due course.

Discussions about the assignment went on late into the night, leaving the sisters with little sleep before they were summoned the next day to 49 Belgrave Square, SW1, the home of Sidney and Mary Herbert. There they met Florence Nightingale. Sarah Terrot of the Anglicans recorded, 'From the first moment I felt an impulse to love, trust and respect her. Her appearance and manner impressed me, with a sense of goodness and wisdom, of high mental powers highly cultivated and devoted to highest ends.'[33] This high praise was later modified when she experienced Nightingale's strength of will. Sidney Herbert gave the whole group a rousing address, in which he spoke some words specifically intended for the nuns. He was keenly aware of the controversy that would follow his decision to send out religious sisters, so he stressed that they must avoid religious proselytizing: 'Keep yourselves to the objects for which alone the government sends you out: administering to the bodily wants, and soothing the minds of the sick.' They had to sign individually a document laying out their conditions of service, including a stipulation that they should be reserved in matters of religion. He urged modesty and propriety and warned them that they would face hardship. Herbert ended by thanking them for taking on a difficult role.[34]

Mother Lydia Sellon had her own words of exhortation for her sisters. She told them to speak soothingly to the patients but be reserved and courteous at the same time, stay neat and clean, and exercise self-control under pressure. She lifted from them any need to observe the traditional periods of fasting. 'When you are attending to the wounds of the soldiers, try and think of the wounds of our Lord. Keep calm, as before the foot of His cross, and remember that you are doing all things in Him.' This incarnational theology, with its emphasis on seeing Christ in others, was shared by both Anglican and Catholic sisters. But then in a strange afterthought, she added, 'You will be greatly watched, and remember that on me will fall the consequences of little indiscretions on your part'.[35] These words betrayed her anxiety. Only six years previously she had started, with no prior experience, a convent of Anglican nuns. If her sisters in the war zone stumbled or failed, then the critics would say that they were vindicated and that there was no place for vowed and veiled women in the Church of England. The following day, Sunday, 22 October, the Anglican nuns went for communion at St Mary Magdalene, Munster Square. On Monday they were on their way to Scutari and the Crimean War.

The nurses in this first wave fell into three groups.

- There were eighteen nuns, ten of them Catholic and eight Anglican. Of the ten Catholic nuns, five were Sisters of Mercy, and five came from the Convent of the Faithful Virgin at Norwood.
- Another six nurses came from St John's House in London, one of the first schemes for professional training of nurses.
- And fourteen nurses were from open recruitment, having responded to an advertisement seeking women with experience in nursing to go out with the others to Scutari, where they would be paid for their work.

Nurse training was in its infancy. Nursing itself was widely regarded as low-status work. Helmstadter describes British nurses in 1854 as basically 'charwomen who also attended to the wants of bedridden patients, and in less important cases made and applied poultices'.[36] Yet nursing was entering a period of transformation as it moved towards a more professional basis. Some doctors in hospitals like St Thomas's in London understood the difference that good nursing could make, and worked with women of ability who were interested in learning more. In 1840 Elizabeth Fry had started an Institution of Nursing Sisters, with a three-month period of training at London teaching hospitals.[37] In 1848 St John's House in Fitzroy Square London W1 began its own programme of nurse training. It kept the distinction between ladies, who maintained their social class by regarding their work as a voluntary charity, and working-class women, who were paid.[38] Its programme lasted two years or more and offered intensive training in nursing and hospital management, including lectures given by physicians.[39] These developments were still in their infancy and progress towards nursing professionalism was slow.

Women did not nurse in military hospitals, where the care of patients was in the hands of orderlies, usually men seconded for the duty with no training.

Until the Crimean War brought a change of mind, the idea of women nursing in British army hospitals was unthinkable. It was assumed that the sights and sounds they would encounter would be too much for them to bear, and the soldiers too primitive in their manners. The whole idea seemed strange. Lieutenant Richard Godman of the 5th Dragoon Guards, hearing of the arrival of Nightingale's party at Scutari, wrote: 'I think ladies are very much out of place as hospital nurses, however kind their intentions may be; it is better left in other hands. I must say I should not like a lady to attend me if I knew it. I look upon it as a sort of fanaticism.'[40]

Although St John's House was a Church of England foundation, its sisters were not nuns. They could be married or single, keep their own property and live in their own homes. Hence, they have not been treated as nuns in this book. Eventually, in a long and complicated history, St John's House did become an Anglican sisterhood, the Nursing Sisters of St John the Divine. This sisterhood established clinics and hospitals in London's East End and was the institution behind the television series *Call the Midwife*.[41]

Despite a flood of volunteers, it was not easy for Nightingale to find able, reliable and experienced women to accompany her as nurses to Scutari. Some who put themselves forward were widows or servants who could not make a living in any other way. Excessive drinking was a problem for many nurses and contributed to their low status.[42] Nightingale knew that she could rely on the Anglican and Catholic nuns because they came from a structured, well-ordered community life. Many had acquired some experience in nursing during cholera outbreaks in the teeming slums. Beyond them, however, she needed more hands, which required a selection process. Nightingale entrusted this to her sister Parthenope and three friends: Selina Bracebridge, Mary Herbert (wife of Sidney) and Mary Stanley. Selina and Parthenope found it a dispiriting process. Nightingale was looking for women with the dedication and knowledge that she had found in the Deaconess institution at Kaiserswerth, and in the Maison de la Providence in Paris of the Sisters of Charity, where she had studied the theory and practice of nursing. It seemed instead that some of those who offered their services were looking for a bit of adventure and a soldier husband. Others were barely literate or had rough manners. Many were attracted by the pay more than anything else. But, as Anne Summers points out, 'Working women who had a secure livelihood were not very likely to sacrifice it for dangerous employment of uncertain duration.'[43] There was a rough and ready element in these nurses who had been found through open recruitment. For many of them, their lives had been hard and the Victorian class system unforgiving.

The second party that went out, led by Mary Stanley, brought a total of forty-eight more women. Among them were fifteen nuns, all of them Sisters of Mercy, eleven from convents in Ireland and four from convents in England (for convenience they will sometimes be referred to in this book as Irish sisters). There were also twenty-four paid nurses and nine ladies. The latter were women considered to be of a higher class, who came out on their own recognizances.

Before they left London, Dr Manning had written a careful letter of advice and encouragement to this second group of Sisters of Mercy. He said that they might face 'the slights and injustice of adversaries, the rudeness and censure of many who are good in many ways'. It was an allusion to possible Protestant opposition. Manning, like Sellon, gave a strong message that their nursing work did not take them away from Christ but in fact brought them to Christ: 'God is able to make the hospital a cloister and your own heart a choir. . . . If you leave Him in the silence of your convent, it is to find Him by the bedside of the wounded. You leave Christ, for Christ, and wheresoever you go for His sake, he will be with you.'[44] The Stanley party left London on 2 December and arrived at Constantinople on 17 December on the *Egypt* via Marseilles. Mary Stanley was the leader of the party as a whole, but Francis Bridgeman was very much in charge of her nuns. Bridgeman had a strong sense of the dignity of their vocation, which included the maintenance of class distinctions. She was doubtful that it would be possible 'to raise the moral character of the nurses by placing them on an equality with the ladies'. On board the ship from Marseilles she was shocked to find that most of the nuns would have to travel second class, along with the paid nurses. She complained about 'the evil consequences of being thrown thus into domestic contact with this class of people'. On the first day when they sat down to dinner 'a crowd of coarse men rushed in and sat down without ceremony'. Mother Francis Bridgeman signalled to her sisters to retire to their sleeping quarters rather than eat under such circumstances.[45] This sense of the dignity of her sisters must have made their chilly reception by Florence Nightingale all the more painful after the *Egypt* reached Constantinople.

Information about their arrival was sent up to Barrack Hospital and they waited. Eventually, Charles Bracebridge came to the ship from Scutari on behalf of Nightingale. He bore the unwelcome message that in her view the War Office had misunderstood the situation. Mary Stanley, her ladies, her nurses and her nuns were superfluous. Their services were not required and there was no accommodation for them. Two emissaries, a doctor and an MP were then sent from the boat to ask Nightingale to change her mind, but she was adamant. There was no place for this new and unexpected party.

'This was an indescribable shock to us all', Bridgeman wrote later.[46] The news angered and bewildered her. They had answered an urgent call to help sick and wounded soldiers. The British government had encouraged them and authorized their going out. Negotiations to this effect had been handled on their behalf by Dr Manning and therefore had the approbation of the highest levels in the Catholic Church. Now they were being told that there was no place for them in the hospitals under Florence Nightingale. Nightingale had not suggested that they go back, but for the moment Mary Stanley's party was left in limbo. Bridgeman acted to preserve the distinctness of her sisters. Accommodation had been found for lay members of Mary Stanley's group along the coast at Therapia, where a villa belonging to the British embassy had been put at their disposal. Bridgeman and the Sisters of Mercy went to stay with the Sisters of Charity at Galata. However, although the Irish sisters were made welcome they were in an uncomfortable situation. To accommodate them the Galata sisters had to suspend their small day school, a major source of income. Tensions must have developed. In Bridgeman's words, 'our position became extremely unpleasant'.[47] She realized that somehow she would have to come to an arrangement with Nightingale.

Francis Bridgeman had a strong personality. She has been called 'charismatic'.[48] This ability to inspire, plus energy and a sense of vision made her a natural leader. Francis Bridgeman was also proud, with a tendency to imperiousness. As we have seen, she had a keen sense of propriety, careful to guard the dignity of her sisters and their social standing. When seeking sisters to volunteer, the Mother Superior of the Dublin convent had written, 'The eyes of the world will be on the poor nuns.'[49] Bridgeman and her sisters had left Ireland in a blaze of publicity and goodwill, with coverage which the *Times* picked up from Irish papers. The *Cork Reporter* considered the commissioning of the sisters to be 'a proud testimony in favour of our conventual institutions'.[50] The *Galway Packet* reported 'an immense concourse of people' at the railway station to bid their nuns farewell, the men all raising their hats in respect as the train pulled out.[51] It was the same when the sisters left Kingstown on the ferry for Holyhead. Aloysius Doyle recorded, 'There are great crowds to see us off, Sisters of Mercy *en route* for the seat of war, and then, as the vessel moved off, a fervent "God Speed You" arose in one loud cry.'[52] Later, when the final eight sisters were summoned to join the others already assembled in London, the *Cork Reporter* described 'the enthusiastic joy of the good sisters . . . on their mission of mercy, although well aware of the hardships and privations they will have to endure'.[53] It would have been an unthinkable humiliation for the sisters to return having accomplished nothing. There was also the wider social situation to consider. A large proportion of the soldiers in the British army were Irish. Poverty in Ireland provided a fruitful recruiting ground. The Bridgeman party was well aware of this, and the Sisters of Mercy from Ireland keenly anticipated a caring ministry among their fellow Irish.

Nightingale wrote a wrathful letter to Herbert, reminding him that nurses were to be sent out only when she requested them. It had been difficult enough getting good order into the initial group of nurses, and winning the trust of the doctors, who repeatedly told her that 'more women cannot be usefully employed'. She waxed bitter: 'You have sacrificed the cause so near my heart. You have sacrificed me, a matter of small importance now.'[54] Another letter to Herbert on Christmas Day showed no lessening in emotion. 'We have not the slightest doubt that this woman [Bridgeman] not only intends to turn our house out of windows, but to trample upon and disperse the ruins when out.' Bridgeman, she said, 'is obviously come out with a *religious* view – not to serve the sick, but to found a convent, completely mistaking the purpose of our mission'.[55] The strength of feeling shown by Nightingale to a government minister was only possible in the context of their long friendship. The extremity of her language might reflect her exhaustion. For several weeks now she had been working up to twenty hours a day. But it also reveals her fears. Nursing, its reform and professionalization, had been her lifetime ambition. Now, given this opportunity, she was concerned that religious tensions could undermine everything that she was trying to achieve.

Nightingale worried about the religious balance. The arrival of fifteen Catholic nuns added to the ten originally present could have provoked suspicion among those who suspected a Catholic plot. She also feared that Bridgeman wanted to establish a local convent, which would give her a degree of autonomy at odds with Nightingale's leadership. Her fears were not unfounded. Back in London, before sending the Bridgeman party out, Manning had noticed Bridgeman's spiritual ambitions when he experienced her zealousness. He told Bishop Thomas Grant that at a meeting with Bridgeman he found her 'full of difficulties'. She had insisted that a chaplain travel with them. Manning demurred, but she insisted 'with some heat'. Manning stood his ground and was on the point of replacing the Irish Sisters of Mercy with others when Bridgeman gave in. 'I have my fears' he wrote, 'She is zealous, ardent, resolute, but very quick and I fear not controlled enough for the difficulties at Scutari.'[56] Behind this relatively trivial point about a chaplain lay Manning's apprehension that the Irish Sisters of Mercy saw themselves as a distinct unit, negotiating with the authorities on their own terms.

Eventually Nightingale asked Bridgeman to meet her at Barrack Hospital on 22 December. The plan was that five of Bridgeman's sisters would be under Nightingale's managerial authority as nurses, but under the spiritual authority of Clare Moore as nuns. Bridgeman declined the offer. She was determined that her sisters would remain under her authority alone. She maintained that she had been given this authority by her ecclesiastical superiors, and could not cede it to anyone else. But there was another factor at work. She had seen the living conditions of her fellow Sisters of Mercy at Scutari and was appalled at their spartan poverty. The sisters in the Bermondsey group were, she later reported 'all soiled and neglected looking'. At that point, their cramped accommodation was still shared with the Norwood nuns, with only 'a soiled white calico screen hung in the centre' to divide the two communities. The untidy room was near 'a thoroughfare of dirt and confusion'. Bridgeman even complained about the scanty fare of the lunch she shared with Nightingale.[57]

These were extraordinary statements for a religious superior to make about sisters of her own order. They were the more surprising given the Rule of the Sisters of Mercy told them to imitate the poverty of Christ, homeless and ultimately naked on the cross. The Rule also said they should be content with the food and clothing given to them.[58] It seems strange then that Francis Bridgeman looked disdainfully at sisters from her own congregation because they were living in actual poverty out of necessity. Bridgeman seemed to have little understanding of the pressure on the nuns as they nursed at Scutari, and the conditions they necessarily endured out of a desire to nurse the men.

A compromise had to be found. Bridgeman's position was weakened when the patience of her hosts at Galata ran out, and the Irish Sisters of Mercy had to join the rest of the Mary Stanley group at Therapia. Nightingale asked Moore to negotiate with Bridgeman. On 6 January 1855, Moore was rowed in an open boat in a snowstorm to meet Francis Bridgeman at Therapia, where an agreement was reached. Mother Francis and four of her sisters would nurse at General Hospital, Scutari and would share the accommodation of the Bermondsey sisters at Barrack Hospital. The remainder of Bridgeman's sisters would remain at Therapia until something else was found for them. Frustrated at not having any way to fulfil their mission, they offered up novenas and hid religious medals in buildings they thought might be assigned to them as a base for their nursing.[59]

The earlier dismissal of the Norwood nuns was evidence, in Catholic eyes, of Nightingale's anti-Catholic bias, despite the fact that their departure made limited room for Bridgeman's party. Two priests visited Nightingale and told her that the dismissal of the Norwood nuns was 'an affront to Catholicism'.[60] One of the priests said her conduct was like King Herod causing the Virgin Mary to flee across the desert.[61] Now Nightingale's dour response to Bridgeman seemed to confirm to the priests that she was anti-Catholic and not to be trusted. The chaplains turned on the Bermondsey nuns, who they knew supported Nightingale. One of the priests even used the sacrament of confession for partisan purposes. When the Bermondsey sisters went to him for confession he 'harassed their minds – suggested dangers at every step'. Clare Moore remembered, 'the good Priests attributing . . . unkind motives on the part of Miss Nightingale, [they] expressed their displeasure loudly & condemned our Sisters with her.'[62]

The Bridgeman sisters were assigned a Jesuit priest, Fr William Ronan, as their chaplain, 'a fine, strong young priest', noted Aloysius Doyle, 'and also cheerful and good'.[63] With the self-assurance of a young priest, he decided that Clare Moore was a deleterious influence. Writing to the archbishop of Dublin he declared: 'Miss Nightingale is easily dealt with if she had no evil advisers. Mrs Moore is one of those.' He further complained that Moore was supported by an English priest.[64] This occasional tension between the English and Irish Catholic contingents was never resolved throughout the war. Nightingale said that the situation was developing into 'a Roman Catholic storm' and began referring to Bridgeman as 'Brickbat' and her sisters as 'the Brickbats'.[65]

Mother Clare Moore quietly resisted the attempted manipulation by the priests, which was an abuse of the sacrament of confession. She and her sisters had shared the gruelling first two months at Scutari with Nightingale, and would not abandon their quiet support of her. They knew what challenges they had faced together. The English sisters did not scheme or agitate on behalf of Nightingale. They simply refused to be involved in any campaign against her. Nightingale was aware of this and wrote to Herbert that they were 'the truest Christians I ever met with – invaluable in their work – devoted, heart and head, to serve God and mankind – not to intrigue for their church'.[66] A very different perspective developed within the communal memory of the Irish Sisters of Mercy. Their tradition held that the sisters led by Clare Moore were tainted by their co-operation with Nightingale. A century later the Mercy historian, Evelyn Bolster, accused Moore of 'unfriendliness' towards Bridgeman. She attributed this to Moore being 'so well established in [Nightingale's] good graces that she seemed to have resented sharing the "privilege" with any other'.[67] Bolster offered no evidence for this. In fact, any chilliness would seem to have emanated from Bridgeman with her distaste for the poor living conditions accepted by Moore and her sisters. A legacy of bitterness was forming.

In standing their ground, both Moore and Bridgeman displayed formidable strength of character. Despite their differences, it could be argued that both superiors were drawing upon the spiritual tradition of the Sisters of Mercy. The congregation was still young, the first sisters having made their professions in 1831. The congregation began in poverty and obscurity, but grew quickly and would continue to do so for a century and a half. This owed a great deal to the leadership of its founder, Catherine McAuley. Mary Sullivan, the historian of the Sisters of Mercy, notes that when McAuley composed the rule of the congregation, it was 'a conscious though indirect affirmation of women and of their mature capacities . . . she would not treat her sisters as children'. The tradition of the religious life for women had sometimes inculcated an 'unthinking submissiveness to others . . . and self-denigrating assessment of oneself'.[68] By contrast, McCauley encouraged humility in the sense of transparency, openness and honesty before God and others. She saw Christ as the pattern of this, and, as Sullivan puts it, humility, therefore 'could not be a matter of always deferring to the judgment of others'.[69]

By the end of January 1855, five sisters led by Moore were working willingly in the hospitals under Nightingale. Another five led by Bridgeman worked reluctantly and shared the accommodation at Barrack Hospital. Ten more of the Irish Sisters waited across the Bosphorus and prayed for a better outcome. The five remaining Anglican nuns worked well with Nightingale though they were depressed, and missed the companionship of the three who had been sent back to England.

All parties were operating in unfamiliar horizons, moving between the world of the British army on the one hand and the alien unfamiliarity of Turkey on the other. Tensions easily flared and disagreements could become exaggerated. The ripple effects of this controversy carried on and would haunt Nightingale, distracting her at intervals over the next eighteen months. Bridgeman would not only outwit Nightingale but would also quickly establish herself as an alternative pole of nursing power. Soon their leadership would be tested further when winter broke on the Crimea in all its fierceness.

3

Winter ordeal

As the end of 1854 approached the nuns who accompanied Nightingale were entitled to a sigh of relief. Together with the other nurses, they had made a vital contribution to the hospital as the Inkerman wounded arrived. They had also managed to survive the rigours of poor food and indifferent accommodation. In early December, the *Manchester Guardian* reported that 'The hospital department is now in a state of great efficiency, and the nurses and Sisters of Mercy sent out have been found extremely valuable.'[1] This alleged efficiency of the hospital was about to be put to the test.

The deteriorating health of the army owed much to a lack of supplies. The purveying department was badly organized. Initially purveying was handled by the Commissariat, which came under the aegis of the Treasury rather than the War Office, which ensured a degree of civilian control over the military. What had worked in the Napoleonic Wars no longer worked in the Crimean War, and in December 1854 Sidney Herbert put the Commissariat under War Office. The Commissariat operated in layers of forms, following a strict and unimaginative system that failed to comprehend the urgency of the situation. It did not help that Lord Raglan, the army commander in Crimea, resisted pressure to replace Lord Estcourt, his adjutant general, and Lord Airey, quartermaster-general.[2] As the war progressed, cumbersome administrative requirements would result in needless deaths.[3] Even simple requisitions could require a lengthy form in duplicate that then had to be countersigned by someone else 300 miles away.[4] Evidence to the Hospitals Commission gave many examples of the ineptitude of the purveyors. Purveyors would tell the inquiry that particular items were not available, but, on conducting an inspection, the commissioners would find those very items in the army stores.[5] Similarly, Florence Nightingale would be told by the purveyor that something necessary could not be obtained locally, whereupon she would go out that same day and buy it herself.[6] Men fell ill from scurvy in the Crimea because of a lack of vegetables. Hearing of this Lord Stratford sent up a boatload from Constantinople, but because the vegetables were not included in the daily rations neither the quartermaster-general nor the Commissariat would issue them, and they were tipped into Balaclava harbour instead.[7] A fierce storm in the Black Sea on 14 November 1854 worsened the situation. Over twenty British ships sank, including the *Prince* which was carrying medical supplies and enough winter coats and boots for 40,000 men.[8]

Even when supplies arrived there were problems with transport. Until a railway was constructed in late March there was only one muddy track from the harbour at Balaclava up to the plateau, where most of the troops were stationed. Provisions could not be brought up in sufficient quantity and were often left rotting on the harbour quays. The *Times* noted in January that within 8 miles of the soldiers there could be found 'clothes, food, material for house-building, fuel, and many other comforts; but the soldiers have been in rags, have been placed on half-rations, have been reduced to burrow in the ground for shelter'. The paper blamed 'our incurable national self-complacency'.[9] The French were much better supplied from their own harbour at Kamiesh. Sometimes hungry British soldiers begged the French to give them the dregs of their mess tins.[10]

Frostbite was soon added to the army's miseries as the Crimean winter grew fiercer. The men were housed in tents which offered little protection from the howling wind. They had no spare clothing and would lie down to rest in the wet clothes in which they had stood guard for hours. George Bell, an officer with the 1st Battalion of the Royal Regiment, wrote in his diary, 'They go down to the trenches wet, come back wet, go into the hospital tents wet, die the same night and are buried in their wet blankets the next morning! Nine of my good men lay stretched and dead this morning outside one tent.'[11] Gales blew a fine, drifting snow that penetrated into the tents. In January it covered the ground to a depth of 3 feet, rising to 5 or 6 feet in the drifts, and the temperature would drop at night to well below freezing. On a few occasions, sentries were found frozen to death at their posts or died soon after.[12] A hard frost and snow in January meant that even men sheltering in their tents could be found dead in the morning. Two doctors died in this way.[13]

Seriously ill men needed to be evacuated from the Crimea to the hospitals at Scutari, but transport was part of the problem. Between 600 and 1,200 men at a time would have to wait on the beach at Balaclava, exposed to foul weather. They would then be put on board vessels that were badly overcrowded. Although the sea journey was only a few days, the time from embarkation to disembarkation could stretch to two or even three weeks.[14] The process of putting injured men on and taking them off was slow: the anchorage at Constantinople was crowded, and the wharf at Scutari unusable in windy weather. Not surprisingly, mortality on the journey was high. Samuel Wells of the Coldstream Guards told the Hospitals Commission that after his arm was amputated (without chloroform) he was put on a ship that spent four or five days in Balaclava harbour, followed by another two weeks at sea before disembarking. The men had to lie on the bare planks of the deck. 'The air was very foul at night . . . owing to so many men having diarrhoea and lying so close.' Of 227 on board his ship, 23 died en route to Scutari.[15] George Bell wrote: 'Soldiers are sent from the Balaclava Hospital in shiploads, to die at Scutari. Hundreds are thrown into the Black Sea.'[16] A soldier of the Rifles invalided to Scutari on the *Orinoco* wrote that of 300 wounded on board, 120 died on route. He described the journey as worse than the slave trade.[17]

This was the background to the winter crisis facing Nightingale, her nuns and the other nurses. The situation rapidly became alarming. Not only were the patients already seriously ill when they were admitted, but the hospital itself became badly overcrowded. From mid-December 1854 to mid-January 1855, Barrack Hospital could reasonably accommodate a daily average of around 1,600 patients. In fact, it held a daily average of around 2,200.[18] Such was the fear of cholera that the spirits of the men sank. Margaret Goodman noted that normally patients who were able to leave their beds would gather in groups for conversation. By contrast, 'during the continuance of the cholera, the buzz of voices was entirely hushed, and an oppressive and death-like stillness pervaded the whole of that immense building.'[19]

That winter was a harrowing time for the nurses. Sarah Anne Terrot of the Anglican sisters remembered that things changed towards the end of December 1854. Some of the wounded patients were sent home or back to the ranks, to make room for sick and dying men, whose death rapidly made way for others again. A bed could fill and empty several times in a week. The soldiers admitted were now 'in a very bad state – some dying, some in a state of filth no words can describe, miserable skeletons devoured by lice'. Several of them died within an hour of their arrival, some never spoke. Asked by orderlies to bathe a skeletal young man they had left on the ground Terrot 'could hardly believe the thing lying on the ground was a human being, much less a man still young'.[20] One evening she was asked to sit up with eight seriously ill patients. Before the night was over, all were dead.[21] Another Anglican sister, Margaret Goodman, noted that in one bed twenty successive occupants died.[22]

In a time before antibiotics, there was little that could be done for patients with bowel infections or cholera. The importance of oral rehydration was not realized, and this was before the invention of the intravenous method. Most of the active nursing at hospitals like Scutari was aimed at relieving the symptoms and keeping the patients clean after the repeated loss of bowel control. Patients with bowel disease would often experience terrible stomach pains or muscular cramps that made their limbs rigid. Doctors ordered poultices of mustard, and also 'stuping'. For the latter, a square piece of blanket would be sewn up at each end so as to allow a stick to be inserted. The cloth would be dipped into a large tub of boiling water, taken out with tongs and then all the water wrung out. A preparation of chloroform would be sprinkled onto the blanket, which by now would be tolerably hot, and applied to the patient's stomach. The patient would also be given a spoonful of brandy and a piece of ice in hope of settling the stomach or muscular cramps. Other remedies involved rubbing the stomach with mustard or turpentine. But, noted Aloysius Doyle sadly, 'cholera is proof against all. Rarely, very rarely, anyone got over it.'[23] In fact, their labours were not entirely in vain, because 40 per cent of those admitted with cholera to Crimean War army hospitals survived.[24] It must have been sweaty, tiring work for the Sisters of Mercy in their thick serge habits, who also had to cope with the frustration and distress of seeing so many men die despite their best efforts. Nobody knew that the treatment, by making the men perspire, might have worsened their dehydration and hastened their end.

Soon bowel diseases were overtaken by the ravages of frostbite. When they left Britain or Ireland the sisters could hardly have imagined the scenes they now witnessed daily. An army surgeon, Henry Bellow described a group of casualties arriving at Scutari as covered in grime and dried faeces and alive with vermin. 'One poor fellow had lost both feet by frostbite; another had lost the fingers of both hands. . . . In all these cases the gangrene is far advanced and the whole air of the hospital is tainted with a dreadful stench.'[25] Frostbite could affect ears, toes, fingers or feet. When the affected part of the body thawed out, mortification was likely to set in, followed by a slow rotting of the part affected. 'Great numbers now came in dying', recorded Sarah Terrot, 'some rallied for a little, and then sunk suddenly, their feet turning black sometime before death; others never rallied, but sank at once'.[26] The pain could be excruciating. Amputation to stop the necrosis was one of the few treatments that worked, provided the patient survived the amputation and its aftereffects.

The help given by nurses could mean further, unavoidable pain. One of Bridgeman's sisters wrote home to Ireland saying that sick men were coming in constantly from the area around Sevastopol: 'They suffer beyond description from the cold and frost; their feet are sometimes in such a state that in the attempt to remove their boots parts of their feet remain in them.'[27] This was not hyperbole. Florence Nightingale wrote in February 1855 to a schoolboy who had, it seems, had sent her a jingoistic letter:

> If you could see the feet of one poor frostbitten soldier, the flesh dropping from the bones and the rest black and broken to be cut and sawn off, you would prefer mercy and benevolence to honour and valour. . . . Some are unconscious, worn out and weary, and stretch out their hands and say 'Sister', the last word – and then they move no more and have no more pain.[28]

In one of the attempted cures, large linseed meal poultices could be placed over the whole foot and ankle. But sometimes when the poultices were removed pieces of decayed flesh, and even toes were found in them. Hardened veterans told Goodman that in the freezing conditions of Crimea some of the younger soldiers, tested beyond their endurance, preferred to lie down in the snow and die.[29] Aloysius Doyle, one of Bridgeman's sisters nursing in the General Hospital at Scutari wrote back to her convent in Carlow, Ireland, that she witnessed scenes that would haunt her forever. Beds were ranged down long corridors, as far as the eye could see, and still, there were frostbitten soldiers lying on the floor. Their nursing never seemed completed: 'We are in the wards late and early. When we go to our apartment, to get a couple of hours rest, we groan in anguish at the thought of all we had to leave undone.'[30]

An undated fragment of a letter from Moore outlined a typical day for her nuns. They were called at 6.00 am, said the Little Hours and Morning Prayer, followed by Mass and 15 minutes of spiritual reading. They nursed in the wards until 1.00 pm when after their meal they said the Angelus, Litany and Act of Contrition. In the afternoon the sisters visited the Catholic patients to instruct or pray with them until 5.00 pm, evening meal and vespers. They then returned to the wards to nurse again until 8.00 or 8.30 pm, and compline. In the afternoon Moore would be in the stores and in the evening in the kitchen until 10.00 pm. She admitted that they were rarely in bed before 11.00 pm.[31]

The soldier patients in the hospital showed a stoicism that touched the nuns deeply. The cries of anguish could be harrowing but generally were suppressed. Goodman found that a maternal gesture towards a baby-faced drummer-boy was not entirely welcome. On ward rounds with a doctor she noticed a 'feeble little drummer, who, notwithstanding his weakness, tried to answer the doctor in a brave tone . . . [later] almost without thinking, I put back the hair from his face and kissed him' whereupon the boy burst into tears. He was ashamed of it and thereafter treated her with marked coolness.[32] Sarah Terrot saw young men turn red and weep with pain, 'but without cry or moan'.³³ Goodman said that they steeled themselves 'to meet unflinchingly the probes, forceps or caustic'.³⁴ The men often tried to conceal their pain 'lest we should be distressed'³⁵ and shrank from admitting their weakness even as death approached, 'but they would often ask us to be near them in their last moments'.³⁶ The masculine code of stoicism and resignation did not entirely preclude the consolation of a female presence.

In theory, much of the work assigned to the nuns and other nurses were the province of the orderlies. These were generally men assigned to the task by their regiments, without any training or regard for ability. The nuns quickly discerned that the orderlies could not be trusted, and kept a sharp eye on them because there were many incidents of orderlies stealing from the patients. Terrot wondered if the poor quality of the orderlies derived from a feeling among them that this was woman's work, to the extent that they would even prefer the danger and hardships of active duty to the work they were doing in the hospital.³⁷ Some did not hesitate to rob the dead or dying. The orderlies were frequently drunk, as doctor after doctor testified. 'The orderlies all drink', said a senior staff surgeon at Barrack Hospital, 'I have to send some to the guard house every day for it.' Another medical officer said that he found them drunk when he went round at night.³⁸ The Hospitals Commission said that the quality of service rendered by the orderlies was 'most unsatisfactory'.³⁹

Nursing included such tasks as spoon-feeding those who could not help themselves, washing the men who were debilitated, and attending the medical officers on their rounds. This latter task included unbinding bandages, dressing wounds or bed sores, and bandaging them up again. This required a sister to have 'a stiff apron, with pockets, scissors and surgical instruments at her side'.⁴⁰ After the departure of the Norwood party and the three Anglican sisters, the remaining nuns became reliable workhorses for Nightingale. This was important because the turnover in nurses continued. Although sixteen nurses had been selected before departure, Nightingale had arrived with fourteen – one had been dismissed before embarkation as clearly unsuitable, and another had turned back on the way after falling ill. By the end of January 1855, another seven nurses had been sent home.⁴¹ In addition, Nightingale had sent back four of the six nurses from St John's House, an unfortunate decision given their training and experience: it seems that she had been fed slanders about them by someone she trusted.⁴²

One of the duties entrusted to the sisters was the administration of alcoholic beverages. At a time when there were so few treatments available for men in pain, the hospitals floated on a sea of officially prescribed alcohol. With both nurses and orderlies prone to drunkenness, the nuns were an obvious choice for the doling out of what were coyly referred to as 'stimulants'. Clare Moore was in sole charge of the extra-diet kitchen established by Nightingale, and on an average day might issue 21 bottles of wine and 100 bottles of port.[43] The latter might then be mixed into arrowroot, a bland staple of the patients' diet. The amount of alcohol being consumed in military hospitals can be gleaned from the quantities given for shipments. In May 1855, 2 vessels arrived at Scutari carrying between them 144,000 bottles of port wine and 500 gallons of brandy.[44] The Hospitals Commission fretted that 'the quantity [of alcohol] which has been used, as we are informed, in these hospitals, has been in our opinion greatly excessive, and wholly disproportionate to the real wants of the sick'.[45]

Alcoholic beverages could be administered neat, or as brandy beaten into egg, but the memoirs of the sisters make most frequent reference to preparing negus, which was a gently warmed drink made of wine or port, mixed with hot water, orange or lemon juice, spices and sugar. The men also received a daily ration of one glass of rum each. The nurses including the nuns could have a daily allowance of one and a half pints of ale or porter (a dark, heavily malted beer); alternatively they could choose one pint of porter plus either wine or brandy.[46] The sisters did claim their portion but usually, it was not all used and what was left was given to the men, a practice frowned upon by Nightingale. Eight years later, when Nightingale heard that a sister at Bermondsey was recovering from typhus, she offered to send six bottles of port to the convent.[47]

One inescapable curse of nursing was the presence of vermin, lice especially. The nuns were infested too. The Sisters of Mercy found that sometimes they had to stay up until midnight to free themselves of infestation acquired during the day, only to be kept awake by the large rats scampering around.[48] The nuns also took responsibility for simple tasks of personal maintenance such as washing the men and cutting their hair, when the patients were incapable of doing this for themselves. Such unavoidable contact further exposed them to infestation. Sarah Terrot remembered caring for one man in this way whose flannel shirt seemed to be moving with lice.[49]

The daily realities of hospital life meant that the sisters shared the risks associated with nursing. They were well aware that in dressing wounds, they had to be sure there was no cut or nick in their own skin. The consequences of cross-infection conveyed in this way could be disastrous. There were several other sources of risk, such as the effluvia of men with cholera, or infected water that conveyed dysentery. The wards were both physically and emotionally draining. They worked long hours. The supplies crisis meant that many necessities had to be obtained from the stock of goods purchased through a fund organized by the *Times*. As nurses converged on this store there was shouting and shoving, which Moore had to control.

Among the Bermondsey sisters, Anastasia Kelly became dangerously ill with fever, and Stanislaus Jones caught it too. It was thought they were dying and Anastasia was anointed. For a time the fever affected Stanislaus mentally – she was described as 'suffering in her head'. Part of the problem was that the sisters could not get hold of the nourishment that they needed, until medical officers had a discreet word with Nightingale about this, a sign that the nuns were now on good terms with many of the doctors who were concerned for their well-being. Nightingale told Clare Moore to use anything from the stores that was necessary for the good health of the sisters.[50] Despite a dispensation, the nuns fasted for Lent. Both Anastasia and Stanislaus had recovered by Easter.

The Anglican sisters Bertha Turnbull, Sarah Terrot and Margaret Goodman were assigned duties down the hill at General Hospital, Scutari, where they shared a room with three ladies from Stanley's party. In this room they slept, cooked, ate, said their prayers and received visitors. Terrot said that given the sick men around them, they felt an obligation to keep well. To be ill and confined to bed was not to be thought of – 'it would be a capital crime against decency and order'. In this conviction, she struggled on, 'weak and weary' until around the middle of February she began to feel more unwell than usual. Soon she was unable to rise, went deaf and felt a searing pain in her head. For a time she was only dimly aware of the world around her. Terrot later realized that it was not only exposure to contagion but also 'fatigue, and mental anxiety' that had brought her to this state.[51] Margaret Goodman reported to England at the end of February that while Terrot was out of danger, 'She is so very deaf that it is impossible to hold any conversation with her and this may account for the vacant impression which is in her face. She is very weak.'[52] She was taken to Barrack Hospital and watched over by Nightingale until she recovered. During her slow recovery, Terrot felt 'increasing anxiety and grief', worried that she would be sent home and never see her patients again.[53]

This was almost certainly the same fever that had affected Anastasia and Stanislaus, because in a letter to her superior in England, Goodman wrote: 'Sister Sarah Ann has "The Fever" but there is every reason to hope . . . Four nuns, 2 ladies and 4 nurses are ill, two of them very dangerously. The poor men are taking it in great numbers and also many of the doctors.'[54] It was probably typhus, which typically presents with headache, joint and muscle pain and high fever, and sometimes loss of hearing. It is spread by insects, typically fleas, and as indicated above, there was a problem with rats, which were frequently flea-bearing. Nightingale reported at this time that several of the hospital staff had contracted a malignant type of typhus.[55] The sisters might have been lucky to survive: it had a high mortality rate. Its lingering effects on Terrot meant that she was unable to continue nursing at Scutari. Nightingale was reluctant to let Terrot go, for she was conscientious, purposeful and always a willing worker. However, as with Stanislaus, the fever had affected her mentally, with Terrot at one point showing a touch of paranoia, and medical advice was that unless she went back to England the balance of her mind might be affected. 'There is not one in the whole sisterhood whom I shall miss so much', wrote Nightingale.[56] On 9 April 1855, Terrot watched from her ship as the lights of Scutari slowly vanished, and envied those left still ministering to the sick and suffering.[57]

Later that month two other Anglican sisters returned to England, Emma Langston and Harriet Erskine. On 23 January they had been sent together with seven nurses and two ladies, to take charge of the General Hospital in Balaclava. Emma Langston was the designated leader of the group. She had been there only six weeks when Nightingale decided that she lacked the necessary powers of leadership. Unlike Clare Moore or Francis Bridgeman, Emma Langston could not maintain the unity and focus of her group, which became prone to feuds and complaining. It was also a physically draining place for someone like Langston who was not robust. In that desperate winter, the Balaclava nurses shared the deprivations with the rest of the army. One doctor remembered a lunch at General Hospital, Balaclava, when a large iron cauldron was carried into the middle of the ward, with the contents defying description. The sheep provided for the seven surgeons one day was 'like a skinned greyhound' which they could not eat and threw onto the roof instead. 'We were practically without medicines ... the base hospital at Balaclava was devoid of opium, quinine, ammonia, and indeed of all important drugs.'[58]

Langston seems to have fallen ill as well – in Nightingale's words, 'losing her money, her head and her health'.[59] Balancing this there is the testimony of Goodman. A patient who arrived from Balaclava told her that the nurses had effected 'a vast improvement in the Hospital there. During the time that he was in his fever, they brought him things and watched him night and day.'[60] But Nightingale decided that Langston had to go, and Harriet Erskine with her. Perhaps the rigours of the situation were simply beyond endurance for all except the toughest of women. At their departure Langston received a note from Nightingale: 'I wish to say how much I regret losing the services of yourself and Sister Harriet for the work's sake, how much I regret that both you and Eldress Sarah Anne [Terrot] should have lost your health in this work.' But medical officers had warned her not to risk exposing those two to another attack of fever. We may wonder whether the swiftness of Nightingale's judgement was judicious. Emma Langston and Harriet Erskine were joining an increasing line of dismissals by Nightingale: the Norwood nuns, Elizabeth Wheeler and two other Anglicans, four capable St John's House sisters, and several nurses. This fresh round of dismissals left only a small group of nurses in Crimea without clear leadership, a vulnerability that Nightingale would come to regret.

The wards were both physically and emotionally draining, which took its toll in the form of stress or depression. Margaret Goodman found that even her faith was shaken. In February she wrote from Scutari to Sister Catherine Chambers, her superior in the Anglican convent at Devonport:

> Our work, as we say, has prevented us from attending prayer or even H. Com. I am afraid, Honoured Madam, that the hearty desire has been wanting in my case. It seemed that I couldn't bear to say my prayers. I became almost an unbeliever. I can scarcely make myself clear. I seemed to cling to Holy Truths only my mind was so full of doubts. I suppose to rid myself of this pain I forbore to think at all.[61]

Feelings of dissociation are a typical coping mechanism for those coping with trauma. After being criticized for her slackness by one of the ladies, Goodman attended chapel the following Sunday. The cruelty and suffering of war, which she saw daily in the broken and dying men around her, had raised questions in her mind about divine providence. Sarah Terrot, too, had grappled with the same questions. It helped, she said, that she and other nurses caring for the soldier patients had been 'granted a calm and quiet temper and a sort of stunned feeling, for had we realized all their sad sufferings, all their bright hopes and young lives, all the love and care of wives and mothers all quenched in misery and death, we could not have borne it . . . we saw them crushed to death by cruel improvidence and neglect'.[62] This is a remarkable passage, witness both to pathos and to suppressed emotion arising from her new awareness of the awfulness of war. She coped by trying to dissociate her feelings from the reality around her, but this repression had taken its toll. It is significant that she blames the poor organization of the army, its 'improvidence and neglect' for so much death and disablement. She had not been blinded by jingoism or patriotism.

Even privacy was in short supply. Early one morning when the Anglican sisters were dressing, an Irish soldier passed through their room to enter the tower above and raise the Turkish flag. Terrot detested 'living and resting under the flag of infidels & indeed since it has been hoisted we have not had one quiet night, violent storms shake the whole building'.[63] For the Bermondsey Sisters of Mercy also there are hints of stress in the *Annals*. The sisters were ordered by the medical officers to go out into fresh air each day as it was feared their health would suffer from constant confinement in the hospital. Clare Moore accepted that the Sisters of Mercy shared the same difficulties as everyone else, but felt that these were more trying because of 'the strangeness of their position: as Nuns dwelling amongst more than three thousand Soldiers: – mixed up with foreigners from all countries'. They were keenly aware of being observed, which meant they had to be extremely cautious at all times. It was impossible for them to obtain a moment's solitude. There was very little privacy in their quarters at Barrack Hospital, where, said Moore drily, 'the Soldiers walk in and out freely; it is one of the "advantages" of living in a Barrack'.[64] Yet this same trust allowed the sisters to build a close relationship with the soldiers, who called on them not only for prayer books or rosaries but also for a wide range of assistance: to write letters home for them, to intercede with the authorities, to supply a remedy or even articles of clothing. She noted that sometimes sick men came to them instead of going to the medical officers, afraid of being looked on as cowards looking for a deferment when others were being sent to fight.[65]

One of the strengths of the Sisters of Mercy was their disciplined prayer and sacramental life. This not only centred them with daily reminders of God and their vocation, but also gave them a sense of unity in which they realized they could depend on one another. There was daily Mass in the priests' quarters. The nuns were more disciplined about early rising than the priests, which Fr William Ronan, one of the chaplains felt created a scandalous situation: 'Mass is celebrated in a room where two or three priests sleep and it was not unusual for some of the clergy to get up at the same time that the nuns were assembled at the Holy Sacrifice. This abuse, I felt, could not be tolerated.'[66] He meant it as a criticism of the sisters, not of the priests. A permanent chapel was not provided at Scutari until late summer. Soldiers clubbed together to buy a crucifix and some ornaments, and the community at Bermondsey sent out candlesticks, a ciborium, a thurible and some other articles. The sisters treasured their prayer times in front of the Blessed Sacrament, the twinkling light reminding them of the hidden presence. Recitations of the rosary and litanies could be shared with the soldiers.

The Anglican nuns said evening prayer together, and when a chapel was set up they found that some of the men attended and participated heartily. The Sunday service they attended was not always a eucharist, and being intended for the soldiers, might be broad-based in its approach. The men ended up detesting the parable of the Prodigal Son because Scutari had a succession of Protestant chaplains who turned first to this parable as their scripture reading of choice. One chaplain gave fifteen discourses on it and was succeeded by another who started with the same parable, to loud protests.[67]

There was no joint worship to unite the Catholic and Anglican nuns, or even shared prayer. Catholic teaching forbade this until the Second Vatican Council. Ecumenism had not yet been invented. One telling incident occurred when Catholic and Anglican sisters found themselves temporarily snowed in at General Hospital, Scutari. Their transport back to Barrack Hospital did not arrive, and they had to spend the night in a shared room at General Hospital. Sarah Terrot listened to the Catholic nuns say compline, the last office of prayer of the day, which is short and relatively unvarying, and which she knew off by heart. She joined them in prayer, but silently, knowing that it would have caused difficulties if she as a fellow Christian said the prayers out loud.[68] Terrot was generous in praise of the Sisters of Mercy. Her memory of the Catholic sisters was one of 'affectionate admiration; their invariably patient, cheerful, gentle manners, their constant, considerate kindness ... a beautiful picture of true and practical Christianity'.[69] But she was uncomfortable with Gonzaga Barrie being put in charge of the nurses at General Hospital: 'I had a feeling of national and ecclesiastical independence that I would rather not be under the command of a Roman Catholic nun'.[70] Even though she shared with the Sisters of Mercy not only the Christian faith but also a vocation to the religious life, Terrot's Anglican background meant that she still viewed the English national community as properly represented by the Church of England. Between individual Catholic and Anglican nuns there was respect, but a strong sense of distinctiveness remained.

Gonzaga Barrie was originally Anglican and had been received into the Catholic Church. She understood the diverse schools of theological doctrine that federated under the Anglican banner but remained sceptical about their compatibility. She wrote back to England reporting, 'There are several Anglican ministers here and two are High Church, one Evangelical and one Doubtful – at least so I heard Miss Sellon's disciples say who were discussing their respective merits. I was greatly diverted by the discussion and thanked God that I was out of all that inconsistent work.'[71] Gonzaga thought the Anglican sisters were excessively proud and hoped for their conversion to Catholicism.[72]

In their writings, the sisters practised Victorian reserve about their religious feelings, but where their spirituality is mentioned, it was often strongly incarnational. Sarah Terrot reflected that although the soldiers often came from the poorest ranks of society, indeed were sometimes recruited in a stupor from the pubs, they seemed 'better Christians, more Christlike, more patient, more humble, more unselfish' than men from the better-off elements in society who had been well tutored in Christianity. It made the sisters recall the passages in the gospels where Jesus preferred the sinner or the low born to the prominent believer.[73]

In their nursing of the soldiers, the sisters were fulfilling their mission to care for some of the poorest and most vulnerable in society. Recruitment into the British army in the mid-nineteenth century was often an escape from poverty or a life of petty crime. Recruiting sergeants were known to hang around the judicial quarter sessions, where malefactors might be given the alternative of the army or prison. Some regiments were proud of local ties or had higher standards, but others accepted whoever was available. Sometimes the man was the black sheep of the family looking for a way out of a difficult situation. Orlando Figes quotes a letter from a French soldier to his parents giving his opinion on the British soldiers he met in the early stages of the war: 'The English recruiters seem to have brought out the dregs of their society, the lower classes being more susceptible to their offers of money. . . . In England, the soldier is really a just a serf – he is no more than the property of the government.' The Frenchman was particularly shocked at the sentences of flogging inflicted on British soldiers for indiscipline or drunkenness, which the French army had abolished in 1789.[74]

A large proportion of the UK soldiers came from Ireland. Estimates generally put the Irish proportion at around 30 per cent, but Brian Griffiths estimates that it was as high as 40 per cent if Irish Protestants were included. Some regiments recruited almost entirely in Ireland and one, the 18th Foot, was largely Irish-speaking to the extent of being addressed in Irish by its commanding officer before going into battle. Even nominally Welsh, Scottish or English regiments might contain a large number of Irishmen in their ranks.[75] One Irish MP observed that 'starvation is a good recruiting sergeant', although it was also true that there was a pull factor of possible adventure and escaping the narrow confines of rural Ireland.[76] The government was aware of the Irish numbers, most of them Catholic, and had already provided chaplains. The presence of Irish nuns was intended as a contribution to hospital care but could bolster the wider sense of making provision for Catholics.

Joining the army as a soldier might have been an escape from poverty or some other problem, but it was an escape into a harsh environment and one where class distinctions could keep the men in low regard. Officers bought their commissions, and came from the aristocracy or landed gentry. Although there was, again, a variety of officer–men relationships across regiments, many officers regarded their men as brutes. Nightingale was told that she was spoiling 'the brutes', and heard the troops described by their officers as 'animals', 'blackguards' and even 'scum'. A doctor with the Scots Greys told the Hospitals Commission that during his time in the Crimea no general officer had interested himself in the sick.[77] When nuns nursed those same men, they were not only ministering to some of the poorest in society but also were implicitly resisting any upper-class blindness towards the humanity of the common soldier. Some officers, it should be added, had great respect for the courage and loyalty of their men.

The nuns at Scutari were little different from the other Westerners in their attitude to local Christians. In their minds, there was a simple identification of Christianity with the Western interpretation of its faith and practice. It is striking how little meaningful contact the Catholics and Anglican nuns had with local Orthodox Christians. The Greek Orthodox remained a substantial minority in the Constantinople region. Many of the hospital servants were Greek, and across the water from Scutari lay the seat of the Ecumenical Patriarch at the Phanar in Constantinople, but Orthodox Christianity hardly seemed to figure in the consciousness of the nuns. When a small party of Anglican sisters went to visit a large Christian village damaged by fire about a mile from the hospital, their attitude seemed to be one of detached curiosity. 'We had some opportunity of observing the manners of Greek Christians', wrote Margaret Goodman, with nothing more to say about them.[78] While waiting at Therapia, Frances Taylor, one of the ladies in Mary Stanley's party, went to a Greek service on a Sunday. She found the liturgy 'most curious and picturesque' but the chanting of the two priests 'sounded like the most dismal howling'.[79] Sister Joseph Croke, too, had a poor opinion of the local Christians. She believed that there were about two million Greeks in the empire and added: 'They are very cunning and are said to be great thieves.'[80] Four years previously Nightingale had been similarly unimpressed. On a visit to Athens with her parents she had pronounced that

> The Greek Church is dead, it seems to me: the priests are her undertakers, the churches her vaults. The priests are so ignorant that they can hardly read. They neither are fit nor wish to be treated like gentleman. . . . I prefer the most intolerant fanaticism to this. . . . What a contrast to the liveliness of the Roman Catholic Church. I never go into a [Greek] church without being disgusted.[81]

It is possible that Nightingale and the nuns' understanding of Orthodox Christianity had been coloured by a tendency in England to see 'the Greek Church' (a designation that included Russian Orthodoxy) as a corrupt form of Christianity, trapped in fossilized ritual and obscurantism. Russia itself was often portrayed as barbaric, with a false or inadequate understanding of Christianity. The *Times* aired these prejudices in an editorial which at the same time betrayed some unease. 'The Russian is hardy, obstinate and fanatical', said the editorial. 'He is told that he is fighting for orthodoxy, for the Holy City, or the Christian faith. . . . The Emperor is reduced to the pitiful necessity of proclaiming a holy war, and calumniating two nations of Christian Europe [Britain and France] as enemies of the faith.'[82] Figes notes that at the outbreak of war, 'Church leaders seized upon the war as a righteous struggle and crusade'. They spoke of Britain 'promoting the cause of religious liberty', of Russians as 'the hordes of the modern Attila', who were 'a hopeless and degenerate people'. Some saw it as a war for the true Western religion against its Greek debasements.[83]

At the end of the war, Florence Nightingale still held similar sentiments. Her experience of warfare and the wastage of men had not led her to doubt Britain's denunciations of Russian barbarism. She wrote to her urging her family not to give in to sentiments of pity for Russia. Sevastopol represented, she said, 'aggressive fanaticism' on the part of the Russians. Nightingale felt sorry for the poor Russian wretches who had died, but their cause had been 'To make Russia the tyrant of the world. I should like to have seen the Crimea held by us as the outpost of civilization, the Russians driven beyond the Caucasus and the Caspian a sea of British trade.'[84] She did not doubt the superiority of British culture, nor the righteousness of its imperialism.

The challenges faced by Nightingale and her nurses, and the broader scandal of the supply situation, continued to arouse public opinion in Britain where the newspapers kept up the pressure on the government. This incompetence was the focus of opposition attacks on the government of Lord Aberdeen, in which Sidney Herbert was serving as secretary at war. A motion passed in the Commons calling for an investigation into the state of the army, and the performance of the government departments responsible for it. Aberdeen resigned on 30 January

1855, and a new government was formed under Palmerston. Sidney Herbert served for a few weeks in the new administration as secretary for the Colonies and then resigned along with two Peelite colleagues over Palmerson's decision to allow a Radical MP, John Roebuck to lead an inquiry into the conduct of the war.[85]

Nightingale no longer had her friend at the centre of power. Yet the changes still worked in her favour. Members of Parliament kept up the pressure on Palmerston, accusing him in the Commons of allowing aristocratic favouritism to run the army rather than talent. On 19 February, he appointed a commission under Dr John Sutherland, to investigate once more the state of the hospitals, this time with a special focus on sanitary arrangements. It arrived at Scutari in March and acted swiftly, describing the sewers at Barrack Hospital as 'cesspools of the most dangerous description' while it noted that at the General Hospital the human waste sometimes backed up from the sewers into the corridors.[86] In the thinking of the day, it was believed that pollutants carried in the air were the cause of illness, rather than faeces infecting the water supply. But the sewage improvements, and water filtration that the commission demanded, effectively eliminated many of the problems created by contamination of the hospital's water. Mortality rates began to fall from the end of March onwards, also because there was less overcrowding, and the weather improved. Another commission set up at the same time investigated the breakdown of supplies. Its report in June 1855 left no doubt about the incompetence of the authorities and again brought improvements in its wake, although the senior officers deemed to have failed in their responsibilities were swiftly exonerated by the army, which put all the blame on the government.[87] These investigations and reforms meant that for the nuns and all the nurses, the Scutari hospitals became less stressful. There would be other crises, such as an outbreak of cholera in August, but from spring 1855, the pressure on the nurses slackened appreciably. The fall in the death rate at Scutari was dramatic. From January to March 1855, the ratio of deaths to admissions was 33 per cent; from April to June, 6 per cent; and from July to September, 2 per cent.[88]

In January 1855, Bridgeman's group of Sisters of Mercy were in a situation that weighed heavily on her mind. She and four others were busy at Scutari, but the remaining ten were in the British embassy villa at Therapia, wondering if a useful role would ever be found for them. She wrote later that her group of five had been given little to do, which she blamed on Nightingale, 'against whose whim we had no appeal'.[89] This is difficult to square with Doyle's words about the sisters retiring to bed at night tormented by the thought of all they had to leave undone after an already busy day. Bridgeman's account, though, is part of her polemic against Nightingale. By the end of January, a solution of sorts was at hand. To relieve the overcrowding at Scutari, other hospitals were being made ready. One was at Koulali, a few miles further along the Black Sea coast. It seems to have been Lord Stratford, the British ambassador, who suggested that this hospital should be allocated to Mary Stanley's party, including Bridgeman's Sisters of Mercy.

Koulalai Hospital relieved Nightingale of the dilemma of what to do with Mary Stanley's party. Nightingale had a low opinion of her capabilities but knew that a solution had to be found for the Stanley group. Their return home would have been bad publicity for Nightingale, and moreover, Mary Stanley had been lobbying hard at the British embassy where she had gained the sympathy of Lady Stratford, the ambassador's wife.[90] On 27 January, Bridgeman and her Sisters of Mercy moved to Koulali, thus giving a nursing role to the ten who had been waiting impatiently at Therapia. They joined the rest of the Stanley party at Koulali Hospital, full of thanksgiving and relief.

4

Vocation and resistance

The growth in the number of convents and sisters in the mid-nineteenth century bears witness to the number of women with a sense of vocation, and a yearning to harness their abilities. This same expansion of the religious life also produced a reaction of alarm in some British politicians and commentators. Their fear was so strong that they launched a campaign to control and resist this religious development in British society. But why did the religious life appeal to so many women? And why did it produce such fear in some of its opponents?

Certainly, the growth in the number of nuns and convents in Britain was remarkable. Thomas Chambers, a lawyer and Liberal MP, regarded their growth with hostility. He told the House of Commons that whereas in 1843 there had been fifty-six convents in the UK, by 1853 this had grown to 220 convents, 203 of which were Catholic and 17 Anglican.[1] The growth continued throughout the century. Carmine Mangion's research shows that the number of convents in England and Wales grew from 24 in 1800 to 596 in 1900.[2] These convents were both enclosed ('contemplative') and apostolic ('active') but numerically the latter were far more numerous. By 1850 there were over twenty different Catholic congregations teaching the children of both the middle classes and the poor.[3] Charitable work in the slums was undertaken by sisters coming from the ranks of the Franciscans, Sisters of Mercy, Little Sisters of the Poor, Sisters of Nazareth, Daughters of Charity and other communities. A Jesuit historian reckoned that one of the most striking features of the nineteenth century was 'the incredible growth and multiplication of congregations of religious women'.[4] One of the congregations, the Poor Servants of the Mother of God, had been founded by Mother Magdalen Taylor, who as Frances ('Fanny') Taylor had gone out with Mary Stanley's party and worked closely with Francis Bridgeman and the Sisters of Mercy at Koulali Hospital.

Becoming a nun appealed to women at a time when their opportunities were very limited. This was not, of course, the only avenue to social engagement. The picture needs to take into account women like Josephine Butler who campaigned nationally for social reform, and the many who sought to ameliorate conditions locally. The historian Kathryn Gleadle warns that while the limitations on women were real, the picture should not be reduced to one of misery and limitation. Among upper-class women, there were a few who were captains of industry, some in partnership with their husbands, others in their own right. But for most upper- and middle-class women the expectation was that their duties and responsibilities would be limited to the domestic sphere, while men pursued careers or some form of public life. Generally, 'women were portrayed as financially, intellectually and emotionally dependent upon their male kin'.[5] In England and Wales, before the Married Women's Property Act of 1870, if a woman married, her personal property passed into the possession of her husband. For young impoverished single women from genteel backgrounds, the options were extremely circumscribed, basically to becoming either a governess or a school teacher, each with complications of social class and expectations.[6] A contemporary best-selling book about the role of women in England mentioned no duties outside the home, but said that a woman's influence on her family affected national destiny, for it was 'the minor morals of domestic life which give the tone to English character', and 'over this sphere of duty it is her peculiar province to preside'.[7]

For middle-class women, entering a convent would have given them the mutual support and encouragement of other women, in a structured and recognized role which made possible a public ministry. In some of the teaching orders, a limited degree of professional development would have been possible as the sisters acquired the necessary knowledge and skills. These fledgling developments opened up new possibilities for women. Cornelia Connelly, for instance, founded the Society of the Holy Child Jesus in 1843. Her confidence in the powers of women would have gladdened Nightingale's heart. Connelly told her sisters, 'We have to learn to make strong women, who while they lose nothing of their sweetness and gentleness, should yet have a masculine force of character and will.' Today's critic might wonder at the gender stereotyping, and why she reached for the language of masculinity to describe purposeful women, but there is no doubting her intent. One of her favourite maxims was, 'Anyone can do anything until proved to the contrary.'[8]

For working-class women in mid-nineteenth-century Britain, the picture was different, characterized by an urgent need to provide for their families and to avoid a descent into poverty. Growing industrialization meant that by 1847 there were around 300,000 women in factory work, sometimes with wages that allowed them relative autonomy. But more often factory pay was poor, and the conditions bad or even dangerous. Piecework at home was necessary for many women in addition to domestic duties, but here the pay was even worse than in factories, so much so that in London, for instance, many women in dressmaking were forced to supplement their earnings through prostitution.[9] In Ireland, the famine of 1845-9 had left a significant number of men unable to earn a living that would support a family. Consequently, in the post-famine period, there was a growing number of single women.[10]

Working-class women might look to the convent for an escape from drudgery or an alternative to marriage, one that offered a sense of usefulness and protection. It was not always an escape from drudgery: lay sisters usually undertook housekeeping roles within convents and sometimes felt that they were exploited. Their poverty and station were symbolized in the fact that lay sisters were not expected to bring a donation or 'dowry' to the convent. But Catherine McAuley understood that women were coming forward with minimal education, but who as lay sisters could be generous-hearted, excellent at household management, able to teach sewing or manage a large laundry.[11] English Catholic convents drew from a wider social base, with a tendency towards vocations from lower-middle-class backgrounds such as skilled tradesmen or clerks.[12] Some communities had only one class of sisters, while others maintained the tradition of choir and lay sisters. Susan O'Brien concluded that where there was two-status membership in this way, 'it shaped much else about the ethos, culture, and organization of congregations, and was used to uphold the existence of a two-class society'.[13] Even so, there was no discernible difference 'in the attraction of the religious life for women of particular social backgrounds and in their own perception of their vocation. In this sense, vocation seems to have transcended class'.[14] She also notes that the apostolic congregations provided the opportunity for some women, often working-class, to receive professional training as nurses and teachers.[15] All the sisters from Bermondsey in the Crimean War were choir sisters. Of the group led by Bridgeman, twelve were choir sisters, two were lay. Although some Anglican convents had choir and lay sisters, many did not. Most of the Anglican nuns were from the upper classes. A survey of entrants into 28 Anglican communities up to 1900 showed that 51 per cent came from families with a father in the professions, and 15 per cent from the aristocracy or gentry.[16] None of the Anglican sisters at Scutari were working class.

One of the most remarkable apologias for religious life came from the art historian and early feminist writer, Anna Brownell Jameson. Her account also testifies to the suffocation that middle-class women could feel within lives that outwardly looked comfortable. She was inspired to write by learning about the Sisters of Mercy and their role as military nurses in the Crimean War. Jameson regarded them as examples of what women could achieve when freed from the shackles of convention. The achievements of these sisters pointed to new possibilities that should be open to a large number of women 'in every country, class and creed'.[17] The world of work drew upon the highest human faculties and brought fulfilment. Yet while men's work related them to the world around, women's work was limited in scope. The health, strength and progress of women was 'wasted in desultory, often misdirected efforts, or perishing inert, or fermenting to evil and despair'. It was assumed that women needed to be 'always protected, under tutelage, always within the precincts of a home'.[18] Nor was there any training to bring out the capacities of women. Catholic institutions by contrast offered an example of 'a well-organized system of work for women'.[19] It had taken, she said, the crisis of the Crimean War hospitals to break the self-defeating cycle, in which it was acknowledged that women were needed to step into new roles while simultaneously asserting that they could not be found.[20]

When Nightingale went to the eastern hospitals, along with public relief and gratitude, there was, said Jameson, 'fear . . . incredulity . . . amazement, as if it were a thing unheard of, unknown, and now for the first time attempted, that women . . . holding a certain position in society, should, from motives of piety and humanity, become nurses in a hospital'.[21] If the achievement of Nightingale and her assistants seemed amazing it was because women were being denied a 'sphere of activity commensurate with the large mental powers or passionate energy with which God had endowed them'.[22] Greater openings for women to employ their energies and abilities were one of the reasons so many educated women were going over to the Catholic Church.[23] Jameson hoped that Florence Nightingale and her band of devoted assistants had now broken through a wall of religious, social and professional prejudices, opening the way to new opportunities for women.[24]

The frustrations voiced by Jameson were shared by Nightingale herself. They emerge strongly in *Suggestions for Thought*, a long and rambling series of meditations that she began to compile around 1852 and resumed after her return from the war. These reflections on human nature, God, religion and society were printed and circulated among a small circle of friends she trusted, among them John Stuart Mill and Benjamin Jowett. In the section known as 'Cassandra', her anger blazed as she described the obstacles put in the way of women's fulfilment. Or at least, in the way of some women. Nightingale was speaking about her own social group when she complained that women were condemned to waste away their lives with 'frivolous duties' and a socially mandated 'conventional idleness'.[25] Working-class women would not have recognized this description of their life. But otherwise, her words would have spoken for many when she asked, 'Why have women passion, intellect, moral activity – these three – and a place in society where no one of the three can be exercised?'[26]

Women longed to enter the professions open to men but were cut off by convention and by being denied the time necessary for study and professional preparation. 'That man and woman have an equality of duties and rights is accepted by woman even less than by man. Behind *his* destiny woman must annihilate herself, must be only his complement.'[27] Nightingale's words draw their strength, and their occasional asperity, from the pent-up frustration that she experienced during the years when her parents initially would not permit her to train for nursing, and then reluctantly allowed her limited periods away at places like Kaiserswerth: 'Women dream until they no longer have the strength to dream. . . . All their plans and visions seem vanished, and they know not where. . . . And they are left without the food either of reality or of hope.'[28] This constant beating against the prison imposed by expectations of others could leave women ashamed of their dreams of a better and more positive way of life. It required strength of purpose to accomplish anything, for it was a 'fierce and continued struggle'.[29]

From the knowledge of her own struggles, Nightingale understood the attraction of the religious life. She also realized how the co-operative spirit and disciplined life of the convent could bring fulfilment. In June 1852, when she was still searching for an avenue that would allow her to train and practice as a nurse, she wrote to Henry Manning: 'No one can tell . . . what she [the Catholic Church] is to women, their training, their discipline, their hopes, their home. . . . For what training is there compared to that of a Catholic nun?'[30] She would later change her mind on this. Her Crimean experience of working with nuns would considerably modify what she thought about the utility of a Catholic nun, and bring about a more negative perspective.

Nightingale admired the way that 'religious orders' tried to obey directly the commands of Christ to sell all and give to the poor, and to allow nothing to come between them and God. This note of respect crops up several times in *Suggestions for Thought*.[31] But Nightingale was also critical of the fussiness of religious orders when they put so much stress on the devotional life. She was aware, too, of the contrast between the high ideals of their founders and the pettiness of some of the superiors who followed them: 'Great minds found [religious orders]; little minds spring out of them.'[32] In Clare Moore, Nightingale had found a nun she could respect and trust. Moore was no 'little mind', but one of those she admired as trying to put into direct action the words of Christ.

The picture of the convent as a place of female freedom and development was an idealized one. The reality was that a nun's life brought both gain and loss, freedom and restriction. A religious sister could teach, nurse, visit the poor and move purposefully through the slums; but she would have no social life. She might be encouraged to develop and use her skills and intellect; but her day was strictly regimented. She no longer had to meet the expectations of her family; but she was subject to obedience to a superior. A cartoon in *Punch* showed a lady from Belgravia in the process of changing her mind about becoming a nun because she has seen one of the sisters on her hands and knees scrubbing the floor. Yet Nightingale wrote admiringly after the war, that visiting the convent at Bermondsey, she had found Clare Moore cleaning out the gutter with her hands.[33] This was the reality of the religious life. The poverty could be real, not metaphorical, especially in some of the new, indigenous English foundations. Nor was it a life free of male clerical control,[34] although women's communities had considerable leeway in mid-nineteenth-century Britain, where the Catholic Church, struggling to look after its rapidly growing numbers of urban poor, depended greatly on the work of women.[35] Even when the negatives were put into the balance, this life appealed because it affirmed a woman's innate worth. Carmen Mangion says 'It offered a spiritual idealism that had an element of social action. The philanthropic work . . . appealed to many women.'[36] Similarly, Ann Stott points out that a large proportion of eighteenth- and nineteenth-century feminists were Christians, and many 'who would never have thought of themselves as propounding women's rights, found in their relationship with God a validation of their separate identity and integrity'.[37] Many first-generation nuns were moved by their awareness of the injustices in society. One nun when asked what motivated her replied simply, 'The Poor Law'.[38] Anglican nuns used the metaphor of 'metaphysical motherhood', seeing themselves as mothering the poor.[39]

Spiritual factors were at work as well as sociological ones. Evangelicalism created a self-aware devotional and moral culture that flourished in nineteenth-century England.[40] Although much of this came from non-Catholic traditions such as Methodism or the Salvation Army, its effects were felt in the Catholic Church too, where by the mid-century there was a new emphasis on a sense of direct relationship with God and the accessibility of the supernatural world. There was a striking resemblance between the new Catholic piety and evangelical enthusiasm.[41]

Women had their own spiritual yearnings, and in considering the vocational 'pull' which drew women to the convent it is also worth remembering the high levels of religious practice. The mid-nineteenth century saw levels of church attendance that would astonish the people of the early twenty-first century. A government-approved census of religious attendance in 1851 showed that out of a population of 17.9 million in England and Wales, around 10.9 million were in church on the sample Sunday at the end of March. Of this, only 383,000 church attenders were Catholic.[42] A careful estimate of the overall Catholic population at this time says that it numbered 679,000, so the rate of Catholic attendance was also high. Given its relatively small base, the achievements of the Catholic Church around this time in terms of vocations and buildings look all the more remarkable.[43]

The very year that these census results were published (1854) saw a campaign launched against convents, on the grounds that communities of nuns were undermining the Protestant establishment, and even the traditional Christian family. In segments of British society, there was a general fear of Catholics and a special fear of nuns and convents. Suspicion of Catholicism derived in large part from the self-image of Britain as a Protestant island, an island, moreover, with a history of resisting invasion by tyrannical Catholic countries. To this was added the memory that sometimes Britain's own Catholics had proved to be unreliable in their sympathies, whether plotting to destroy parliament like Guy Fawkes or supporting Stuart efforts to supplant the Hanoverian kings. Until 1859, the Book of Common Prayer of the Church of England still contained an official service of thanksgiving on 5 November for deliverance from the Gunpowder Plot. Bonfires and fiction showed that anti-Catholicism was not just an intellectual movement but also drew strength from a populist anti-Catholic groundswell. There was a sense of divine providence in Britain's Protestantism, a conviction, as Linda Colley puts it, 'that Britain's physical identity, its very shape and place on the map, had been laid down by God . . . its inhabitants saw themselves, particularly in times of emergency, as a people apart'.[44] This shared Protestantism became part of the glue that held together the component nations of England, Scotland and Wales.

By the mid-nineteenth century, the fires of anti-Catholicism were beginning to lose some of their intensity. There had been considerable sympathy for priests, monks and others who had sought refuge in Britain during the French Revolution.

Catholic emancipation in 1829 had extended to Catholics the qualified right to vote, serve in parliament, take office under the crown and be councillors on town corporations. It is less often remembered that the furore over the passing of the Catholic Relief Act had led to a compromise, in which clauses were inserted to impose fresh controls on Catholic life, including restrictions on male religious orders.

Some of the more conservative politicians were disconcerted by the geographical and numerical growth in the number of convents. Nuns had been specifically exempted from the clause intended to control religious orders, but by 1850 nuns and convents were part of the increased visibility, in the literal sense, of the Catholic Church. In 1840, the architect A. W. Pugin was involved in the building of seventeen new churches.[45] His preferred neo-gothic style emphasized Catholicism's pre-Reformation history. Pugin had designed a new convent for the Sisters of Mercy in Bermondsey that was blessed in December 1839, said to be the first purpose-built religious house for women in London since the Reformation. Their founder Catherine McAuley disliked its 'old heavy monastic style'.[46] It was destroyed by a V2 rocket in March 1945.

This increased visibility of Catholics and their growing confidence animated a political counter-reaction aimed at limiting Catholic influence. The campaigners were sometimes anti-Catholic evangelicals, drawing on the rhetoric of the Reformation. More often, however, those opposing Catholic expansion were motivated by a particular understanding of English identity descended from sixteenth-century theorists like Richard Hooker, in which church and nation were regarded as two sides of one coin. There was also fear about the influence of the Tractarians who were viewed as Romanizers in the Church of England, making its members more susceptible to Roman Catholicism. A stream of converts, with Newman the best known, showed that this fear was not groundless. Antipathy towards nuns was part of this broader anti-Catholicism. At the demotic level, there was a concern, even a lurid fear, that nuns represented something profoundly unnatural. To their critics, the life of the convent undermined the traditional family and especially the rights and privileges of the father, as head of the family. This was expressed in a flood of novels and tracts. At the political level, criticism of nuns drew on this same fear, by portraying convents as profoundly un-British. A parliamentary campaign, supported in the newspapers, sought to bring in legislation for government inspection and regulation of convents.

Fiction became an outlet for these concerns about Catholicism in general and about religious orders in particular. Probably the best known was Charles

Kingsley's novel of derring-do, *Westward Ho!* which describes the adventures of a Devon boy in the Elizabethan era. The plot includes dastardly Jesuits, the Spanish Inquisition and the defeat of the Armada. Even here the Crimean War lurks in the background. Kingsley was worried about what he considered Britain's deficient masculinity, and *Westward Ho!* allowed Kingsley to suggest that nineteenth-century Britain needed to find once more the greatness and courage with which it had defeated Catholic Spain. Susan Griffin says this novel 'provides a venue in which Kingsley can voice his concerns about Britain's military weakness, as evidenced by the Crimean War, as well as his anxiety about the health and hygiene of British bodies'.[47] Kingsley's writings are credited with the origins of the phrase 'muscular Christianity'.[48] From this point of view, Catholicism lacked the necessary virility.

There was a spate of novels about nuns and convents, usually to their disadvantage. Examples would be Frances Trollope, *Father Eustace: A Tale of the Jesuits* (1847, 3rd edition); Jemima Luke, *The Female Jesuit: Or, the Spy in the Family* (1851); and Charles Frothingham, *Six Hours in a Convent: Or, The Stolen Nuns!* (1854). There were also works of polemic like Catherine Sinclair, *Popish Legends or Bible Truths* (1852); or Richard Blakeney, *Popery in its Social Aspect. Being a Complete Exposure of the Immorality and Intolerance of Romanism* (1854). Some of this literature was American in origin and found avid readership in Britain. Probably the bestseller purported to be a memoir by Maria Monk, *Awful Disclosures of the Hotel Dieu Nunnery* (1836, many editions). These novelists would typically portray Protestantism as a family religion, based on domesticity rather than ecclesiastical fervour. It was the responsibility of a British father not only to teach his children the principles of Protestant Christianity but also how to defend them. Catholicism threatened this domestic religion by encouraging an interiority, a spirituality which by a morbid focusing on self, loosened a person's sense of belonging to the family or society.[49] Contained within this narrative was the fear that fathers might lose control over their daughters. Indeed, when convents were discussed in the House of Commons, stories about daughters defying their fathers to enter the convent were cited as evidence of the need to institute some kind of inspection or licencing of convents.

Novels about convents often depicted superiors as establishing a reign of terror over their nuns, who were portrayed as immature or timid. Many of the stories were ostensibly by, or about, nuns who had been trapped in the convent and had managed to make their escape. The novels were both titillating and at the same time served as a warning about convent life. The witness of the escaped nun now back in the world was presented as proof of the falseness of the Catholic religion.[50] Authors went to great lengths to include 'corroborating' evidence of their book's authenticity, such as footnotes, cross-references and appendices drawn from theological, historical and even fictional works.[51] Imprisoned or psychologically terrorized nuns symbolized a wider threat to the freedom of the nation as a whole. Often this was ascribed to machinations by the Jesuits. One of the most widely read novels of its time was *Beatrice: Or, the Unknown Relatives* (1852) by Catherine Sinclair, which was set in the Scottish Highlands. In its plot Jesuits seemingly want to improve the conditions of British Catholics but in fact, are seeking political dominance. One character describes them as 'a spiritual army at war with the individual interests of all mankind . . . Shall free-born Britons allow such coils to be thrown over their hearts and their homes?' And another exclaims in alarm, 'A convent is the only spot in her Majesty's wide dominions to which the law of British liberty does not extend.'[52] Even Nightingale was suspect. In May 1855, a Scottish lady who had returned to Britain from Scutari wrote to Francis Bridgeman from London: 'It is altogether very strange . . . the various opinions one hears among people. The commonest belief here still I think is, that Miss Nightingale is a Roman Catholic, a Jesuit in disguise and is secretly scheming with powers of Rome.'[53]

Beneath the concern for a Reformation political establishment, the concern about nuns and convents suggests other fears at work. The inspection and control of convents meant inevitably the inspection and control of women. The fictional stories about escaped nuns assumed that some women could not rationally make a free choice to enter a convent, and must have first been duped and then silenced and restrained, thus needing the intervention and protection of men. There was also a concern for wider liberties. Freedom of speech was associated with Protestant nations and control of speech with Catholic ones. Women in the apostolic, or active communities were not really silenced or restrained, but the belief that they were, worried those who saw religious and political freedoms as intertwined and dependent upon true Protestantism. In short, for many different reasons, there was a strong element of resistance to Catholicism in general and to convent life in particular in mid-nineteenth-century Britain. Women who chose to enter the religious life would do so knowing that it offered spiritual fulfilment and perhaps the possibility of personal development. But they also did so knowing that while their vocation was respected within the Catholic community (or in the case of Anglicans, within Tractarian circles) in British society as a whole they might be regarded with suspicion or even hostility. Against this background, it took courage and steadfastness to become a Sister of Mercy, or an Anglican to join one of the fledgling communities.

Political anti-Catholicism was galvanized by the restoration of the Catholic hierarchy in 1850 when thirteen dioceses were created to replace the previous system of eight vicars apostolic. Suddenly it seemed that the Catholic Church in England and Wales had its own hierarchy to rival that of the established church. The Catholic bishops were headed by Nicholas Wiseman, the first archbishop of Westminster. It did not help matters when he issued a flamboyant pastoral letter in which he spoke of the counties where he would 'govern, and would continue to govern' as bishop. To his critics, it seemed as if he was infringing the sovereignty of the monarch. Lord John Russell wrote an open letter protesting against 'a pretension of supremacy over the realm of England, and a claim to sole and undivided sway, which is inconsistent with the Queen's supremacy ... and with the spiritual independence of the nation'.[54] Gladstone said in the House of Commons that the language used by both pope and archbishop 'was not only unfortunate, but of a vaunting and boastful description'.[55] The resulting controversy was dubbed 'Papal Aggression', a phrase that Nightingale would pick up and use herself when she was contending with Catholic clergy and nuns during the war.

Opposition to this resurgent Catholicism was expressed at both parliamentary and popular levels. One focus was on convent life. Thomas Chambers, Liberal MP and barrister, was one of those who believed that nuns were prevented from leaving their convents and were in effect prisoners. In May 1853, he proposed legislation that would empower the home secretary to investigate convents where restraint was suspected and release the inmates.[56] His initiative petered out, so he tried again in February 1854, when he asked the Commons to appoint a select committee 'to inquire into the number and rate of increase of conventual and monastic institutions in the United Kingdom, and the relation in which they stand to existing law; and to consider whether any, and if any, what further legislation is required on the subject'.[57] He portrayed convent life as unhappy and constrained: 'No man ... could venture to deny that, as a matter of history and of fact, the cloister has in all ages enclosed within its walls many of the most miserable of womankind.' There were sadistic practices, 'penances of all sorts, varying in degrees of torture; a girdle, with sharp points inside, drawn tight around the person – a cap, called bonnet rouge, which, when placed on the head of the victim, produced in a moment or two the most excruciating pains, ending in a very few minutes in insensibility, from excessive agony'.[58]

He told the house stories well known in the press of the day, alleging that fathers had lost their daughters to convents through deceit or coercion. Anglican convents too were part of his concern. Chambers quoted from a letter written to Priscilla Lydia Sellon, not long before the sending out of her sisters to Scutari. An aggrieved father had written to Sellon, 'You have robbed me of my daughter; and here I am, an Englishman, a father, and in my own native land, one of my daughters is seduced from me, and I have no redress. I say to you, give me my daughter whom you have stolen – give me my daughter back!'[59] Here Chambers touched on two themes that would recur again and again in the debate about convents: that fathers were being deprived of legitimate control of their daughters, and that the whole institution of convent life was alien to the British way of life and would insidiously work against its traditional character.

Irish MPs pushed back against Chambers in the debate. One referred specifically to the work of the Sisters of Mercy and the Sisters of Charity, 'ladies whose services were well known throughout England and the whole civilized world'.[60] Another said that Chambers had managed to insult every Catholic in the Commons, and quoted a physician to the royal family who said of the convents in Ireland that they were 'fountains of good to the localities in which they were situated, and might not only be permitted but encouraged'.[61] It was a past and future prime minister, Lord John Russell, who identified a key issue with the Chambers proposal. His motion, by asking for convents to be investigated, insinuated that there was a problem in the first place. The appointment of a committee by the house would imply that a prima facie case had been established, when in fact all that had been adduced was 'the most worthless gossip'.[62] When it came to a vote, the Commons supported by a majority of sixty-seven the call by Chambers for a select committee, but obstructive tactics by members prevented the committee from being formed, and the suspicion that engendered the fear of convents lingered on.

Anthony Trollope satirized the campaign in his novel *The Warden* by creating the character Sir Abraham Haphazard. Encouraged by a newspaper, the *Jupiter* [i.e. the *Times*] Sir Abraham was 'deeply engaged in preparing a bill for the mortification of papists, to be called the "Convent Custody Bill," the purport of which was to enable any protestant clergyman over fifty years of age to search any nun whom he suspected of being in possession of treasonable papers, or jesuitical symbols'.[63] Given this lampoon, it might have been wise to refrain, but the cause was taken up by another MP, Charles Newdegate, who repeatedly tried to bring it back to the House of Commons. In 1865, he was reminded in a debate that 'nuns had bravely served in the Crimean War'. Convent schools were already inspected by the government, and he was persecuting women who educated the poor, visited the sick and performed works of charity.[64] Attempts in parliament to legislate for convents continued until 1874 but these led nowhere. Even the eventual appointment of a select committee in 1870 backfired on Newdegate when it listened sympathetically to the evidence submitted on behalf of convents, and recommended rectifying legal anomalies which disadvantaged convents.[65] The witness of the charitable work of the sisters, and the memory of Scutari and Crimea, still stood them in good stead.

This influence on public opinion was what had been hoped for by Bishop Grant and Dr Manning when the Sisters of Mercy left for the theatre of war. In fact, in May 1855 when the hospitals had improved and the sisters were wondering whether to return to England, Bishop Grant wrote to them begging them to stay, telling them that it was a good witness to the work of nuns at a time when there was yet another attempt to bring a convent bill to the House of Commons. He was so concerned about this that he even tried a little emotional blackmail: if they came home now, it would be said that they had abandoned the poor soldiers.[66] He wrote to Moore again on the same subject in August: 'Bless the Sisters for me, and tell them that during this last session of Parliament no one has dared to say a single word against convents or religion, although the bigots have otherwise been very active. This silence is attributed, through the divine blessing, to the Sisters.'[67]

Women with the strength of a community and the sense of their own calling had won over a large section of public opinion that had previously been suspicious of, or even hostile to, their whole way of life. But the material above shows the context in which they had to operate, and the size of their achievement. There was a national memory of their religion as something alien. Legislation was threatened that would have left convents under a cloud of suspicion. Novels and other books portrayed convents as sinister places and nuns as pitiable victims, or, differently, as women who manipulated and schemed. Things did not change overnight, but the narrative about nuns had a new dimension. There had been public praise for their good works. They had been associated with a national hero, a household name, Florence Nightingale. A visceral anti-Catholicism took another century to fade away – but the weight of public opinion had shifted.

5

Irish nuns at Koulali

The compromise worked out by Bridgeman and Nightingale had found employment for only five of the Irish nuns. The other ten were left languishing at Therapia, but not for long. To the relief of Bridgeman and these sisters, their waiting period came to an end at the close of January 1855. Five sisters were to remain at General Hospital, Scutari. The larger party of ten nuns joined other nurses and ladies in a party led by Mary Stanley, which would take charge of the hospital at Koulali. This hospital was under the patronage of Lady Stratford de Redcliffe, wife of the British ambassador. Koulali Hospital had been opened at the beginning of December 1854 but its capacity was now being greatly expanded. It was originally intended to take convalescent patients from other hospitals, but instead, it was pressed into action to care for the sick and wounded from Crimea. The Irish nuns felt that at last they were being given a responsibility commensurate with their abilities.

They also had in mind a model hospital that would, through its efficient operations, show up the inadequacies of the hospitals at Scutari under Florence Nightingale. They had been watching her modus operandi and they were not impressed. Mary Austin Carroll, chronicler of the Sisters of Mercy, wrote that Nightingale did not seem to know 'how to go about the complicated business entrusted to her'. Moreover, the 'well-intentioned' Nightingale was poorly endowed with a talent for governance.[1] These retrospective comments come after the fact when the Irish sisters were contending for control of the narrative, but there is little doubt that they described the feelings of the Bridgeman sisters at the time.

Koulali Hospital was about four miles north of Scutari, close to the water's edge on the Bosphorus. The road journey there from Scutari meant a slow, jolting carriage ride, so travellers often preferred to sail along the coast. Koulali was another instance of converting barracks to serve as a hospital. The hastily repurposed barracks were built on a narrow strip of land along the shoreline, with the ground behind rising steeply. The great advantage of the location was the adjacent quay at Koulali which could be used in all weathers, unlike the rickety dock at Scutari, which was unusable in high winds. This made it much easier to land the sick and wounded swiftly and efficiently. The civilian dockside crowds at Koulali differed from the rackety mass of hustlers, soldiers, pedlars and others at Scutari. Frances Taylor, one of the ladies in the Stanley group remembered seeing 'Turkish ladies in their yahmacs, attended by their slaves, women of a lower rank with bundles and babies, Greek ladies with uncovered heads, their hair wound round in long plaits and adorned with artificial flowers . . . men and boys in crimson fezs'.[2]

The hospital was a square red building, three stories high in front. An archway led into a quadrangle with wards to right and left.[3] Local tradition said that the hospital was built on a site of an earlier church dedicated to St Michael. From the windows of the wards, there were views of trees and water, of hills and villages, in what was said to be one of the loveliest turns of the Bosphorus. The situation was good in so far as those able to walk could get outside the hospital and catch the fresh breeze from the sea. Frances Taylor recalled: 'Here we could see the men, just able to crawl out of their wards, basking in the sun or trying their returning strength in walking on the grass.'[4] Above this former barrack was another hospital block, built on a shelf jutting out of the hillside.

Despite its advantageous site, the building was not a good choice for a hospital. Sanitation, ventilation, heating and kitchen arrangements were all defective.[5] When the sisters and other nurses moved in they found the hospital filthy. It also lacked a proper kitchen. Hot water came from boilers so immense that the water had to be drawn by using a ladder to reach over the top.[6] The Sanitary Commission noted that the hospital basement contained 50 Turkish privies and stables for 200 horses. The stench from these pervaded the building until the works ordered by the commission were undertaken, during which 2 tons of 'filth' was removed.[7] Mary Stanley's nursing party had already been at work there for about two months before these recommended works were completed.

Mary Stanley was appointed lady superintendent at the hospital by Lord William Paulet, the commanding officer at Scutari. She had no nursing experience and the stress of this role quickly took its toll on her. On 2 February she put Mother Francis Bridgeman in charge of the upper hospital where all the nursing was now undertaken by the nuns, meaning that they had a unit to themselves. 'We were glad to get away from the secular party', wrote Bridgeman.[8] Two rooms were assigned as accommodation for her Sisters of Mercy, and they turned a small closet into an oratory complete with the Blessed Sacrament. Their arrival at Koulali coincided with the winter crisis. Along with the other Scutari hospitals, bed provision had to be rapidly expanded and by February 1855 Koulali had a potential maximum of nearly 1,200.[9] Early in February transport ships from Crimea unloaded 490 starving, freezing and sometimes dying patients at the quay. This was the first of many such transports. A shocked Aloysius Doyle felt that 'such desolate worn out looking patients never before entered any hospital'. She wrote to the sisters back in Ireland that these men had endured 'sufferings beyond what you can imagine... where the cold is so intense that a soldier described to me the Russians and the Allies in a sudden skirmish, and neither party able to draw a trigger'.[10]

More of the sick from the trenches began to pour into Koulali Hospital. There were very few wounded. Fever, dysentery and frostbite were the main illnesses, and by the time the men arrived the rigours of life in the trenches had broken their constitutions, leaving them with little strength. At first, the patients had been mostly English, but in March 'the Irish soldiers began to come down in shoals'. It was supposed that their constitutions were more inured to hardship than the English, allowing them to hold out longer. Even so, frostbite often led to amputations, and the constitutions of many of the soldiers were so broken that they were unable to rally from the post-operative shock.[11]

After a few weeks as superintendent at Koulali, Mary Stanley decided to step down. She had overestimated her powers of administration and found her hospital role drained her physically and emotionally. She left on 2 April, but before doing so was received into the Catholic Church by Fr Ronan, the Jesuit priest at Koulali, who was chaplain to the nuns. Nightingale had always feared that Stanley was advancing the cause of Koulali as part of a wider scheme to promote Catholicism. She worried about it to the extent of sleeplessness. Writing to her family she described Mary Stanley as having been 'overexcited and literally, for a time, insane', adding: 'She has done me and the cause as much harm as if she had been a cold-hearted liar. But... she is not deliberately false.' Nightingale immediately contradicted herself by going on to say that Mary Stanley had played 'her little black part' and succeeded 'by dint of lying' in winning the co-operation of the embassy and Lord Paulet.[12] Nightingale's emotive language showed her dislike of anyone exercising autonomy in matters of nursing management.

Nightingale contemplated taking over the management of Koulali herself, but aware of Bridgeman's power there, changed her mind and wrote to London disclaiming any authority over Koulali. Nightingale's letter to Benjamin Hawes, deputy secretary at the War Office, was quite specific: she wanted no association with the Irish nuns, asking that she 'should be in no way responsible for the conduct and expenditure of the Sisters'.[13] The coolness and perhaps even distaste that she had shown towards the Irish sisters on their arrival had not diminished.

Nightingale never visited Koulali during the time the nuns were there.[14] Amy Hutton, one of the ladies, was appointed superintendent in place of Stanley by Lord Paulet. This meant that from April to October 1855 Bridgeman effectively shared the administration of Koulali Hospital with her. Hutton had great confidence in Bridgeman and made no important decisions without consulting her.[15] Hutton, who was a Protestant, remained a friend and defender of the nuns. This was one more example of Bridgeman's gift for building alliances. Bridgeman was a good networker too among her fellow Catholics, always aware of where a word could help advance things.

For a short time after Stanley's departure, the Sisters of Mercy had to assume the greater part of nursing at Koulali. Many of the nurses had been dismissed for drunkenness or other problems. At one point there were only two paid nurses left, one of whom fell ill. One of the Sisters of Mercy was also ill. That left one lady (Frances Taylor) and nine sisters to keep the whole hospital running, during a week of 'intense anxiety'. Taylor wrote that she would never forget 'the indefatigable manner in which the Sisters of Mercy carried on the work of the hospital'.[16] On 9 April a fresh party of six ladies and fourteen paid nurses arrived, taking the pressure off the exhausted nuns.

It helped that the winter crisis had passed, and pressure on the hospital system was easing. For the rest of 1855 Koulali, like the hospitals in Scutari, would be admitting mostly wounded soldiers from the front in the Crimea, or those who had been weakened by sporadic flare-ups of cholera. Scutari and Koulali would no longer be as important as formerly, because hospital provision had been expanded in the Crimea. There, a network of general, regimental and temporary field hospitals had been created closer to the action. This largely obviated the necessity of the journey across the Black Sea to Scutari or Koulali, with all its hazards. As Shepherd noted, 'The policy of admitting casualties to hospitals within relatively easy reach of the front line, and of holding them there until convalescent, ensured much better results than previously.'[17] The number of patients arriving at Koulali began to diminish as soon as spring arrived, and would diminish further in summer.

The fact that Bridgeman and two-thirds of her party were removed to Koulali did not guarantee peace with Nightingale. Nightingale resented the independent spirit and initiative of the Bridgeman group. The five sisters who remained at Scutari nursing at General Hospital managed to obtain better accommodation during one of Nightingale's absences. The purveyor gave them a larger room, which they divided to create a small oratory where they could pray and reserve the Blessed Sacrament. On her return, Nightingale launched into correspondence with the nuns, criticizing them for acting without her permission. The question of who was in charge was always a neuralgic point with Nightingale, and she was alarmed by their 'independent action' and by a casual remark of one of the doctors that he supposed the Sisters of Mercy 'did not belong to Miss Nightingale's party'.[18] Nightingale blew the matter out of all proportion, but she used it to raise another concern, namely that the five sisters still at Scutari were giving spiritual counsel to patients and NCOs, away from the wards where they were nursing.[19] This was the beginning of a recurrent accusation that Bridgeman and her sisters were proselytizing among the soldier patients to win converts for the Catholic Church. There was public concern in the UK that soldier patients should not be subjected to proselytizing when they were at their most vulnerable. Sidney Herbert had a politician's awareness of public opinion. In some quarters in England, his loyalty was already under suspicion for another reason: his mother was Russian. It was not long before Protestant fears of Catholic proselytizing by the nuns were aired in the correspondence columns of the *Times*. Manning was called a 'pervert . . . said to be constantly at the War Office', and Mary Stanley was described as 'an Anglican Papist'. One letter writer said he was convinced 'that a Jesuit conspiracy is in active operation for the subjugation of England and the ruin of her church; and a Popish and profligate government . . . have played the game of the conspirators'.[20]

Nightingale had been alerted earlier by reports of proselytizing by an Irish Sister at General Hospital, Scutari. Sarah Anne Terrot had been puzzled and dismayed by a deathbed conversion, where it was alleged that the Sisters of Mercy had persuaded a young man to accept conditional baptism and reception into the Catholic Church. Terrot was surprised because she knew the young man in question to have been a communicant Anglican. The Irish nuns insisted that he had changed allegiance freely, but soldiers in beds nearby insisted that the Irish sisters had shown 'constant and peculiar attention to this young man' at a time when his spirits were weakening.[21] A complaint by the Revd John Sabin, the chief Church of England chaplain, reached the War Office in London. It was a delicate moment. In his letter of appointment to Nightingale, Herbert had charged her to guard against any of her nurses attempting to 'interfere with or disturb the religious opinions of the patients ... and at once to check any such tendency, and to take if necessary severe measures to prevent its repetition'.[22] When Bishop Grant negotiated their terms of service with Herbert, the bishop had been careful to specify that 'The greatest caution being necessary on all hands, in the matter of religion, the Sisters of Mercy will hold themselves free to introduce such subjects *only with patients of their own faith*'.[23] In the end, Nightingale squashed a move for an inquiry into the incident.[24]

Nightingale was not only concerned about Catholics. She also had her eye on other errant forms of Christianity. In the same letter to the War Office complaining about Catholic activity, Sabin also consulted them on an attempt by Nightingale to dismiss Miss Tebbutt, the lady superintendent at General Hospital, Scutari, on the grounds that she was a Unitarian. There is a hint of dignified exasperation in Hawes's reply:

> I am directed by Lord Panmure in the first place to say that ... he deeply laments to find that religious differences have arisen to such an extent as to mar the united energies and labours of those who are devoting themselves with such disinterested and heroic courage and success, to the relief of the Sick and Wounded Soldiers in the East.
> ... it is his duty to state that he cannot allow the Hospitals to become schools of controversial theology, and the scene of religious dissensions and animosities.[25]

The initial accusations that the Irish Sisters of Mercy were proselytizing were at General Hospital, Scutari. Bridgeman blamed the Anglican nuns for this upsurge of accusations. They had, she said, been 'gnawed by jealousy' when they saw the great influence of the Catholic nuns. In response to these rumours of conversionist activities, Fr Ronan wrote to one of the accusers, the Revd A. Hobson, an Anglican chaplain. Fr Ronan SJ announced himself the 'guardian and protector' of the Sisters of Mercy and demanded to know 'when and in what instances these Sisters have interfered in the religious affairs of Protestants. The charge of violating a solemn engagement is too serious to be lightly passed over.' Hobson retreated behind obfuscations.[26]

Soon the accusations spread to Koulali. With their control of the upper hospital at Koulali, and their influence felt throughout, the Irish Sisters of Mercy became more confident in pastoral zeal. Bridgeman again attributed these complaints to the jealousy, this time of the 'parsons', that is, the Protestant chaplains, and said that the sisters were subjected to 'unceasing persecution'. Even so, 'no one whom we had nursed could ever be found to aid in substantiating any of the reports set afloat'.[27] Given the mythical role of Jesuits in popular opinion, it probably did not help calm English fears that she had Fr William Ronan, a combative Jesuit, taking her side. Ronan had accommodation at Koulali. When complaints were made she adopted the same tactic as Ronan and asked for specific details: which patient had been approached with conversionist intent, when and by whom? Who was the eyewitness and what was said? In the face of such searching inquiries, accusations tended to melt away.

The War Office tried to tamp down on this confessional civil war, which it regarded with a degree of incredulity. Panmure's office wrote to the military commander at Scutari, Lord Paulet, asking him to issue 'clear and distinct orders' instructing chaplains, nurses and nuns not to 'interfere with the religious opinions of any person whatever'.[28] Paulet took the maximum interpretation of this and ordered the nuns to limit their duties to nursing. If they spoke of faith matters to anyone, they would subsequently be forbidden to enter the wards.[29] This brought the sisters great distress. Bridgeman's response was to write a long and careful letter, notionally addressed to Fr Ronan, but knowing that he would ask for an interview with Lord Paulet and present the letter to him. Her letter was written in an affective language, mentioning the suffering of soldiers in pain or approaching death, and longing for a consoling word.

> Not to speak on religious subjects to the Catholic ... To see the approach of death and not speak of the awful judgment soon to be gotten! To be disbarred from speaking a word of consolation or hope to the poor Catholic soldier or from breathing a prayer for the grace then much needed by him. This is a restriction to which we can never submit.... the poor Catholics often say that when we can spare them a few moments it affords them more comfort than all we can do to relieve their corporal wants.[30]

She stressed that she regarded it 'as a point of honour and conscience' not to interfere in the religious concerns of Protestant soldiers. Bridgeman said that she could not yield up the freedom to offer this kind of consolation, and closed with an allusion to public opinion: 'I feel satisfied, at least, that neither God, our superiors, nor our country will expect it of us.'[31] The letter showed her shrewdness and the determination of her will. Its reference to public opinion was a master stroke, given the widespread anger about the conduct of the war and poor treatment of the nation's soldiers. With so many Irish soldiers in the army, and Palmerston's government dependent on Irish votes in the House of

Commons, Bridgeman's threat was not to be treated lightly. An exasperated Paulet gave in and allowed the nuns to continue as before.

Bridgeman dissembled when she said that she and her sisters refrained from discussing faith matters with the Protestant soldiers. In practice, the nuns allowed themselves some leeway. One of her sisters, Aloysius Doyle hinted at this when she wrote back to Ireland that 'there are many who linger on the household and the faith, and a word of encouragement or advice may help them into the fold'.[32] Bridgeman was more explicit: 'Notwithstanding our strict adherence to our engagement many were quietly received into the church and admitted to sacraments both in Scutari and Koulali and many apostates reconciled'.[33] Later, when Ronan was back in Ireland, he read Bridgeman's account of the controversy, and added a marginal note in the text: 'Every one received by me into the church at Koulali attributed his conversion under God to the Sisters of Mercy'.[34] The implication is that these changes of ecclesial allegiance occurred after the men had taken the initiative as inquirers about Catholicism, but the situation is opaque, and certainly, the nuns had not restricted themselves to speaking about religion to Catholic patients only.

What emerges from this struggle is Bridgeman's sense that she and her sisters had a distinctive mission. They saw their nursing role as part of a larger pastoral ministry. There is a stark difference between the account of the war years written in the Bermondsey community Annals by Mother Mary Clare Moore, and the one written by Francis Bridgeman. Moore's account highlights vicissitudes overcome in order to nurse sick and dying men. Bad food and poor accommodation have to be endured, shortages of hospital supplies have to be solved, so that the men may be properly nursed. Bridgeman's account features, again and again, tussles with a stubborn and prejudiced English establishment, one of the chief aims being that Catholics might be succoured in their faith. She and her sisters also had a quietly vigilant eye for Protestants who might be wondering whether to become Catholic themselves. Bridgeman portrays Nightingale's exercise of her authority as one more example of English control, with the Protestant chaplains complicit. The Irish Sisters of Mercy tended to identify England as an enemy, and uphold Catholicism as inseparable from Irish identity. Sister Aloysius Doyle had written to her convent in Carlow on the eve of departure for Constantinople, proclaiming, 'We travel in our veils, in the face of *proud, bigoted* England, no disguise whatever. *Will this not be a triumph for our holy religion. Everything seems conducted by the hand of God*'.[35]

It was not, of course, an either/or, preaching versus nursing. The Bermondsey sisters under Moore spoke of faith to those who asked them, and the Bridgeman sisters nursed with equal assiduousness both Catholic and Protestant patients. Doyle recorded that they treated equally the 'temporal wants' of the Protestant patients. Later the sisters might even have been a little embarrassed by their even-handedness because when Doyle's account was published for a largely Catholic readership, this affirmation that they looked after the everyday needs of Protestants was omitted.[36] But Bridgeman and her sisters, in asserting their rights to speak of religious matters, created a different kind of nursing ministry at Koulali. They made sure that the hospital had an attractive chapel, with daily Mass, two Masses on Sundays and Benediction in the evening. Mass was attended by men off duty and convalescent patients. Doyle noted that 'the Sisters had the satisfaction of knowing that no Catholic ever left Koulali without receiving the sacraments, nor did a simple Catholic die without the consolation which Mother Church reserved for her dying children'.[37] This was easier to achieve because their influence ran large throughout the hospital at Koulali. In the bigger and more pressured establishment at Scutari, the nuns under Clare Moore had to make do with whatever opportunities came their way, in a hospital with complex layers of authority. At Scutari, they were only one group among many, with a much lower profile.

The role of the Irish sisters at Koulali also demonstrates their confidence in pastoral ministry, which was usually a male and clerical preserve. Nightingale had quizzed Bridgeman about this, asking her, 'Do you think it suitable for a woman to take upon her the duty of a priest?' Bridgeman's reply was to distinguish between the sacramental authority of the priests, and that of her sisters, which was 'gently to instruct the ignorant, to advise and influence the erring, negligent and wayward, in short to do for, or supply to those Catholics what a good mother might or should have been to them'.[38] Bridgeman's retrospective account of this conversation is too neat, as so often in her presentation, but there is no doubting the confidence of her nuns in their own sphere of ministry. Here were women commending and explaining Christian faith at a time when this role would have been forbidden to them within the walls of parish churches.

In the Crimea itself, after the stalemate of the winter months, the coming of spring 1855 saw the allied armies still bogged down in the siege of Sevastopol, which was protected by formidable fortifications. Two bastions known as Malakoff and the Redan seemed the key to capturing the city. The allied armies planned a joint assault on these to begin on 18 June, with the French attacking the Malakoff and the British forces the Redan. The assault on the Redan required British soldiers and sailors to run uphill carrying ladders across 400 yards of open ground, under withering fire from the Russians. The first wave of attackers was quickly dubbed the Forlorn Hope Men. The attack failed, despite courageous efforts. One officer compared the men being felled to crops being steadily levelled by a reaping machine. The British lost just over 1,500 men, the far greater French losses estimated at 7,500 dead and wounded. Lord Raglan, the British commander died a week later, officially of cholera but, it was rumoured, from the effects of the anguish he felt following this attack.[39] The French also failed to take the Malakoff.

During the attack, some of the British troops penetrated a few houses near the Redan. Henry Clifford wrote that he had been told how these soldiers rushed into a house 'expecting to find Russian soldiers, but on bursting in the door, there sat three Sisters of Charity who went on working quietly and never once lifted up their heads . . . the rough soldiers withdrew and left in peace and with respect these Sisters of Mercy'. The soldier who told Clifford the story added that he would have killed anybody who lifted a hand against them.[40] These were almost certainly the Sisters of the Exaltation of the Cross, formed by the Grand Duchess Elena Pavlovna at the request of the army surgeon Nicolai Pirogov to look after the Russian army sick and wounded. They sent 161 nurses to the Crimean War where they nursed assiduously.[41] Their duties were similar to those of the British nurses, with the addition of assisting at operations which could include ligaturing blood vessels.[42] Seventeen of them died of disease, and several were injured during the repeated allied bombardments of Sevastopol.[43]

Another joint attack on Sevastopol on 8 September resulted in further losses, and another British failure to capture the Redan, although a section of it was temporarily captured before the Russians drove the British out. Richard Godman, a witness to the carnage, heard from survivors that in the captured section, 'the fighting was desperate, and when too close for muskets, they dashed each other's brains out with stones'.[44] However, the outcome of the 8 September attack was the French capture of the Malakoff bastion, and with that, the key turned that would soon open Sevastopol to the allies, who finally entered the city on 12 September. The withdrawing Russian troops had destroyed or set fire to what remained of the city following months of allied artillery bombardment. It was a scene of utter devastation. When news of the capture of Sevastopol reached Constantinople, warships and merchant vessels decked themselves with flags and bunting. 'The roar of guns from the different vessels was tremendous', said Emily Hornby. The celebratory cannonades died down but started up again at about eight in the evening, the sound of the explosions rattling the windows of the city. Ships in the Bosphorus were illuminated, and lanterns were hung around the palaces and minarets. Bands of Turkish musicians paraded the streets, playing loudly.[45]

The capture of Sebastopol marked the end of major military operations in the Crimean War, although this was not immediately apparent. Some British opinion wanted to restore the military prestige that had been lost in the failure to capture the Redan and to neutralize permanently Russian naval power in the Black Sea. Tsar Alexander II, who had succeeded Tsar Nicholas six months previously, visited his army in Crimea. Gazing at the ruins of Sevastopol he vowed to stand firm, but the reality was that he had neither the money nor the trained troops. Yet negotiations for peace did not begin in earnest until January 1856.[46]

Figure 1 Convent of Sisters of Mercy, Bermondsey, opened in 1839. Designed by A. W. N. Pugin, it was destroyed by V2 rocket in 1945. Credit: © RIBA Collections.

Figure 2 The *Illustrated London News* depicts a Sister of Mercy making her vows at the Bermondsey Convent, November 1839. Credit: © Illustrated London News Ltd/Mary Evans.

Figure 3 Anglican sisters left for the Crimean War from St Saviour's Convent, Osnaburgh St, London NW1. Designed by William Butterfield, it opened in 1852. Now demolished. Credit: © City of London/Heritage-Images/Getty Images.

Figure 4 Aftermath of the Battle of Inkerman, 5 November 1854, sketched by *Illustrated London News* artist Constantin Guys. Credit: © Chronicle/Alamy Stock Photo.

Figure 5 The vastness of Barrack Hospital, Scutari (now Selimiye Barracks) is shown in this picture of the building today. Credit: ©Alexxx Malev/Wikimedia Commons.

Figure 6 Detail of a lithograph showing one of the wards at Barrack Hospital, Scutari, after an original watercolour by William Simpson. Credit: ©Historical Picture Archive/CORBIS/Corbis via Getty Images.

Figure 7 At times of pressure, corridors at Barrack Hospital, Scutari, had to be turned into wards. Credit: © Wellcome Collection.

Figure 8 A ward in Koulali Hospital, 1856, sketched by a patient, showing a Sister of Mercy on the right accompanied by an orderly. Credit: © Wellcome Collection.

Figure 9 Amputees at Chatham Military Hospital, photographed by Joseph Cundall, 1856. Frostbite as well as wounds led to the loss of limbs. Credit: © Royal Collection Trust/© Her Majesty Queen Elizabeth II 2021.

Was Koulali Hospital better than those directly under Nightingale at Scutari? Those around Bridgeman believed as much. Aloysius Doyle said that Koulali was hailed by doctors as 'the model hospital of the East'.[47] Frances Taylor similarly recalled that 'the hospital so improved that it became the admiration of all who visited it, and the pride of the ladies and nurses who worked in it, and we used to call it "the model hospital of the East"'.[48] Bridgeman believed that because they were free from 'secular' interference in the upper hospital, they could put into effect 'obedience, system, order and good nursing'.[49] She said that Koulali's good name, 'and the totally different system of nursing adopted there, with the full approval of the doctors, seemed to have keenly excited Miss Nightingale's jealousy'. Koulali, then, was adduced as a demonstration of the superior nursing offered by the Sisters of Mercy. Nightingale's alleged jealousy was now added to that of the Anglican sisters and the Protestant chaplains. The figures, however, show a more nuanced outcome.

Limited statistics are available. In February 1855, the ratio of deaths to admissions at Koulali was 52 per cent, as against Scutari's 40.6 per cent.[50] Further direct comparisons are difficult because the data periods are not directly comparable, but from April to June 1855, Koulali had a death rate of 25.9 per cent of admissions; at Scutari, for the far longer period from June 1854 to June 1856, the figure was 11.9 per cent.[51] In many ways, Koulali *was* superior after the Sanitary Commission reforms. Its location was better than Scutari for landing patients, there was a more unified system of command for both medicine and nursing, and the religious influence of the nuns seems to have helped create a calmer, more humane atmosphere. Being smaller also made it more manageable. But like the other hospitals, it struggled during the winter crisis of 1855, and for the same reasons. Its poorer outcomes were not the fault of the nurses. McDonald points out that the Sanitary Commission considered Koulali to have the worst drains of all the hospitals. Yet, 'Nightingale never blamed the nurses at the Koulali hospital for their high death rates, doubtless considering that they were no more responsible for the sewers and drains at "their" hospital than she was at "hers"'.[52] Nightingale understood that nursing was only one of many factors involved in improving outcomes.

Koulali Hospital saw needless deaths in one of the strangest incidents of the Crimean War. The Sisters of Mercy in the hospital were forced to participate in a grotesque medical experiment, as a result of which patients were starved to death. The experiment came about as a result of agitation by civilian doctors working in Constantinople. These civilian doctors insisted that British military doctors were adopting the wrong course of treatment for dysentery. The accusation was that British medical officers by giving their patients stimulants like wine, brandy and nourishing food were making things worse. According to local lore, good nutrition like this had the perverse effect of making dysentery worse, and in consequence soldiers under their care were dying needlessly. These civilian dissidents gained the ear of the *Times* correspondent who wrote an inflammatory article about their concern. He alleged that it was widely talked about in Constantinople that British military doctors were 'killing their patients' through their 'wrongheaded adherence' to an unsuitable treatment in which men 'were sacrificed to their incompetence'. The Constantinople doctors recommended instead the Turkish practice of treating dysentery by greatly reducing the food intake of the patient, and applying leeches. In reply, the army doctors protested that while this might have worked for men in strong health, if applied to 'the enfeebled wretches who arrive from the trenches . . . it would kill them in 12 hours'.[53]

Andrew Smith, medical director-general of the Army in London, decided to put the Turkish 'cure' to the test. He sent out Dr Andrew Bryce, a civilian doctor who had previously practised in Constantinople. Bryce was allocated 100 beds at Koulali. Frances Taylor, who does not name him, described him as 'a very eccentric person' who greatly admired the Turkish way of doing things and was determined to show its efficacy by sharply reducing the diet of his military patients. He also forbade the nurses to give the patients any of the comforts available from the extra stores. The nuns had to implement this policy. Their distress is hinted at by Taylor, who notes that the sisters did all they were permitted to do for their patients, but felt unable to make any remonstrance. They saw the nurses in other wards pleased with the number of patients who were convalescing, while their task was to watch 'the slow progress of disease and death' as their patients succumbed to medically induced starvation.[54] The number of patients who died in this way is not known.

Nightingale knew about Bryce's experiment. She wrote that he 'was allowed a fair and ample trial at Koulali, when he let his patients die' until he finally adopted the usual English practice of good nourishment and stimulants.[55] His starvation treatment had limited nutrition to small quantities of linseed meal with rice water.[56] Bryce may have recognized the enormity of his conduct because there is an implicit echo of guilt in his memoirs. He does not refer to this incident directly. But in a general description of hospital care, he claimed that he had 'never heard . . . of a diet cancelled on grounds of excessive liberality. . . . And the truth is, that fowls, fish, the best of soups, eggs, milk . . . champagne, claret, fruits – indeed every kind of luxury that could be afforded in high life at home – were dispensed medically to the soldiers.'[57] This unlikely suggestion of high-living soldiers seems designed to hide his experiment which in reality deprived a cohort of his patients of food and condemned them to death. And in an interesting example of association, Bryce proceeded almost immediately to praise the Sisters of Mercy for their 'prudent nursing' which had saved many lives.[58] Perhaps he worried that they knew the truth, and hoped that his praise would forestall any possible future criticism.

The general context encouraged unquestioning obedience. In his letter of appointment to Nightingale, Sidney Herbert had stressed that the nurses must obey the instructions given by the medical officers: 'You will impress upon those acting under your orders the necessity of the strictest attention to the regulations of the Hospital, and the preservation of that subordination which is indispensable in every Military Establishment.'[59] Nightingale initially won a place for her nurses at Scutari in exactly this way, by demonstrating how they could work under military command. Reflecting on her experiences, Nightingale wrote that she 'took service on the grounds of being under the principal medical officer' and there was no independent power. There were instances when nuns gave food on their own initiative, and she immediately put a stop to it. 'That the medical officer is the sole master of diets is an axiom of medicine, and of common sense.'[60] She and Bridgeman likewise expected those they commanded to accept their instructions. It was a strictly hierarchical system. At a time when there were few options for drugs or invasive treatments, the administration of food was regarded as one of the doctor's tools. In our own day, there is still an echo of this in the saying, 'Feed a cold, starve a fever.' Bridgeman maintained that when it came to food, the patients at Koulali were well cared for and the doctors were satisfied. But significantly she added that 'nothing by way of food was given by the Sisters without a general or particular permission from the doctors'.[61] Nightingale certainly agreed with the principle, saying: 'The only system by which female nursing establishments can be made of permanent use is that of issuing every article, whether of food or clothing, upon the written requisitions *only* of the medical officer in charge.'[62] The silence of the Sisters of Mercy watching their patients starve to death has to be seen in this atmosphere of command and obedience.

Taylor makes it clear that Hutton knew about the policy of starvation imposed by this doctor, and sympathized with the nuns having to implement his orders. Bridgeman must have known what was going on. Starvation takes time. There would have been the emotional toll of watching men fade away. Bridgeman repeatedly demonstrated her understanding of power relations, her articulacy and her courage. Yet when patients were starving to death in plain view, she and her sisters felt there was nothing they could do except make them comfortable. We might wonder why she did not see this as a moral issue that should have been challenged. On the other hand, the experiment underlines how the rigid role expectations of the day left so little room for the women to express themselves. In a system where the men themselves were under authority and those in charge did not brook questioning, the women were often left voiceless. Nightingale was resented earlier for speaking the truth publicly about Scutari, but had some protection first from Sidney Herbert and later from her public standing. Bridgeman and her sisters did not have these advantages. Nightingale knew what was going on with Bryce's 'experiment', and she as the ultimate nursing authority could have intervened, and chose not to do so. If she felt unable to do so, it is not surprising that Bridgeman did not do so either.

In the summer of 1855, with her characteristic astuteness, Bridgeman realized that the time would soon come when Koulali was no longer necessary to the British army. The creation of hospitals in Crimea greatly reduced the flow of patients to Koulali. When Koulali closed where would Bridgeman and her sisters apply their talents and energies? To go to Scutari and put themselves under Nightingale was unthinkable to her. She and her sisters could have returned to Ireland, but they had been out less than a year, and she was aware of how the hierarchy valued the good name they were winning for Catholic Church. The solution was to offer their services as nurses in Crimea, and she apprised Sir John Hall, the principal medical officer in the east, of this possibility.

In mid-1855 nursing provision in Crimea was fragmentary and in a state of flux. In January, Nightingale had sent a party of eight nurses to Balaclava led by the Anglican Mother Emma Langston, accompanied by Sister Hannah Erskine. The departure back to England in April of these two Anglican sisters and later of other nurses had left only a handful of nurses in Crimea without clear leadership, although Jane Shaw Stewart took an informal lead. Meanwhile, the question of the extent of Nightingale's powers had still not been clarified. She had been appointed in charge of the female nursing establishment in Turkey, but Crimea was part of Russia. Nightingale had visited the Crimea in May when she had been received with acclaim by the ordinary soldiers, but her status was ambiguous. She had fallen dangerously ill while out there (typhus and brucellosis have both been suggested) but she had resisted suggestions that she should go to England or Switzerland to recuperate.

Nightingale had never been on good terms with Sir John Hall. She believed him to be strangely indifferent to the plight of the wounded or sick soldiers. Chloroform was beginning to be used in surgery for anaesthesia, but Hall had sent a circular to the surgeons discouraging its use, on the grounds that the pain of the operation was more likely to stimulate the men to recovery. Hence it was better to hear them 'bawl lustily under the knife'. Some surgeons chose to disobey him rather than inflict needless suffering.[63] When Hall was knighted with the KCB, Nightingale dubbed him 'Knight of the Crimean Burying Grounds'.[64] He in turn resented her high public profile. Her fame implied that the arrangements made by the army medical service were inadequate and that she had rescued the situation.

When Francis Bridgeman made her inquiry about nursing in Crimea, Hall saw a chance to neutralize Nightingale. In September he suggested to Nightingale that she withdraw the nurses in Crimea over whom she might still be said to exercise authority, and she agreed, perhaps seeing this as a first step towards a new nursing plan for Crimea. Hall swiftly gave Bridgeman and her sisters the responsibility of the General Hospital in Balaclava.[65] This scheme had added attraction for the Irish sisters. It would bring together the smaller party still at General Hospital, Scutari, with the larger group at Koulali, in one shared enterprise. Above all, it would support Bridgeman's claim that she was not under Nightingale's authority. Bridgeman could say that she had been appointed to her position in Crimea by Sir John Hall, and was answerable to him alone. As Nightingale's biographer Mark Bostridge puts it, 'Florence had been roundly tricked.'[66]

Nightingale wrote in protest to the War Office, to the ambassador at Constantinople, and to General Sir Henry Storks, military commandant of the hospitals in Turkey, but the situation was fait accompli. With characteristic overstatement Nightingale wrote to a beloved aunt, Mai Smith, 'My cause has been betrayed by everyone – ruined, betrayed, destroyed, by everyone, alas.'[67] And to her mother, she wrote that she was 'wearied . . . by the ill will, incompetence, ignorance and bigotry . . . varied only with occasional flashes of more vehement hatred and ill being'.[68] The offending parties are not named, but she must have had Bridgeman and Hall in mind. She had been outwitted by an Irish nun. But it was disingenuous for Nightingale to complain. Soon after the Bridgeman group arrived, Nightingale had told Bridgeman that she had no power to assign any role to the Irish sisters, save the small party coming to General Hospital, Scutari.[69] Later she took little interest in Koulali Hospital and as described earlier, in April had asked the War Office to 'dissever' her connection with it. Moreover, there is no sign that she recognized the contribution the sisters and others had made to its operational success. In fact, she was prone to misrepresenting Koulali by saying that the nuns had been issuing extras to the patients without medical authorization. She alleged that this had resulted in 'enormous' expenditure and when the authorities put a stop to it, the nuns had resigned.[70] She alleged that this profligacy had led to the end of British nursing at Koulali, but it was simply not true. In fact, the hospital was handed over to the Sardinians and the German Legion because there were no longer sufficient British patients to justify its existence.

To save what authority she could, on 8 October Nightingale joined Bridgeman and her sisters on the *Ottawa* to sail to Balaclava. When the time came for Bridgeman and her nuns to depart, there were tears from some of those they left behind at Koulali. A wry Bridgeman noted that some of the NCOs and orderlies who had worked with them, having 'abstained from drink in a special compliment to us, got drunk to drown grief on this memorable day'.[71] It must have been a strange, tense voyage. Perhaps the seasickness that kept the passengers in their cabins helped avoid a confrontation.

In Crimea, a new chapter would open for the Irish nuns. Their relationship with Nightingale would continue to deteriorate. And two of the nuns would not return home.

6

Balaclava battleground

Balaclava had been the centre of British operations in Crimea since September 1854. Its poor harbour, muddy roads and desolate beach had sent many sick and dying men to hospitals in Scutari. When the Sanitary Commission visited in March 1855 it was appalled to find that the contents of latrines were dumped into the small harbour, which also received waste from ships and the bodies of dead horses.[1] The cemetery had been built in a marshy area, and remains of the dead could be seen protruding above the ground, to the extent, said Nightingale, that portions of extremities and red coats to be seen even above the surface.[2] These were only some of the many sanitary problems that needed rectifying. Six months later Balaclava was a changed place. The Sanitary Commission's actions neutralized the problems of sewage and the cemetery. There were other improvements in the course of 1855. A railway line now transported goods to the British camp on the heights above Balaclava. Mary Seacole dispensed hospitality and traditional medicine from her establishment in the town. In the camps themselves, there were stronger tents and wooden huts, and the men were better fed and clothed.[3] These improvements meant that there would be less pressure on the hospital that the Irish nuns inherited at Balaclava. Winter, however, would still be an endurance test, and the war was never far away. When the nuns arrived on 10 October 1855, they could hear the rumble of distant cannon fire. Sevastopol might be in allied hands but the Russians were still just north of the city, and from the Star Fort were able to shell some of the allied lines. Beyond the nearby Chernaya river, the Russian army mustered fourteen divisions.

On 12 October Dr Hall welcomed Bridgeman and the Sisters of Mercy to the General Hospital at the north end of town and formally inducted Bridgeman in charge of nursing. Including Bridgeman, thirteen Sisters of Mercy were assigned to this hospital (two had already returned to Ireland). For six months a small team, mostly orderlies, had kept the hospital functioning under the medical officers.[4] Jane Shaw Stewart had taken over leadership of the hospital from Mother Emma Langston. Then she moved to take charge of the Castle Hospital, and Margaret Wear supervised while the Welsh nurse, Elizabeth Davis, ran the extra-diet kitchen. But leadership had fragmented and morale was low. The newly arrived sisters faced the task of revitalizing the place. It was an added challenge that General Hospital was, as its name implied, a port of call not only for sick soldiers and sailors but also for the men in other trades such as merchants and muleteers. Among the civilian patients, there were Maltese, Greeks, Italians, Americans and Africans.[5] At times civilians constituted the majority of the patients. When the sisters arrived there were also some Russian prisoners of war. All patients received the same attention from the sisters, regardless of status.[6] A surgeon who was unaware of the nuns' arrival was startled when, on a midnight visit to a critically ill patient, he saw 'by the light of a wretched little lamp' a dark figure gliding from bed to bed. It was one of the nuns, 'attired from head to food in the deepest black; even their heads are carefully hooded. The only relief to this sombre attire is the double string of large beads hanging from their girdle.' But, he added, they were very attentive 'and eminently deserving of the name they bear, "Sisters of Mercy"'.[7]

The dressing of wounds was considered to be properly the work of doctors, or of the dressers who worked under their instruction. Even so, the surgeon in charge could ask the nuns to open bandages or dress any wound if he saw fit. The Irish nuns at Balaclava were usually on hand to cut the linen bandages to the size required for each wound. They also took charge of the preparation of any poultices. They had devised a system for changing the bed linen of patients who were in great pain, folding the sheets in a pattern that minimized their suffering.[8]

The wards of General Hospital Balaclava were in two parallel stone buildings which had originally housed a Russian military school. Only the seaward side of the buildings had windows, as the reverse wall backed onto the sloping hillside. The walls inside and out were limewashed regularly. These wards were supplemented by fourteen huts scattered on the adjacent hillside, which meant a good deal of clambering up and down the hill. At first, the sisters lived and slept in one hut, 24 foot × 10. Meals were taken sitting on their beds. By the end of 1855, two additional huts had been made ready for the sisters, and poles and sheets were used to create individual units for each of them. A third hut was used as a community room, and there was an oratory.[9] However, the problem of the rats never went away. Not only were the huts plagued with enormous rats, but the rats were bold and unafraid and their scuttling about kept the nuns awake at night.

During their first week cholera broke out and they took it in turns to sit up through the night with critically ill patients. When this outbreak subsided the sisters found the work less heavy than previously, which Joseph Croke greeted as a great relief. Their exertions at Koulali and Scutari had taken a toll and they did not have the strength they once had. The sense of relief comes through in the diary kept by Croke. There are moments of release when the accumulated tension is let go in fits of laughter as good-humoured sisters egg each other on, although they were careful not to bring hilarity into the wards.[10] At first, the weather was pleasant enough to allow the nuns to take evening walks on the hillside. During one of them, Croke averred that she had seen the flash of a Russian cannon in the far distance. Before long the weather changed. Winds whistled through chinks in the wooden wall of their hut. There was daily Mass at 7.00 am. Rotas were arranged during a retreat week so that the sisters could make their retreat one by one.

On 20 October it was clear that cholera had spread from the patients to one of the sisters, Winifred Sprey. A chaplain anointed her and gave her communion. After this, she seemed to rally, and for a while, they hoped she might pull through. Winifred herself was confident and pronounced that she was not going to die. Nightingale came to watch with the sisters and knelt with them in prayer. She knew Winifred better than most because she had been one of the five from Bridgeman's group who had not gone to Koulali but nursed instead at Scutari. As they prayed the sisters were shocked to see Winifred's face and hands turn black. Her mind began to wander. She died on 21 October. 'The first gone of our little band and gone so quickly', wrote Aloysius Doyle, 'full of life and energy the day before. We were all very sad, and wondering who would be next.'[11] Bridgeman remembered the scene as a desolate picture, 'The wretched wooden hut, damp and unfurnished with the wind playing freely through the open chinks. The poor, uncurtained bed. The Sister of Mercy extended on it, dying of that fearful disease far from her convent.' After Sprey's death, the sisters took turns to stay up and guard her corpse in case it was attacked by rats. She was buried the next day. Three priests chanting the *Miserere* led the way to the grave, one holding a thurible of incense, the other a processional cross, with a large crowd of soldiers, sailors and hospital officials following. The coffin was borne by four soldiers to a grave on the hillside above Balaclava.[12]

A closer look shows that the accounts of this death written by Sister Joseph Croke and Mother Francis Bridgeman respectively, do not quite tally. Croke's account is contemporaneous, in diary form. In Croke's telling, Bridgeman asks Nightingale to send a mounted orderly to bring a priest as quickly as possible. Nightingale joins in the deathbed prayers and attends the funeral having asked Bridgeman's permission first. In Bridgeman's account, these positive facts are not mentioned, and instead, the funeral becomes one more negative instance of Nightingale's assertiveness, first by Nightingale attempting to assist with the funeral arrangements, then by her offering to have a stone cross erected over the grave. Bridgeman rejected these offers and wrote that these 'acts of kindness' really showed the 'continued surveillance' of Nightingale and were intended as such.[13] It seems that in the eyes of Mother Francis Bridgeman, the motivations of Florence Nightingale were to be regarded as always suspect and possibly malign. Outwardly their relations were conducted with glacial civility, but inwardly there was deepening hostility.

Nightingale was still trying to exert her authority over all nursing in the region. She wrote to Hawes in January 1856, insisting that nursing arrangements should always come through her. In a marginal note written on her letter, Hawes allowed his irritation to show through:

> Is every woman who can aid the sick and wounded, to be forbidden to enter the Crimea, even at the request of the distinguished head of the Medical Department of the Army in the East, unless with the consent of Miss Nightingale? . . . I think it is time we curbed the pretensions of Miss Nightingale to unlimited & almost irresponsible command. . . . When it suited her views, she threw over all those stationed at Koulali.[14]

Nightingale returned to Scutari on 21 November, having renewed her authority over two other Crimea hospitals, the Castle Hospital and the Land Transport Corps Hospital, but still kept at arm's length by Bridgeman and her sisters who continued to run the General Hospital.

The nuns had little time for mourning, as the cholera outbreak lasted well into December. The sisters took in turns to watch their patients through the night. Mustard poultices were applied, and chloroform was rubbed on also, in attempt to save the sick men. Early in November, the snow arrived, and the Crimea winter was upon them. A tough Russian cat purchased for seven shillings put the rats in their hut to flight. On 19 December the day was so cold that Bridgeman ordered all the sisters not working to stay in bed. On returning from the wards on Christmas Eve the sisters found an anonymous gift in their quarters, a basket containing a bottle of champagne. On Christmas Day itself, there was rice pudding for all the patients, and those who had clubbed together were able to have plum pudding. Four Masses were celebrated.

Across the water at Scutari, the approach to Christmas had been marred by the recurrence of cholera in November. Between twenty and thirty patients were dying daily. The German medical corps was particularly hard hit, and Gonzaga Barrie, who spoke German, went to comfort them.[15] The sisters were constantly in the wards and Clare Moore went around at night to help them. When Christmas came spirits lifted. The Scutari Sisters of Mercy found that a party of prisoners had been sent out on Christmas Eve to bring back green boughs. These were arranged to decorate the Barrack Hospital chapel. Soldiers were waiting from 4.00 am for the Mass of the Dawn at 6.30 am. This was followed by another Mass at 7.30 am and Catholic troops were paraded for the final Mass at 9.00 am. The men all enjoyed themselves, recorded Moore, 'some, of course, a little too much and had the misfortune of being taken to the prison cells'.[16]

The vicinity of Balaclava General Hospital was a thoroughly masculine atmosphere in which the nuns had become used to being the only female presence. Croke realized this on 1 February when she noted, 'I saw a *live* women going by! The first since we came here, it was a relief to the eyes. I called the Sisters to look at her.' Women were few in proportion to the men at Balaclava, but in fact, there were other women there. Officers' wives could be seen in the town, and presumably also some of the soldiers' wives who had intrepidly joined their menfolk. Most colourful of all were the French *cantinières* who would ride into town in their colourful uniforms, shocking the British by riding astride the horse in a masculine fashion.[17] The sisters rarely ventured far from the grounds of the hospital except for walks up the hill. In February they were sickened by hearing the cries of pain from one of the orderlies being flogged in the space between the hospital buildings. On another occasion, a patient who was under a charge was freed at the earnest appeal of the sisters.[18]

Although the winter of 1856 was as harsh as usual, the improved supply situation meant that many fewer British soldiers fell ill. It helped, too, that with the capture of Sevastopol, there was less need for soldiers to spend long hours in damp trenches or standing guard in the snow. The army was now better fed and better sheltered. Mortality rates for medical conditions other than cholera were low. Where frostbite occurred it was usually ears or hands, not in the feet or lower leg as before. Cholera, typhus and bowel infections were the main problems.[19] The nursing of the Sisters of Mercy there played an important part in bringing about these improved outcomes.

By the end of January, there was increasing talk of peace, feeding the sisters' hopes that a final treaty would be soon concluded and they could return home. But the negotiations dragged on and it was not until 25 February that the peace conference opened in Paris. An armistice was declared on 29 February. It was all the harder for the nuns that now, with peace almost in sight, they lost another sister. Elizabeth Butler fell ill with typhus on 17 February. She was anointed on the 22 February and died the following day. She was 'in agony' during her last few hours, on a stormy night when the noise of the wind and rain was so loud that the prayers for the dying 'had frequently to be interrupted to let the frightful blast pass over'. The wind blew so strongly through the chinks in the hut that it kept extinguishing the lights, and the prayers 'mingled with the howling of the wind and creaking of the frail wooden hut'.[20]

Elizabeth Butler's funeral was a public liturgy even more impressive than Winifred Sprey's four months previously. Displays of Catholic and largely Irish solidarity were not new. Each Sunday 500 cavalry of the 8th Hussars would ride to Mass led by Viscount Killeen, impressing onlookers with the glitter of 'their brass helmets and long swords . . . The noise of their accoutrements and the capering of their horses.'[21] Now, for the funeral, soldiers with heads uncovered stood in double lines on each side of the path as Elizabeth Butler's body was taken from the hut where she had died, first to the hospital chapel, and then, after the office of the dead, up the hillside to her grave. The 89th Regiment asked to be freed from their daily parade so that they could attend the funeral and carry the coffin. This regiment was originally raised in Dublin and the nuns felt an especially close relationship with it. Aloysius Doyle recorded that over a thousand mourners attended the funeral, where the respectful silence was broken only by the voice of the priest leading the prayers. Eight priests and five or six Italian sisters from the Sardinian army were present.[22] Francis Bridgeman turned down a suggestion that Elizabeth Butler be buried with military honours.

The attention given to the funerals of the two nuns contrasts with the perfunctory treatment of dead soldiers. Before the capture of Sevastopol, Henry Clifford, an officer in the British lines, noted that the daily experience of death had hardened the troops. In fact, they had been desensitized to the extent that the stretcher bearing the dead could pass through the camp, 'taking some poor fellow to his last resting place – unnoticed'.[23] The attention given to the nuns in death by the soldiers suggests that in these obsequies the men claimed in some way a dignity for their own dead. A code of stoicism muted the grief for the deaths in their own ranks, which were anyway too numerous to be marked properly. But they could allow themselves to grieve the two sisters who died.

Throughout the winter months, Nightingale had been pushing the War Office in London to clarify her status. She pressed for a formal declaration that she was in sole charge of military nursing in the region. She was in frequent contact with John Henry Lefroy, an aide to Lord Panmure, the minister of war. Lefroy, probably meaning to help Nightingale, asked one of the officials in the Crimea to draw up a confidential report on the state of army nursing in Crimea. Lefroy gave the task to David Fitzgerald, the deputy purveyor-in-chief. Fitzgerald was an officious character, much given to paperwork and a sense of his own importance, but a key figure in the supply chain and thus essential to the smooth running of hospitals. Francis Bridgeman, with her intuitive understanding of how people and systems operate, had quickly taken the measure of the man. She found him 'most difficult to manage and most penitential to deal with, and yet one whom it was most essential we should win to work with us'.[24] She quickly won him round and he became her devoted ally.

His partisanship was evident in the rambling report he submitted to the War Office on 24 December 1855. He drew attention to the confusion caused by changes in leadership since the departure of Emma Langston in April, and to the wrangling and discontent that had ensued. The problem, said Fitzgerald, was that nursing superintendents disobeyed the medical officers, on the grounds that they were subordinate only to Nightingale. Hence, 'a supreme superintendent' [i.e. Nightingale] would be incompatible with 'local controls, actions, obedience and co-operation'. The report wended its way in purple prose to a conclusion which turned out to be a paean of praise for the Sisters of Mercy:

> The superiority of an ordered system is beautifully illustrated in the 'Sisters of Mercy', – one mind appears to move all; – and their intelligence, delicacy, and conscientiousness, invest them with a halo of confidence extreme [sic]; the Medical Officer can safely consign his most critical case to their hands; – stimulants or opiates – ordered every five minutes, will be faithfully administered, though the five minute labour were repeated uninterruptedly for a week.
> ... a calm resigned contentedness sits [on] the features of all – and the soft cares of the female and the Lady breathes placidity throughout.[25]

The report naturally delighted Bridgeman, although one wonders what she made of this defining male gaze turned on the heroic and sacrificial work of her sisters. Nightingale had not been given a copy of the report. She heard of it through Lefroy at the War Office. She was furious and wrote to London repudiating the implied calumny in the report and challenging the facts it claimed to present, calling part of it 'a malicious and scandalous libel' against the good names of nurses it had criticized. She concluded by challenging the War Office not only to clarify her status but also to instruct Sir John Hall not to oppose her in the exercise of her duties. The appointment and allocation of nurses should be solely her responsibility.[26]

In letters to those she trusted Nightingale wrote bitterly about Fitzgerald and let fly with anti-Catholic and anti-Irish sentiments. It must have been galling for her to find Fitzgerald praising Bridgeman who had challenged her authority throughout. Fitzgerald was Catholic, and Nightingale not unreasonably suspected that Catholics were uniting against her.[27] In a letter to her uncle Samuel Smith she wrote, 'Now Mrs Bridgeman and Fitzgerald are one.'[28] She wrote similarly to Lefroy, complaining that the British government feared inflaming Irish sentiment, and for this reason had passively allowed 'Fitzgerald's slanders and Mrs Bridgeman's insurrection'. She alleged that at Scutari, Bridgeman and her sisters were always called 'The Brickbats'. They were

> the tools of an Irish faction. . . . By strengthening the *Irish* R.C.s here, the government raise up enemies to themselves, the Irish R.C.s hating the English government as they do. . . . I have always said that a R.C. can do everything which we cannot do, lie, steal, murder, slander, because we are afraid of the Roman Catholics. What an advantage it must be![29]

Nightingale's extreme language shows the extent to which 'Catholic' and 'Irish' had coalesced in her mind to figure as her enemy, forgetting that Mother Mary Clare Moore was also Irish. She asserted that others called the Irish nuns 'Brickbats' but the derogatory cognomen was Nightingale's own creation. At the end of 1854, Nightingale was already calling Bridgeman 'Brickbat' in a letter to Sidney Herbert.[30] Now she was extending this derogatory name to the whole cohort of Irish sisters. In her mixture of exhaustion and resentment, Nightingale was resorting to ethnic slurs and slotting her own narrative into a longer-standing one of English–Irish antipathy. But this worked the other way too. The Irish nuns from the outset had seen themselves representing Ireland in the face of an unfriendly England. It could not end well.

Nightingale's request for the backing of the War Office was granted. On 25 February 1856, Lord Panmure wrote to General Sir William Codrington, the Crimean Commander-in-Chief, criticizing Sir John Hall for interfering in the allocation of nurses. Codrington was told to promulgate in his General Orders 'the rightful position of Miss Nightingale in reference to the distribution, situation and power of discharge, or dismissal or all nurses, and sisters, employed in the military hospitals of the Army'. Nightingale had won. Or had she? Her arch-enemy Hall had been censured. She was duly proclaimed in sole charge of nursing in Codrington's General Order of 16 March 1856. Yet it is significant that Panmure's move concurred with progress at the Paris peace conference, which concluded with the ratification of the peace treaty on 30 March. Panmure supported Nightingale in the knowledge that her reign would be limited to the time it took the British army to disengage in Crimea and return home. Moreover, even the ascription of authority to her was qualified by the requirement that she work in co-operation with the principal medical officer – Sir John Hall. If this was a vindication of her, it was a late one and still left room for future friction.

Nightingale sailed once more across the Black Sea and arrived in Balaclava on 25 March. She went to the General Hospital to assure Francis Bridgeman that she and her Irish nuns were welcome to stay. She said that she would not interfere or make any changes as long as Dr Hall was satisfied. This gesture by Nightingale offered a degree of autonomy to Bridgeman but Bridgeman would have none of it. She was afraid, as she put it, 'Once under her control, we would be at her mercy'.[31] Once more, Bridgeman alleged that Nightingale's nursing system was inadequate in comparison with the practice of the Irish Sisters of Mercy: '[Nightingale] knew that neither she nor her system, nurses, etc., was in good order, that our leaving would still more distinctly and publicly mark and distinguish our systems and working from hers'.[32] Nightingale made several visits but Bridgeman did not change her mind. Bridgeman called Nightingale 'the goddess of humbug'.[33]

During the last two weeks of their stay, the Irish sisters distributed great quantities of books, rosaries and religious medals. They were besieged with well-wishers asking for keepsakes, and sisters in turn were looking for soldiers to return money given to them for safekeeping.[34] The Irish nuns embarked on the *Cleopatra* on 11 April, boosted by the knowledge that General Codrington had written to Hall regretting their departure, and asking him to convey to Bridgeman 'the high estimation in which her services, and those of the nurses, are held by us all'.[35] Soldiers, many in tears, came to say goodbye to the sisters, who sailed on the following day.

At General Hospital Balaclava, between October 1855 and July 1856 there were only 27 deaths out of 1,363 patients admitted.[36] October 1855 was when Bridgeman and her sisters arrive. Their nursing must have contributed to this remarkable success rate. The departing sisters left behind them two sisters in graves hewn into a rocky hillside, surrounded by iron railings and surmounted by a white marble cross. The nuns arrived at Portsmouth on 8 May, and after an initial stay in London made their way home to their various convents. While in London, Bridgeman had several meetings with Dr Andrew Smith, the director-general of the army medical department who had often clashed with Nightingale. According to Bridgeman, he made dark hints about gathering material about Nightingale which would expose her failures, 'and that the whole truth of the nursing system would come out. He seemed well aware of Miss Nightingale's character, mismanagement, etc.'[37] In effect, he was pumping Bridgeman for more information, but she was too canny for this and simply reassured him that she had kept careful records of what had transpired between herself and Nightingale. Already Bridgeman had an eye to the battle for the narrative after the war.

The handover at Balaclava descended into recrimination and pettiness. Nightingale had to struggle even to get the keys to the hospital. Fitzgerald continued his hostility to her. After the handover, he tried to frustrate her by withholding supplies. According to Susan Goldie, he showed 'petty and obstructive malice' and 'deliberately set out to be as obstructive as he could'.[38] Fitzgerald's officiousness had previously hindered others. Once an exasperated medical officer had placed him under arrest because of his obstructiveness.[39] Some of the letters Fitzgerald wrote to Hall explaining how he was trying to block Nightingale convey a pathetic toadying to power.[40] Was Fitzgerald's obstructionism part of the Irish and Catholic conspiracy against her that Nightingale believed she had detected? Fitzgerald did feel an innate sympathy with the Irish nuns, but Bridgeman too found Fitzgerald difficult to work with and had set out to win his favour. The obstacles encountered by Nightingale seem to be less due to conspiracy than to the interplay of the personalities involved.

Nightingale declared that the Irish nuns had left General Hospital in a deplorable state, 'a pigsty . . . we must whitewash, scrub, scour, to prevent fever. . . . The patients here are in the most disgraceful state of dirt and filth and bedsores.'[41] Within days Sir John Hall had visited the hospital and now declared that *Nightingale* had let it deteriorate. He wrote angrily to Nightingale, ordering her to restore it to the admirable order it had enjoyed under Bridgeman.[42] In Nightingale's account, the Irish nuns had left the hospital in a deplorable state; in Hall's account, it had declined quickly and shockingly under Nightingale's watch. Both scenarios seem extremely unlikely, but the controversy would flare up again later. The stress of war had taken its toll and patience was snapping. Even the cease-fire and the approaching peace might have contributed to this. In the heat of war, rivalries can be sidelined as an army focusses on its most urgent tasks. When the pressure eases, suppressed tensions emerge.

At the most obvious level, there was a clash of wills between Nightingale and Bridgeman, both of them strong personalities. Their relationship had never recovered from Nightingale's rejection of the Irish nuns when they arrived at Scutari in December 1854. Over the next sixteen months, the Irish Sisters of Mercy and Florence Nightingale had grown in mistrust of each other, which in turn had accentuated ethnic sensitivities.

In her conflict with Bridgeman, Nightingale privately accused the Irish nuns of wasteful expenditure and mendacity. She even hinted at the abuse of alcohol.[43] Some of her accusations are about 'Catholics', but the context indicates that Irishness is at issue.[44] In a controversy caused by a Jesuit refusal to hear the confessions of the English Sisters of Mercy at Balaclava, she wrote that there was 'none so coarse as an Irish R.C. priest'.[45] There was a split in Nightingale's mind between English and Irish Catholicism. English Catholicism represented her friendship with Mary Clare Moore and the good works carried out by her sisters. Irish Catholicism represented untrustworthiness and subversion, characterized by Francis Bridgeman. Nightingale was tapping into the long history of English fears about Ireland's loyalty to the crown. In 1798 Wolfe Tone had sought to raise a rebellion in Ireland with the help of French forces, leaving a residual fear that enemies might use Ireland as a springboard for an invasion of England. More recently, a small localized Irish uprising in 1848 had been inspired by revolutions elsewhere in Europe that same year.

We might also wonder whether Nightingale's resort to anti-Irish stereotypes was fed by fear of the popularity of the Irish nuns. She knew that they had won the affection of many Irish soldiers. The funerals of the two sisters had been public liturgies with the serried ranks of the Irish soldiers demonstrating their solidarity with the nuns. Did she fear that the soldiers would resent her arrival and blame her for the departure of the others? Croke recorded in her diary that the Inniskilling Dragoons and the 88th Royal Irish Regiment were almost entirely Catholic, 'staunch papist heroes', and that its soldiers resented more recent recruits from 'other creeds'.[46] References like this convey an impression of a mutually reinforcing circle of nuns, chaplains and soldiers.

Nightingale had guessed that the Irish nuns might depart rather than work under her. As a precaution, she had taken with her to Balaclava three of the Sisters of Mercy from Clare Moore's group: Stanislaus Jones, Helen Ellis and Martha Beste. She also brought with her the remaining two Anglican sisters, Bertha Turnbull and Margaret Goodman. Within half an hour of the Irish sisters leaving the hospital at Balaclava, Nightingale had moved in with her new nursing team. She soon realized, however, that more help would be needed. She had assumed responsibility for another hospital, the Land Transport Corps (LTC) Hospital at

Karami, five miles away on the heights above Balaclava. This hospital had been established primarily for the large and motley corps of muleteers and others who made possible the endless movement of the vast amount of supplies needed by the army. These drivers and waggoners came from countries around the eastern Mediterranean and their hospital had been rather neglected. Nightingale wrote urgently to Moore back in Scutari asking for yet more sisters to be sent, and on 14 April Joseph Hawkins, De Chantal Hudden and Anastasia Kelly arrived to reinforce Nightingale's nursing team.

Without these six nuns sent to Crimea by Moore – and the two Anglican sisters – Nightingale's final achievement of nursing control could have collapsed. She knew that she could rely on Moore when an urgent response was needed. It was courageous for Moore to respond so generously given that she and Bridgeman belonged to the same religious congregation as Moore. The Mercy communities were autonomous, but they followed the same rule, were inspired by the same founder and belonged to a network of mutual respect and recognition. Moore, in supplying sisters who stepped in the moment the Bridgeman sisters stepped out of the door, could have been construed as implicitly criticizing Bridgeman's decisions. Although for the time being she kept her thoughts to herself, Moore well understood that Bridgeman had been working with Hall to oppose and undermine Nightingale. She also recorded that Purveyor Fitzgerald, in his campaign of petty harassment, had provided the newly arrived sisters and nurses with meals that were almost inedible.[47] The negativity of Bridgeman's departure had not affected the friendship and affection between Nightingale and Moore. Nor was Moore swayed by the prejudice Nightingale had developed against the Irish in general and Bridgeman in particular. Moore was fair-minded. She wrote that the departure of the Irish sisters 'was regretted by all parties. The Sisters had been greatly beloved by the Soldiers, they had laboured efficiently among them, [and] had gone through immense hardships' to fulfil their nursing duties in army hospitals.[48]

Soon the nuns newly recruited to Balaclava were making a difference in the hospitals to which they were assigned. Three Sisters of Mercy were assigned one wing of LTC Hospital and a hut to live in. The wind blew through the gaps and the first morning they woke to find themselves covered with snow in their beds. It was so cold that even the ink froze in their huts overnight. Nightingale was told by a medical officer that the reforms worked by the sisters at the LTC Hospital had achieved more than medicine.[49] The nuns found a friend in one of the Protestant chaplains, a Mr Holt, who surprised them once by galloping up in the middle of the snowstorm to present them with a kerchief full of eggs. He took every opportunity to show them kindness, from procuring fish for them on Fridays to finding a Turkish carpet for their hut. In return, they helped him with the laundering of his neck kerchiefs, the equivalent of a clerical collar in those days, and he teased them that they would have to confess having done an act of charity for a Protestant minister.[50] It was a rare example of friendship and co-operation across the confessional divide.

Nightingale told Clare Moore that at General Hospital, Balaclava, Sister Stanislaus was 'very brave' and was bringing order to the extra-diet system which had been in disarray. Anastasia was 'a very quiet steady helper' while De Chantal was 'commanding and courageous and not easily daunted'. But why was such courage needed? In a strange comment, Nightingale added that whatever she and the nuns achieved they would nevertheless be blamed because there were 'evil eyes all around them'. The implication seems to be that the allies of the Bridgeman sisters were predisposed against not only Nightingale, but also the English nuns too, who, as Nightingale put it, 'go on with their duty steadily, with a single eye to God'.[51]

Nightingale's fear of hostility towards the nuns was not a figment of her imagination. Once again a sacrament was used against them. The Jesuit chaplain at LTC Hospital, Fr Patrick Duffy, having discerned that the English Sisters of Mercy were aligned with Florence Nightingale, refused to hear their confessions. On their first Sunday, even the patients and staff suffered from his ire, when he declined to come to the hospital to say Mass for Catholics in the LTC Hospital.[52] Duffy was an inflexible man of military demeanour. Later in life, he wrote a spiritual book with a bracing title, *The Eleven Gun Battery for the Defence of the Castle of the Soul*.[53] In the practice of the day, confession preceded communion at Mass, and although the sisters were unlikely to be in a state of mortal sin, they would have been reluctant to make their communion without prior absolution. Duffy's polemical use of the sacraments in this way deprived not just the nuns but for all Catholics at LTC of a Mass that Sunday.

The nuns were more surprised because those who had come out to Scutari in January 1856 had found him friendly and supportive during the voyage. They had hoped to find in him a friend and spiritual counsellor, but his mind had been turned by talking to others at Balaclava who were fiercely critical of Nightingale. In the words of the Bermondsey *Annals*:

The astonishment of the sisters was great to receive from him a letter telling him that *he disapproved totally of their coming to Crimea – that he could not consent to connect himself with the transaction in any way whatever.* 'In my opinion, he went on "your Superior had committed a grave error in consenting to your coming here in the manner you have come, as I understand it. Such a proceeding, in my humble judgement, tends to the disgrace rather than to the honour of Religion".'[54]

He declared that he wanted nothing to do with them and called them a 'disgrace to their Church'.[55] Other priests took sides for and against the new party of sisters. Fr Michael Gleeson, a Vincentian priest and chaplain at Balaclava wrote to Bridgeman condemning the English sisters for 'co-operating with Miss Nightingale in her ugly work'.[56] Conversely, Fr John Bagshawe, an English priest and chaplain at Scutari, wrote to Gleeson expressing 'horror and regret' at the treatment of these nuns now working with Nightingale. Gleeson decided not to answer Bagshawe's letter and to have nothing to do with the sisters.[57] Factions pro- and anti- Nightingale seemed everywhere, from clergy in Crimea to officials in the War Office.

Confronted with this male abuse of sacramental power, the nuns recognized it for what it was and did not buckle. Moore wrote from Scutari to encourage them, and there is even a hint of amusement in her letter. She told Stanislaus Jones, 'Do not be the least discouraged about not getting Confession or H. Com. – remember our Bd Lord can supply for all.' Then, resuming the letter the next day, Moore wrote, 'Good morning Miss Heathen. I ought not to be writing to an excommunicate old woman, ought I?' But then she remembers how when they first arrived at Scutari the priests, even then, disliked their rapport with Nightingale and tried to turn them against her: 'Don't forget what we suffered here with those blessed clergy – & all the dilemmas we used to be in about confession – do take courage – pray for old Mother Sr. M. Clare.'[58] Anti-Catholic critics of convents sometimes portrayed nuns as in the thrall of priests. This letter shows a different picture, of how nuns through their self-confidence and mutual support could discern what was right according to their own conscience. But it also shows how priests could misuse confession for polemical or ethnic reasons.

Since May 1855 there had been only two Anglican nuns left at Scutari, Bertha Turnbull and Margaret Goodman. Before leaving Scutari to join Nightingale and the Sisters of Mercy supporting her in the Crimea, Goodman and Turnbull walked through the graveyard at Scutari. As they perused the names on the crosses they recalled the faces of many of the men they had nursed, now lying in those graves.[59] In Crimea, they were assigned to the Castle Hospital which contained an average of 500–600 patients attended by only between five and seven nurses.⁶⁰ This hospital consisted of a row of huts on a mountain ledge above Balaclava. The summit was occupied by the remains of an old Genoese castle. The accommodation hut of the Anglican sisters was so dark that a candle was needed in the middle of the day. There was the usual problem of rat infestation. A large-bodied Scottish nurse visiting them sat on a bed and on rising found that she had crushed to death five or six young rats. To improve their tough mutton stew, Goodman scoured the nearby hills for thyme and wild spinach. She also taught men to read and write in evening classes.⁶¹

Lady Hornby made a visit to Crimea in May with a cousin, a friend, two maids and an orderly. They went up to Castle Hospital. The sea glistened below. Margaret Goodman welcomed the visiting party into the hut she shared with Bertha Turnbull. During their time there the two Anglican sisters had been fascinated by the many types of wild flowers growing on nearby hillsides, an enthusiasm they shared with the visitors. Emily Hornby was impressed by the 'perfect cleanliness' of the house and the 'health, contentment and usefulness' of the sisters. Coming away she mused about their simple wants, their trust in God in a lonely place far away from home. She admired 'these brave, quiet women, who had witnessed and helped to relieve so much suffering'.⁶²

News of the sacramental boycott by Fr Duffy was initially withheld from Clare Moore over in Scutari. In February she suffered a severe episode of dysentery. Scarcely was this over when she came down the following month with 'dangerous pleurisy'. The principal medical officer was called at Nightingale's insistence and his prescriptions helped Moore to cope with the pain rasping in her chest, but it was feared that she might die. This was just before Nightingale set out for Crimea to take over from Bridgeman. Once there she waited anxiously for news about Moore, and wrote urging her to go to Malta to recover enclosing a cheque for £100 for this purpose, adding, 'Your life is the most precious thing we have, both for the work's sake and for the community'.⁶³ But one of the Catholic chaplains at Scutari, worried about her health, had written to Bishop Grant informing him that on medical advice Moore should return to England. In fact, it was 'absolutely necessary & the only hope of saving her, as her health was seriously impaired'.⁶⁴ After an internal struggle, Moore agreed. She paid her first and only visit to Constantinople across the water, where she bought blue silk and candlesticks for church use, and then, accompanied by Gonzaga Barrie, she boarded the *Victoria* on 28 April 1856. They arrived in Portsmouth on 16 May and were back in the convent in Bermondsey that evening.

Moore and Nightingale had been comrades in arms. They had broken through the suspicion that greeted them at Scutari eighteen months previously. Together they had established a nursing system that had to evolve as they learned what worked and what was needed. With the other nuns and nurses, they had shared the rigours of winter temperatures and poor food, and the trauma of seeing hundreds of men dying of injury and infection. Above all, there was mutual trust and respect. Late in April, Nightingale was still assuming that Moore would recover sufficiently to join her in Crimea, and Moore's letter informing her of her imminent return to Britain must have come as a shock.[65] In reply, Nightingale wrote a heartfelt letter:

> Your going home is the greatest blow I have had yet. But God's blessing and my love and gratitude go with you . . .
>
> I do not presume to express praise or gratitude to you, Rev Mother, because it would look as if I thought you had done the work not unto God but unto me. You were far above me in fitness for the general superintendency, both in worldly talent of administration, and far more in the spiritual qualifications which God values in a superior . . .
>
> Dearest Rev Mother, what you have done for the work no one can ever say. But God rewards you for it with Himself . . .
>
> My love and gratitude will be yours, dearest Rev Mother, wherever you go. I do not presume to give you any other tribute but my tears . . . the gratitude of the army is yours.[66]

It signalled not only the end of a remarkable working partnership but also the imminent end of the Crimean venture for all its participants.

The Treaty of Paris formally concluded hostilities. The war was over. News of the treaty reached Constantinople on 27 March even before its formal signing three days later. In celebration, the thunder of cannon sounded from ships at anchor. Muskets were let off and from time to time a rocket went up. All the ships in the Bosphorus were illuminated, and lanterns were hung around the palaces and minarets. Watchmen went through the streets, striking their staves on the ground, like they did during the hours of their watch at night, only this time chanting the word 'peace'.[67] In Balaclava, the celebrations came a little later on 2 April. Relief that the war was over was ignited by celebrations in the French camp at the news that a son and heir had been born to Emperor Napoleon III. French artillery fired a 101-gun salute to the new Prince Imperial from Woronzoff ridge, and not to be outdone, the British artillery lined up and replied with a salute from the hillside. Ships in the harbour joined in the cannonade, and navvies and sailors lined the roads of the town to watch the display. The *Times* reported that 'a general rush was made to the canteens, so that towards even the natural consequences followed . . . the soldiers of the two nations did their best to get helplessly "happy together"'. There was a perpetual fusillade of musketry and rifle fire across the plateau into the night, and several tents burnt down in the excitement.[68]

The army was well aware of the cost of victory, and the tired soldiers were longing to go home. The nuns were tired too, but Crimea still retained a sting. Sister Martha Beste came down with a fever so serious it was thought she might die, and she was given the last rites before recovering. At the General Hospital in Balaclava, the nuns also looked after the sick of the Sardinian regiments who had previously been in the care of the Italian Sisters of Charity but were now entrusted to the English Sisters of Mercy.[69]

As regiment after regiment went home, the need for nurses decreased steadily. On 17 June sisters Helen Ellis, Joseph Hawkins and Martha Beste set sail for England on the *Thames*. They arrived back in England on 9 July. Three of Moore's sisters remained at Nightingale's request for a little longer: Anastasia Kelly, Stanislaus Jones and De Chantal Hudden, but on 29 June they too left Balaclava on the *Ottawa*, arriving in England on 24 July. On board, they found more than 100 sick and wounded men and helped to look after them during the journey. The *Annals* say almost nothing about these homecomings, but we may imagine the relief, joy and thanksgiving which greeted them in the convent at Bermondsey. The Anglican sisters Bertha Turnbull and Margaret Goodman found themselves increasingly impatient as they waited for their turn to come. Margaret Goodman remembered, 'We thought our turn very long in coming, as day after day we watched the vessels leaving the bay laden with troops, who cheered heartily as the scene of so many triumphs and so many hardships receded from view'.[70] The two Anglicans went on a tour of the ruined city of Sevastopol and found it a melancholy experience, although the day was lifted by a surprise picnic tea prepared for them by a sergeant who had been one of their patients at Scutari.[71] In mid-July, they sailed home on one of the last transports carrying invalid soldiers.

One of the duties of a person in Nightingale's position was to provide 'characters' or references to those who had worked under her management. She made notes for herself about many of the nurses, including some of the nuns. About sisters Helen Ellis, Martha Digby Beste and Joseph Hawkins, she wrote: 'It is impossible to estimate too highly the unwearied devotion, patience and cheerfulness, the judgment and activity and single-heartedness with which these "sisters" (who are from Bermondsey) have laboured in the service of the sick.'[72] Nightingale was always sober in her judgements, so coming from her, this was praise indeed. Unfortunately, the pages relating to Stanislaus Jones, De Chantal Hudden and Anastasia Kelly are missing. Nightingale in a private letter wrote of Martha Beste, 'I love her the most of all the sisters. She is a gentle, anxious, depressed, single-hearted, single-eyed conscientious girl, not energetic, but a worker and no talker. . . . And she is honest and true.'[73] When Nightingale was winding up affairs in Crimea, she wrote to Moore, 'In closing this work, I can never sufficiently express how much I feel all that you & your Sisters have been to it. It is beyond expression.'[74]

Nightingale was equally unstinting in her praise of the two Anglican sisters, Bertha Turnbull and Margaret Goodman: 'I cannot estimate too highly the advantage which the faithfulness of these two to the cause has been to us.' Both were, she noted, 'excellent nurses'. And, she added approvingly, they disdained flirtations.[75] On the eve of their return, she wrote to their superior, Priscilla Lydia Sellon, praising their work, and especially Bertha's 'uniform true-heartedness to the duty, her single-minded devotedness'.[76]

On 28 July Nightingale embarked on Constantinople for the return journey. She must have known that publicity and acclaim awaited her, but for now, she craved a period of peace and recollection. She travelled under the name of 'Miss Smith' and arrived back in Britain on 7 August. Before the news of her return could reach the newspapers, she went straight to the convent of the Sisters of Mercy at Bermondsey. The friendship with them, and especially with Clare Moore, that had been forged in the Crimean War was one that would endure.

7

Ireland

Return and aftermath

By the mid-summer of 1856, all the nuns had returned to the UK. After the travails and tragedies of the Crimean War, they might have hoped for a period of tranquillity. Yet their return did not mean that the conflict was over. Resentment grew in Ireland over the way their nuns were overshadowed by Florence Nightingale's fame. Two years later, matters were further inflamed by criticism of the Irish sisters, which Nightingale slipped into evidence submitted to a Royal Commission on army healthcare.

Most of the returning Irish sisters arrived at the Baggot Street convent in Dublin on 22 May. A *Te Deum* was sung in the chapel in thanksgiving for their safe return. The superior declared a first-class recreation day. The following day the sisters from Carlow, Charleville and Cork set out for the respective convents. Word had spread and as they approached their home convents they were greeted with cheering, delegations of welcome and celebratory bonfires.[1] Convents often drew their sisters from local families and there was a strong sense of connection. A local paper reporting the return of nuns to the Cork convent noted with satisfaction, 'After all the fatigue and suffering they have gone through, and the horrors of war they have witnessed, we are happy to say they are in excellent health.'[2]

Ireland had not forgotten the pain and devastation of the famine years. But the country was still in the UK, and for many people, there was a sense of pride in the Irish contribution to the Crimean struggle. A great banquet was held in honour of Crimean War veterans in Dublin on 22 October. A local committee raised the funds and organized the event which required a vast venue. They settled on a dockside warehouse for bonded goods. Here tables were set up in 70,000 square feet of space, which was decorated with patriotic slogans. On the walls were emblazoned the names of significant battles, military commanders –

and Florence Nightingale. Over 4,000 veterans attended the banquet, with the Lord Lieutenant of Ireland, Lord Talbot de Malahide, as the guest of honour. Every regiment in Ireland sent contingents, who were cheered through the streets of Dublin. Vast amounts of food and drink were consumed, including 250 hams, 200 turkeys, 200 geese and 250 joints of beef. Four vans delivered 3 tons of steaming hot potatoes. Each soldier received a quart of dark beer and a pint of port or sherry.[3]

In his speech, the Lord Lieutenant emphasized that the war had been a demonstration of unity. No one, he said, asked whether the blood that was shed in combat was English, Scottish or Irish. All were heroes with one purpose, to defeat the enemy. Among the numerous toasts, there was one to 'The distinguished ladies who ministered to the sick and wounded in the Crimea'. It was proposed by Andrew Carew O'Dwyer, an Irish barrister and minor Liberal politician.[4] His toast demonstrated little understanding of the realities of Crimean War nursing. He praised 'women of gentle birth, of refinement and education . . . assisted by a band of devoted ladies belonging to the Order of Mercy'. These women had not shrunk from the horrors that confronted them. With the end of the war, 'the good and gentle sisters' had returned to their 'convent retreat'. As for the ladies, Carew O'Dwyer surmised that they had returned to 'those circles of society which they had previously adorned'. He hoped that they would be 'blessed with loving husbands, with dutiful children, in whom . . . they shall live again (cheers)'. He urged the men always to defend and protect women, remembering those who had come to their help in Crimea.[5] His speech depicted women as defined and fulfilled by their family role, women as needing protection: it was everything that Nightingale had struggled against. It was, moreover, as if the real work in the hospitals was undertaken by gentlewomen, assisted by the Sisters of Mercy whose life would otherwise have been a retreat from the world. His speech was born of ignorance and rigid role expectation, but it showed that the lenses of the social class could still see female war nursing as a temporary measure outside the norm.

Others in Ireland with better perceptions realized that the contribution of the Sisters of Mercy had been overshadowed by the public acclaim given to Florence Nightingale. This sentiment was shared by Mary Seacole, who in her autobiography described Nightingale dryly as 'that Englishwoman whose name shall never die, but sound like music on the lips of men until the end of doom'.[6] In Carlow, the local paper complained that the nuns had been '*ignored* both by the Protestant public and the British government . . . Protestant bigotry looks on with cold indifference and even colder ingratitude whilst these heroines of

Charity glide once again into the routine of their daily duties to the poor, the infirm and the destitute'. They were forgotten while Nightingale's achievements were 'lauded throughout the land'. Class issues were raised too, with the paper depicting her as 'wealthy . . . in enjoyment of everything that the world can give her' while the nuns might have to live in want. Both sisters and soldiers had been ill rewarded for their sacrifices: 'Such is the recompense which the Catholic religious receive for ministering to the wants of the heroes who battled and bled for England's glory and greatness.'[7] In Dublin, 'Justitia' wrote complaining that Miss Nightingale was admired, while the Sisters of Mercy were ignored. This was attributed to 'bigotry and fanaticism' shown by English Protestants, who were blamed for 'ridiculing, slandering and labouring to uproot [religious orders] since the reformation'.[8] Similar feelings were expressed in papers in Limerick, Wexford and Kilkenny.

In Dublin, Archbishop Cullen in a pastoral letter similarly alluded to Nightingale and the lack of recognition for the Sisters of Mercy when he wrote that the nuns had gone 'With unexampled heroism and devotion . . . to afford relief and consolation to the dying soldier . . . but the merits of the good Sisters, though they are passed over and forgotten in silence by the world, are registered in heaven'.[9] From the careful cadences of Cullen to the more assertive approach of local papers, the message was that a self-referential English worldview had denied the nuns their true recognition and that Ireland was entitled to its share of glory.

The return of the Irish Sisters of Mercy to their convents did not mean that their contention with Florence Nightingale was finished. They were well aware that she had returned to England as a national hero. Mother Francis Bridgeman was determined to contest this narrative which privileged Nightingale's perspective. She wrote: 'An Account of the Mission of the Sisters of Mercy in the Military Hospitals of the East' which has been cited already throughout this book. Originally it circulated among convents and was intended to be read solely by superiors and clerics.[10] Much of the document is dedicated to justifying the Sisters of Mercy in the face of unreasonable behaviour by Nightingale. A pattern develops in the account in which the word 'excited' is deployed against Nightingale. An excited Miss Nightingale criticizes the nuns. A calm Mother Francis Bridgeman rebuts the criticism by presenting the facts. Miss Nightingale subsides. In the last meeting of Bridgeman and Nightingale at Balaclava, where the nuns were preparing to leave the hospital, Bridgeman presents a set-piece confrontation: 'Miss Nightingale was very much excited in this interview. She laughed hysterically.'[11] Earlier, In a particularly revealing passage, Bridgeman says that Nightingale disapproved of the work of the nuns at Koulali. Then she adds:

> So, with her ambitious spirit, it is no wonder she had ever played the part of an insidious, dangerous enemy. So dangerous, propped as she is by human power and English infatuation and bigotry, that only the power of the Omnipotent could have enabled us so often to fail her. Truly in our case has He selected 'the weak things of the world to confound the strong'.[12]

Significantly, Bridgeman wrote in the present tense: 'Propped up as she is by human power.' The implication was that England was an ongoing source of ill-will towards Ireland. Nightingale personified English bigotry and English antipathy towards the Irish. Yet, said Bridgeman, God had been on the side of the sisters in their Crimean War nursing.

Any mention of Irish–English relations at this time has to take into account the terrible events of a few years previously. The Irish sisters and soldiers took with them the memory of the potato famine 1846–9, when the staple crop failed. At least 775,000 died, possibly over a million and there was large-scale emigration of survivors. One result was, says Roy Foster, 'an abiding resentment of "England"'.[13] Another historian, Emmet Larkin, has described the famine as 'a gigantic psychological shock'.[14] Within a decade Ireland's population had been reduced by up to a third through death and emigration. Francis Bridgeman and two others in her party came from the convent at Kinsale in West Cork, where the memory of the famine was still raw. In January 1847 about half the town was destitute because of the famine.[15] Between 1841 and 1851 famine and emigration reduced the population of the area served by the Kinsale Poor Law district from around 41,000 to about 30,000.[16] The Sisters of Mercy at Kinsale convent organized twice daily feeding of starving children. Then, in early 1849 they began visiting the workhouse, where the number of inmates peaked at over 2,400 in May of that year.[17] Initially, they went to bring spiritual encouragement but they were soon drawn into nursing cholera victims. The effects of the famine continued to be felt in Kinsale until the early 1850s.[18] We know that Bridgeman and her sisters went to the Crimean War with the memories of the famine fresh in their minds. Bolster tells us that the sight of carts jolting over rough ground with loads of coffinless corpses 'recalled for Mother Bridgeman the horror and hideousness of famine conditions at home'.[19]

Any suspicion about English intentions harboured by Bridgeman would not have been surprising. There was also political activism in her family background.

Through her mother Bridgeman was a relative of the 'Great Liberator' Daniel O'Connell (1775–1847) who campaigned to repeal the Act of Union, against laws penalizing Catholicism and for the rights of tenant farmers.[20] O'Connell even quoted the work of the sisters among the poor as an example of how Ireland merited its freedom, saying that a country that could produce such sisters was too good to continue in bondage.[21]

Florence Nightingale was at the zenith of her influence in 1857. As Bostridge notes, 'Florence's status as a national heroine remained the most significant weapon in her personal armoury and the source of what in time would become known as "Nightingale Power".'[22] Such was her influence that she was able to negotiate directly with the minister of war, Lord Panmure, about appointments to a Royal Commission of inquiry into the health of the army. The ten-man board 'was heavily packed with her former Crimean allies', with Sidney Herbert as chairman. Nightingale also ensured that her old enemy, Sir John Hall, was not appointed director-general of the army medical services.[23] The commission received its royal warrant in May 1857 and reported in January 1858. The subject of how to improve health care in the army was dear to Nightingale's heart, and she was determined to be allowed her say. The conventions of the day prevented a woman from appearing before the commissioners to give evidence, but Nightingale presented a vast amount of written evidence, much of it in statistical form, demonstrating the army's inadequate provision for the well-being of its soldiers.

Nightingale had not forgotten her abrasive relationship with the Irish nuns, and their victory in winning autonomy from her. The commission's report contained her answers to eighty-nine written questions. In reality, Nightingale had drafted both questions and answers herself. In what can only be described as a sly move, her reply to a question about hospital inspections slid into criticism of the state of General Hospital Balaclava at the time of the handover from the Irish Sisters of Mercy. She alleged that up to twenty men 'of an Irish regiment' were talking and drinking in a kitchen. The wards were untidy and disordered. A patient suffering from frostbite had not been moved for a week, 'and having been neglected, he was found in a state indescribably horrible'.[24] Bridgeman and her sisters were not named, but the target of the criticism was unmistakeable.

There was more. A contrived question about the 'skill and industry of the English labourer's wife' in household management allowed Nightingale to present an ethnic hierarchy of good order and cleanliness. She opined that women of Anglo-Saxon descent in the south and northwest of England were the most capable, followed by women of Danish descent in the east. After them came 'the mixed race in the manufacturing counties'. She placed at the bottom 'the Irish and Highland Celt'.[25] This came as close as possible to saying that the Irish were lacking in cleanliness. It was a cheap slur, but it also drew on some of the academic prejudices of the day. Her language of Anglo-Saxons, Danes and Celts echoed the mid-nineteenth-century debate about putative human typologies among British anthropologists. Some anthropologists posited Anglo-Saxons as an ideal type in terms of innate capability. The Celts were sometimes deemed to be closer to primitive human origins and less endowed with advanced rationality.[26]

The report of the Royal Commission appeared in early February 1858, carrying Nightingale's criticism of the state of Balaclava Hospital. It was not only Bridgeman and Hall who felt maligned by her statements but a wider body of doctors who had served at the hospital felt similarly. Letters to rebut Nightingale were circulated among medical officers who had been there. The correspondence was probably begun by Henry Huish, a staff surgeon at Balaclava now stationed at Chatham barracks. On 3 March 1858, Bridgeman replied to a letter from Huish written on 26 February. Huish had asked Bridgeman if one of the sisters who attended the allegedly neglected frostbite victim recalled the case. Indeed she did, replied Bridgeman: 'She well remembers the resistance he used to make to being disturbed . . . he cried and complained bitterly . . . the least stir or touch even the lifting of his head to place a pillow under it seemed to torture his whole frame.'[27] The suffering of this man named McDonald became the main element in an attempt to rebut Nightingale.

Meanwhile, Sir John Hall wrote to Sidney Herbert pointing out that Nightingale's allegations not only criticized the nuns but were also 'a libel on the humanity of the medical officers attached to the Balaclava Hospital'. If the hospital had indeed been so poorly managed then it implied the complacency of the doctors in the face of poor patient care. As for the Sisters of Mercy led by Bridgeman, they had been 'kind and efficient. . . . I do not believe these good women would have neglected for one single day any human being placed under their care.' The General Hospital was 'a model of neatness and cleanliness for many months before Miss Nightingale joined it, and its condition was the theme of praise amongst both British and Foreign Officers'.[28]

At Hall's suggestion, Bridgeman wrote a detailed memorandum refuting Nightingale's criticism. For example, the man suffering from frostbite who had allegedly been neglected had suffered agonies ('torture') each time his wounds were dressed. Even changing the bedclothes brought him great pain. Doctors had reduced the dressings from twice to once daily, and the bed was changed less frequently. Bridgeman attached a supportive letter from Dr J. Murray, one of the staff surgeons at Balaclava, confirming this explanation and calling the charge of neglect 'utterly false and unfounded'.[29] By now Hall was assembling material, with Bridgeman's assistance, to push back against Nightingale's criticisms. It was a struggle for control of the narrative but it was not a simple English–Irish controversy. Hall was English, while Murray and Huish were probably Scottish.

Nightingale had undoubtedly exaggerated the condition of the hospital at the time of handover. Even so, there was evidence to support her case that the frostbitten McDonald had been neglected. An apothecary at St Thomas's Hospital, Dr R.G. Whitfield, visited Eliza Roberts, one of Nightingale's most capable nurses, to ask if she remembered the McDonald case. Probably Nightingale herself had set the wheels in motion. She was working with St Thomas's Hospital to establish a school of nursing, and she was on good terms with Roberts. Whitfield's report of what Roberts told him gave limited credence to Nightingale's story, but also it testified to the terrible suffering that nurses sometimes witnessed. Eliza Roberts recalled the patient McDonald as being

> in a most fearful condition, greatly emaciated, with a large sloughing sore on the right hip and half-way down the thigh, both feet had sloughed off and neither of the stumps healed. He had evidently been neglected in respect to his personal cleanliness . . . and also as regards the state of his wounds, the linen and the bed were most filthy . . . there was no reason for leaving the bed sores undressed; on the contrary, the cumulation of decomposed and putrescent matter would itself be prejudicial.

Despite his terrible condition, she had been able to dress his sores three or four times and make him comfortable.[30] Hearing about this, a sceptical Bridgeman commented to Hall, 'Clever indeed must she [Mrs Roberts] be if she could make him comfortable.'[31] Roberts was, in fact, one of the most skilled nurses working with Nightingale, who regarded her as 'worth her weight in gold'.[32] Roberts could dress wounds more skilfully than any of the dressers or assistant surgeons,[33] and spent up to six hours a day dressing McDonald's wounds.[34] Even so, these debridements, requiring the cleaning out of decomposing matter, must have been excruciatingly painful.[35]

In the end, the assembly of evidence by medical officers and Bridgeman to counter Nightingale's claims proved of little use. Nightingale was a household name and a national hero. Nightingale had remembered Bridgeman's abrupt departure from Balaclava Hospital and their earlier clashes, and had obtained her revenge with the evidence submitted to the Royal Commission. Hall's letter of protest to Sidney Herbert met with a curt response, and the evidence Hall was assembling with Bridgeman was never published.[36] Perhaps it mattered less than those who had been slighted realized at the time. The allegations about the state of the hospital might have made waves in medical circles, but a search of the newspapers around the time of the publication of the commission report shows little sign of Nightingale's criticisms being picked up more widely. Public attention had moved on.

Historians and cultural analysts give varying weight to three different factors in the emergence of a felt Irish identity: the sense of continuity with a Gaelic past, resistance to English domination and the literary and cultural revival of the late nineteenth century.[37] Resistance to the ascendancy and the crown was occasionally reflected in the sisters' words. Aloysius Doyle referred to 'proud, bigoted England'.[38] Joseph Croke in visiting a Catholic Church in Malta referred to the royal coat of arms in a church as 'a dark spot on its gilded wall',[39] while as mentioned earlier, Bridgeman attributed Nightingale's fame to 'English infatuation and bigotry'.[40]

Irish identity was pluriform and evolving. Paul Huddie has argued that the Crimean War was a 'good' war for Ireland in the sense that it created a greater sense of amity. The war seized the popular imagination and created in many quarters a sense of pride in the Irish military contribution.[41] It helped the Irish comity that Tsar Nicholas I's regime could be seen as oppressing both Catholics and Protestants within the Russian empire. Archbishop Cullen referred to the Tsar as 'a dangerous enemy to the holy religion'.[42] Bishop John Ryan of Limerick said that a soldier in the war would be able to 'discharge his duties in defence of his country, of her liberties and rights'.[43] When the peace treaty was announced Cullen ordered a *Te Deum* to be sung in thanksgiving for victory in Dublin churches. In his pastoral letter, he wrote, 'The late war indeed has shed lustre on our holy religion, and given our Church fresh claims on the affection and admiration of the world.' The Catholic faith had been shown 'to promote discipline, obedience, patience and resignation, and to infuse the soldier with courage and to prepare him to sacrifice his life for his country's good'.[44] The war was proudly commemorated in many Irish town squares, where trophy cannons captured from the Russians were displayed.[45] When the Earl of Rosse installed one behind the high walls of his demesne in Birr, there were protests because it should have been available for townspeople to see. The Crimean War was their war too.⁴⁶ Irish Protestants and Catholics both believed that the valour of their soldiers would strengthen their respective causes in British public opinion.⁴⁷

To this complex sense of Irishness needs to be added the strong local and regional identities that characterized mid-nineteenth-century Ireland. In Ulster, the Protestant presence and the industrialization of Belfast gave the city and parts of the province a strong unionist character. Elsewhere in Ireland Catholics were a substantial majority, forming 86 per cent of the population in Leinster, and more than 90 per cent in Munster and Connacht.⁴⁸ But identity was not always predictable. Philip O'Flaherty, an Irish-speaking soldier from Mayo serving in Crimea was originally Catholic. He converted to Protestantism in his teens. O'Flaherty's Protestantism strengthened his sense of Britishness. A Protestant mentor sent him *A Tract for Soldiers*. O'Flaherty in his reply wrote that the booklet, 'encourages fidelity not only to his Queen and country, but also subjection to those under whose authority he may be placed, especially to the Author of his being'.⁴⁹

Army service for Irishmen could involve them in the imperial project, another layer of identity. Several of the regiments involved in the Crimean War were sent to India in the following years. Paul Huddie draws attention to the ambiguities, and perhaps even the ironies in this situation:

> The popular response of Irish society to the conflict, which was a mix of martial and often imperial enthusiasm combined with substantial local interest, not only exemplifies the ambiguity of Ireland's relationship with the union and the empire, but also demonstrates the complexity and ambiguity of identity-formation in the island of Ireland throughout modern history.... The Crimean War formed a central part of Irish social life in the 1850s during which a large cross-section of Irish people demonstrated an often extrovert interest in and support for it, often with 'British', 'Irish' and 'imperial' sentiments.⁵⁰

Some of these ambiguities have been evident in the popular response to the war service of the Irish Sisters of Mercy. Certainly, there was both local and national Irish pride in the achievements of the sisters, just as there was pride in the courage and steadfastness of the soldiers. Soldiers and others took advantage of opportunities for advancement through the service of the imperial power, but this did not necessarily mean the erasure of their Irish identity or of nationalist desires.⁵¹

Respect and affection for the sisters continued after their return to Ireland. Soldiers would visit the Sisters of Mercy in their local convents to the extent that 'the corridors and chapels of Convents of Mercy were enlivened by groups of red-coats'. Letters of thanks were received and even babies were named after them.[52] In the rigours of wartime, nuns and soldiers had formed a bond through the rituals and expressions of their faith. There was also a sense of camaraderie shared by those who have been through a military campaign together. It is a comradeship of hardships shared, of vicissitudes overcome and of fear that was conquered. Some memories are recalled and shared so often that they become familiar to all. There may be memories that are deliberately buried. The post-war contact between sisters and soldiers hints at a strengthening sense of their shared Irish identity. During the war, the presence of chaplains and nuns, Sunday Mass and the funerals of the two nuns provided a public demonstration of Irish solidarity, expressed in the language and symbols of faith. Even the exasperated, sometimes half-amused stories in which the sisters talk about soldiers over-indulging in drink have an unspoken element of solidarity, even a hint of affection: God love them, these are our boys.

The strong relationship between the Irish Sisters of Mercy and the Irish soldiers fits into the changing devotional temper of Irish Catholicism, a development that Emmet Larkin has called 'the devotional revolution'. For about a hundred years before the famine, the Irish were increasingly aware that they were losing 'their language, their culture, and their way of life'. Education, business, politics and communication were geared to the Anglosphere.[53] The famine intensified this sense of loss and increased the desire to counteract it. Hunger, disease and clearances had left a literal silence in areas now depopulated, added to which the forces of modernity were rapidly changing Irish society. Consequently, says Matthew Campbell, there was a fear of 'the erasure of Irish cultural memory' because 'the Irish language, and its poetry and songs, was in very great danger of being swept away, leaving the land bereft of its Gaelic past'.[54] The response to this danger included cultural, linguistic and even athletic initiatives. Religious fervour was another response. Here Irish identity was expressed by bringing together the Catholic faith of the past with newer, contemporary forms of spirituality.

A key development in this devotional revolution was the ministry of Paul Cullen (1803–78) successively rector of the Irish College in Rome, archbishop of Armagh and archbishop of Dublin. Cullen had been instrumental in getting the rule of the Sisters of Mercy approved in Rome in 1841. Bridgeman wrote to him several times from Turkey seeking his advice at times of crisis. In Ireland, Cullen strongly encouraged the adoption of ultramontane forms of prayer and worship. Confession and communion became more frequent, the Mass more solemn. New devotions were adopted such as the rosary, perpetual adoration and devotion to the Sacred Heart.[55] This spiritual revolution, suggests Larkin, 'provided the Irish with a substitute symbolic language and offered them a new cultural heritage with which they could identify and be identified'.[56] Historians have reviewed Larkin's analysis more critically in recent years suggesting that the Catholic Church was in better health in the first half of the nineteenth century than Larkin allowed. It is said he did not take sufficiently into account the thriving condition of folk religion, the vigour of the clergy, or the way poverty and persecution had earlier inhibited public Catholic observance. According to this revision, it was the application of the Council of Trent reforms from around 1775 onwards which primarily accounted for the devotional upsurge.[57] But overall, concludes Oliver Rafferty, despite legitimate criticism, 'there is sufficient veracity in Emmet Larkin's analysis to see in Cullen the pivotal figure that helped change the religious face of Ireland'.[58]

Nuns were a real force behind the implementation of these changes.[59] Magray says that religious Irish women 'successfully fostered an environment for a new style of religious devotion and behaviour'.[60] The process can be glimpsed in the Crimean War, in which the nuns had a powerful mediating role in religious practice. They set up chapels in Koulali and Balaclava, in the new ultramontane style as far as wartime astringencies allowed. Benediction, which outside Dublin was a relatively new liturgy for the Irish, took place each Sunday or major feast. In Bridgeman's words, 'we sent crowds to confession'.[61] Soldier patients were given prayer books, medals and holy pictures, and a nun might kneel at the bedside to pray with them. Priests would bring holy oils and communion for the dying. The sisters were a powerful humanizing force in a dehumanizing environment, which would have increased the impact of their witness. This promotion of devotional changes was all part of a far larger movement that quickly shaped Irish spirituality along ultramontane lines. This was then carried by Irish missionaries across the world. According to Colin Barr, the Sisters of Mercy, in general, played a key role in this: 'Without what soon became thousands of Mercy Sisters, the vast infrastructure of Ireland's spiritual empire would have been entirely impossible'.[62]

The newspaper reports and public acclaim cited earlier show the high reputation of the Sisters of Mercy in Ireland after the Crimean War. Given this respect, it is surprising that the sisters sometimes overreached in defending their cause. A lie about Nightingale was recycled as truth: Bridgeman claimed that when food was scarce in the early days at Scutari, 'Miss Nightingale had a grand French dinner of several courses served up to her and the Bracebridges daily.'[63] Bridgeman is probably repeating a canard put about by the nurse Elizabeth Davis who disliked Nightingale. Davis's accusation seems in turn to derive from a garbled account of the improvements in military cooking accomplished by the French chef, Alexis Soyer.[64] Bridgeman would have taken this allegation at face value.

There is also a strange instance of what looks like mythopoeia. It occurs in *Leaves from the Annals of the Sisters of Mercy*. Authorship was simply attributed to 'A Member of the Order of Mercy'. In reality, *Leaves* was the work of Sister Mary Teresa Austin Carroll, a native of Tipperary who transferred to the United States in 1856. *Leaves* is written for a broad readership and depicts in lively style the work of the Sisters of Mercy on different continents. Carroll drew on the memoirs of Croke, Doyle and Bridgeman when writing about the Crimean War. She lifted whole scenes from them, sometimes directly quoting, sometimes rendering them in simpler language. One incident described by Carroll is said to have occurred when the returning sisters and soldiers disembarked in England on 8 May 1856. We are told that the commanding officer invited the nuns to head the procession from the ship to the barracks.

> On the way the people who had assembled to cheer the soldiers began to *groan* at the religious, whereupon one of the men became so exasperated that he sprang from the ranks and called upon his comrades to defend the ladies who had stood so faithfully by their dying brethren-in arms. The regiment to a man placed themselves in a threatening attitude, with their rifles levelled at the crowd – a serious position, as all were supplied with ball-cartridges.

The commanding officer then stepped between the men and the crowd, and having explained to them the labours the nuns 'had endured for love of humanity', managed to turn the crowd from hooting to cheering. Since then, said Carroll, 'Sisters of Mercy can walk through London not only unmolested but respected'.[65]

There are several oddities to this account. It would have been a severe breach of discipline for soldiers to aim loaded weapons at their fellow citizens without an order. The Bridgeman party landed at Portsmouth, so the reference to London makes little sense. Their arrival was reported in Hampshire newspapers, but no parade was mentioned.[66] This story is repeated by Bolster with embellishment: 'How little the events of the Crimean War had helped to water down the anti-Catholic prejudices of England . . . the crowd began to hoot and pelt the Sisters until the soldiers lifted their rifles to the rescue.'[67] Bolster gives as her source the Croke journal, but the original journal does not mention the incident.[68] No doubt the story was believed to be true, perhaps drawing on actual incidents when nuns going about the streets of London were jeered and stones were thrown at them. The story of the hostile reception is significant even as an urban myth because it voices a fear among the sisters, namely that the English were contemptuous of nuns, arising from a broader denigration of Irish faith and culture. The imagined defence by the soldiers of the nuns was symbolic protection of Irish identity.

There were other ways Bridgeman's account manipulates the truth. To strengthen her case she had to insist that the dislike of the Nightingale felt by the sisters was shared more widely in the army. For instance, Bridgeman held that many soldiers in Crimea had contributed to the Nightingale collection under duress, or in the mistaken belief that it was intended for the Sisters of Mercy.[69] Against this exaggerated claim stands the widely reported dismay in the ranks over Nightingale's critical illness in Crimea in May 1855, when soldiers wept openly because they feared her imminent demise.[70]

Although both Nightingale and Bridgeman each put forward their own narrative, there was an important difference. Nightingale had a public pulpit. She knew that publicity would attend almost any comment of hers. By contrast, Bridgeman wrote mainly for an internal audience of her sisters and some priests, though with an eye to posterity. Her account, together with the journals of Aloysius Doyle and Joseph Croke, circulated within Mercy convents until Carroll used the material in her *Leaves from the Annals of the Sisters of Mercy*. Despite her desire to set the record straight, Bridgeman's sense of propriety shrank from publicity. In June 1856, she heard that 'an influential committee' was being formed to launch an appeal for the work of the sisters, and she promptly wrote to Archbishop Cullen in Dublin saying that the nuns had undertaken their duties to serve the poor and not for reward. Bridgeman distinguished between the selflessness of the Irish sisters and the vainglory of Nightingale:

> Let the soldiers be able to reflect when all is over that the Sisters who served them did so without honour or profit. Let them feel that while England heaped her honour and her riches on the Lady or ladies whom the emergency sent forth, 'The Sisters of Mercy' served them and received neither.[71]

For the time being, nothing more was heard of this particular appeal, but, as will be shown, the Crimean War record of the sisters did play a part in fund-raising.

In 1858, Bridgeman again declined to court public opinion after Nightingale's criticism in the *Subsidiary Notes*. She told Hall that she preferred to await the judgement of God. 'Oh! How clearly shall we then see the little importance we should attach to what is thought or said by our poor fellow creatures.'[72] Even so, her account meticulously argued her case, supported by the letters and other documents she had carefully marshalled. Refusal to enter the public arena did not mean that Bridgeman was indifferent to how posterity would perceive the caring ministry of the sisters she had shepherded through the Crimean War.

Did Nightingale's experience with the Irish nuns negatively affect her view of nuns as nurses? The answer can be found in *Subsidiary Notes as to the Introduction of Female Nursing into Military Hospitals in Peace and War*. These notes were written at the request of Lord Panmure, the war minister, and complemented the information she had already submitted to the Royal Commission on military health. *Subsidiary Notes* was printed separately. It contains Nightingale's practical advice on issues such as pay, pensions, diet, ward routine and even the scrubbing of floors, as well as the question of whether nuns should be employed as nurses in army hospitals. She concluded that it would be unwise. Nightingale conceded that some nuns had proved invaluable. But others were 'decorous, not very useful'. She was afraid that their close association with the priests encouraged intrigues and proselytizing: 'Where you have the Roman Catholic sister, you cannot be secure from the Roman Catholic direction, with all its many strings and machinery of opposition.' On the whole, concluded Nightingale, 'I must think Roman-Catholic Sisters are better out of, than in, the Army Hospitals.' If they had to be employed in a wartime emergency situation, they should be dispensed with as soon as practicable. As for Anglican sisters, they might fit in more easily, but it would be easier to refuse Catholic nuns as nurses if Anglican sisters were similarly excluded.[73] In 1852 Nightingale had contemplated becoming both a Catholic and a religious sister, impressed by the training offered by convents. Now, only six years later, she was recommending with a note of asperity that military hospitals should not employ nuns as nurses. During the Crimean War, Clare Moore and her team had rendered steadfast service in military hospitals. But this was outweighed in Nightingale's mind by her negative memory of Bridgeman and the Irish sisters.

Nightingale wanted to see the development of an autonomous nursing profession with its own respected place in the hospital system. Nurses would continue to be under the medical authority of the doctors. But the recruitment, training and conditions of service should be regulated within the profession itself, and the nurse would have her own sphere of authority. In Nightingale's words, 'The physician prescribes for supplying the vital force – but the nurse supplies it.'[74] Her war experience was an important step towards this professionalization, and as such, it meant that her approach was incompatible with that of Bridgeman.

Nightingale wanted to deliver nursing free from the control of higher authorities, whether it came from the church or from an army system that refused recognition. Bridgeman, by contrast, saw her religious mission as paramount, and herself as under ecclesiastical obedience. Bridgeman emphasized that a religious community should never yield to the oversight of secular authority. It would be objectionable 'To place Sisters under any Secular Lady, especially a Protestant'.[75] Bridgeman feared lay oversight. It was as if laypeople could never be trusted.

There is a striking difference in how Nightingale and Bridgeman assessed the impact of their work. Afterwards, Nightingale would cite statistics about outcomes such as mortality and life expectancy. When Bridgeman assessed their success she reached for religious language: 'The amount of good that has arisen from the mission is far beyond human calculation, in numberless sinners reconciled to God, souls saved, prejudices removed, the true Catholic spirit enlivened or enkindled in the hearts of the soldiers, who became proud of being Catholics in place of being ashamed of it.'[76] It sounds like an implicit rebuke to the colonial power and its power to make Ireland's Catholics feel ashamed of their own faith and culture.

In the war, Bridgeman kept her team together. She anticipated difficulties, forged alliances and understood intuitively where power lay in the military system. Like other women leaders, Bridgeman was constrained by an androcentric culture, but she found a way through it. This was not unquestioning acceptance of a lower status. Her powers of leadership were demonstrated not only in the Crimean War but also afterwards when she was repeatedly elected superior of the convent in Kinsale. This convent attracted so many vocations that it was able to send teams of nuns to found other convents as far afield as San Francisco. The advancing years smoothed away an occasional 'suggestion of dictatorialism and imperiousness' in Bridgeman's character and she died in Kinsale on 11 February 1888 aged seventy-four or seventy-five.[77] It is hard to square the dynamic leadership of Bridgeman and other women superiors with Caitriona Clear's assessment that nuns won their position in nineteenth-century Ireland 'only by unremitting work, undemanding service, and unquestioning acceptance of second-hand status both for their work and for themselves'.[78] As Magray points out, in conflicts between controlling bishops and convent leaders, the latter, 'though they were always careful to acknowledge episcopal authority, were also quick to defend their own'.[79]

The experience of nursing in Crimea gave further impetus for expansion into nursing by the Irish Sisters of Mercy. They opened the Mercy Hospital in Cork in 1857 and the Mater Misericordiae in Dublin in 1861. It was a natural step for nuns who were already committed to visiting poverty-stricken people in their homes. Soon after the return of their sisters from the war, the Sisters of Mercy placed newspaper advertisements appealing for funds to build the Mater Misericordiae.[80] These advertisements envisaged a 500-bed hospital with medical and surgical wards for both fee-paying patients and the indigent poor. There was no allusion to the work of the sisters in the war, but others made the connection. An editorial in *The Tablet* said that donations would acknowledge the Crimean War work of the Sisters of Mercy 'in a befitting manner by providing the poor and afflicted with a hospital. . . . This will be a Crimean testimonial.'[81]

The Medical Charities Act of 1851 had encouraged poor law unions in Ireland to establish workhouse hospitals or dispensaries. In 1861 the Sisters of Mercy began nursing in the Limerick workhouse. Bridgeman's two fellow journalers, Aloysius Doyle and Joseph Croke, at different times both took charge of workhouse hospitals, drawing on their Crimean War experience. By 1873 six of the eight workhouse hospitals in Ireland where nursing was entrusted to nuns were under the Sisters of Mercy. Nursing sisters were not formally trained as nurses and learned the profession through experience and from the shared wisdom of the order. Because they worked for little or no pay, they were an attractive option for Poor Law Guardians, and by the end of the century, the sisters dominated nursing in poor law union hospitals. These hospitals or dispensaries were where most medical or nursing care was accessed by the poor.[82] The Sisters of Mercy trained within their own hospitals, without a professional assessment from outside. But as the century progressed, so did the pressure for professional nurse training. Nursing historian Gerard Fealy says that by the early 1880s the nurses from the Sisters of Mercy in Dublin saw sick nursing as part of their overall vocation, and believed that teaching nursing to others 'was a product of devotion, care, and good basic education rather than technical training'. Initially they were reluctant to accept technical training and relied more upon 'their considerable corporate knowledge, which they developed from their extensive experience of nursing the sick poor in their own homes'.[83] The Sisters of Mercy eventually established training schools for their own sisters and lay probationers in 1891.

Not long after the Crimean War Sisters of Mercy found themselves on another battlefield. Around 640 Catholic sisters served during the American Civil War (1861–5). Of these, about 100 were Sisters of Mercy (though none of them were from the Crimean War group). They cared for Union and Confederate soldiers alike.[84]

In sum, the nuns who went out under Bridgeman returned to the esteem of their country and church. They had nursed steadfastly in situations of difficulty and danger and they had also strengthened the ties linking Irish soldiers to the Catholic Church. Soldiers, priests and nuns recognized a common identity, in which the Irish and Catholic components strengthened each other, partly in opposition to all that was English and Protestant.

The Irish sisters' dislike of Nightingale also distanced them from their English sisters. The Sisters of Mercy led by Clare Moore showed that it was possible to be both Catholic and loyal to Nightingale. Moore was born in Ireland and had worked with their revered founder, Mother Catherine McAuley. But Moore was a convert of Anglo-Irish descent, and this plus her friendship with Nightingale and residence in England meant that the Bridgeman nuns never really accepted her as Irish.[85]

We might wonder why official and public recognition mattered so much to the Irish Sisters of Mercy and their proponents. They had a key role in the efficient management of Koulali Hospital. They had successfully run the nursing at Balaclava Hospital on their own. They had helped maintain the nursing at Scutari, under challenging wartime conditions. Above all, they were held in esteem by the common soldier, especially the Irish, who felt that the sisters were there in solidarity with them. The occasional barbs from Nightingale must have rankled, without much credence in Ireland. But the Irish sisters would have been acutely aware of the cost of what they had achieved. Two of their party now lay in graves in Crimea. Within a year of their return, two other sisters were dead, one never having recovered from the exhaustion of the war.[86] Perhaps there were other sisters with mental or physical scars that were kept hidden under the reserve and spirit of endurance that often characterized the convent life of the period. With courage and steadfastness, these Irish sisters had brought nursing care and the consolations of Catholic spirituality to suffering soldiers who esteemed them. It was not only the famous Lady with the Lamp who had shed light in a troubled time but also the Irish Sisters of Mercy who had held up the light of hope, and brought healing.

8

England

Return and aftermath

The returning Sisters of Mercy at Bermondsey quickly settled back into their daily routine of prayers, the Mass and charitable work. The work of the nuns to alleviate the suffering caused by the poverty in the slums around them took its toll on them too. Clare Moore confessed to feeling tired: 'Each day brings so much to be done and looked after that I feel almost worn out.'[1] A new recruit to the community was shocked by poverty when she encountered it in reality. Moore wrote to Bishop Grant, 'We have lost our last postulant who was frightened away last Saturday by the sad state of filth in which she saw some poor people.'[2] The sisters scarcely had time to draw breath before they were asked to lend their nursing skills to a projected new hospital. In time, the decision would draw them into a painful controversy with the head of the Catholic Church in England. As for the Anglican sisters, their turmoil would be more personal, as they wrestled with the question of whether or not to continue with their vocation.

There was little formal recognition of the achievements of these nuns. In London Cardinal Wiseman in a Lenten letter noted that 'Florence Nightingale receives, from every side, the loud applause of her countrymen and women'. Why, he wondered had 'charity long nourished in the secret of the cloister' been denied tribute by those who were quick to praise charity elsewhere. He recalled the labours of the Sisters of Mercy even in 'the seat of war' and was pleased that their numbers had increased to meet the demand for their labours.[3] Five months later, a *Tablet* editorial article returned to the subject, contrasting the acclaim given to Nightingale with the treatment of the nuns, which had been 'base, shabby, mean and despicable'.[4]

Cardinal Wiseman contacted the Bermondsey Sisters of Mercy soon after their return. He was looking for nuns to found a new hospital north of the Thames. Wiseman valued the experience gained by the Sisters of Mercy both in Crimea and in an earlier cholera epidemic. He said that it singled them out as well qualified to undertake the service he had in mind.[5] The Bermondsey community acceded to his request and Clare Moore sent five sisters to begin an autonomous community at the new hospital, with Gonzaga Barrie as their superior. Barrie had been in the forefront of nursing at Scutari, and her capabilities had always impressed Nightingale. Four of the five sisters sent to the new hospital had served in the Crimean War, and the link was made explicit in public appeals, where the new hospital was advertised as 'under the immediate care of Sisters of Mercy just returned from the East'.[6]

With Wiseman's encouragement, a committee of wealthy donors bought a house in Great Ormond Street, next to the now-famous Children's Hospital. The new Hospital of St Elizabeth opened in November 1856. It soon expanded into an adjacent house which was bought with the help of a mortgage.[7] Wiseman wrote to Gonzaga Barrie in warm terms that made it clear how important the hospital was to him:

> You have sacrificed much to come to the help of my poor. . . . I can only assure you of my constant and affectionate support and encouragement. . . . I hope, therefore, that you and your zealous Sisters will not be discouraged at the bleakness of your new situation and the difficulties and troubles which always accompany and consecrate a new work of charity.[8]

At his request, the hospital was dedicated to caring for patients with a terminal illness or long-term conditions. There was a pressing need for such a hospital because incurable patients were usually not admitted to ordinary hospitals.[9] It considered applications from the public at large, not just Catholics. At first, the hospital had only twenty beds. Most patients suffered from tuberculosis, neurological diseases or chronic disease of the spine and joints.[10] Funding the hospital was always difficult, but this became easier in 1862 when Sir George Bowyer, a Catholic lawyer, forged a link between the hospital and the Knights of Malta, also known as the Knights of St John. Sir George was a barrister and at that time Liberal Member of Parliament for the Irish constituency of Dundalk. He had become a Catholic in 1850 and an enthusiastic promoter of Catholic causes.[11] Both Cardinal Wiseman and Sir George were Knights of Malta and keen to see the English Grand Priory of the Order re-established.[12] Bowyer agreed with the hospital trustees that a chapel for use of both the hospital and the Knights would be built in front of the hospital. 'St John' was added to its name, and nurses would wear the St John Cross on their uniforms. Bowyer gave the hospital trustees £1000 to pay off the mortgage, £1000 to enlarge and improve the hospital and in addition to the church, he built a convent for the sisters, who were living in the attic.[13] The church was designed with a gallery that allowed patients to be wheeled into the church in their beds, and so share in the Mass. The church was opened by Wiseman in June 1864.

Cardinal Wiseman died in February 1865, having been nursed through his final illness by Gonzaga Barrie, who was seconded from her hospital duties. Henry Manning was already bishop coadjutor and in May was appointed archbishop of Westminster (he would have to wait another ten years for his cardinal's hat). It was a shock for the nuns when, within months of taking over at Westminster, he played an instrumental role in closing the hospital. Manning was chairman of its management committee, and on 17 November he called a special meeting of the committee. After hearing a statement from him it immediately adjourned, an indication of the seriousness of the matter. The contents of the statement are not known, but there was already concern about the financial state of the hospital, which could not meet relatively modest liabilities. The next meeting of the committee on 22 November asked the archbishop to make any necessary changes to restore the efficiency of the hospital. Manning declared in early January that he was unable to do so because governance of the hospital was divided between the committee and the Knights of St John. Until its administrative arrangements were reconstructed, he could not achieve the necessary changes.[14] The committee decided that the hospital would close by the end of March. Strictly speaking, it was the committee that closed the hospital, not Manning, but of its twenty-seven members, seven were clerics, with Manning as chair. His voice would have been a strong one in its decision-making. The evidence suggests that he took over what could have been a temporary financial crisis, and orchestrated it with the aim of reshaping the governance of the hospital to suit his own ends. It came as a great shock to the nuns, who now found themselves facing an archbishop who wanted them out.

Sir George Bowyer wrote to the *Tablet* protesting that the financial reasons given for closure were inadequate. He reminded readers that 'the hospital doomed to extinction' was founded by Cardinal Wiseman.[15] The committee secretary replied in detail about the financial situation, but the 'divided governance' of which Manning had complained hardly featured.[16] Meanwhile, the controversy was picked up by the *Times*, which summarized the committee's case but then concluded with Sir George Bowyer's comment that the closing of the hospital was 'cruel, unwise and mischievous'.[17] The *Tablet*, probably the most influential Catholic publication in Britain at the time, weighed in on the side of the critics, saying, 'The whole transaction appeared to us shocking and deplorable.' It described a report issued by the committee to justify its decision as containing 'deliberate obscurity and obvious inconsistency'.[18] Bowyer had on his side William Maskell, a wealthy country gentleman, ecclesiastical antiquary and polemicist.[19] Maskell marshalled the evidence and issued a pamphlet arguing on behalf of Bowyer. The *Tablet* quoted liberally from Maskell's pamphlet. Maskell estimated that Bowyer had spent about £18,000 in total on the hospital, church and convent. He reported that the Sisters of Mercy community at the hospital had offered to pay off the £500 debt and but the offer had been rejected. Closing the hospital had meant turning out sick adults and children. Maskell quoted an eyewitness who described the sending-away of the patients as 'a harrowing scene . . . callous'.[20]

The debate about the future of the hospital was carried out over the heads of the sisters, despite the fact that they would be drastically affected by the hospital closure. The shutdown removed their livelihood and put their home at risk. From the convent in Bermondsey Clare Moore told Bishop Grant,

> Nightingale is as much grieved and astonished as we are. . . . I have ascertained that [the sisters] have had no communication at the Hospital from Dr Manning since he first intimated his intention of placing the French Sisters there
>
> Our poor Sisters are ready to submit to any arrangement & they can see God's goodness in it, but we do not know whether we ought to represent [sic] the unfairness. Card. Wiseman executed a Deed by which he thought he had secured them the possession of that Convent.[21]

Nightingale described Clare Moore as 'broken-hearted'.[22] Nightingale was outraged at the way the sisters were treated: 'He [Manning] has turned my nuns – the nuns who worked so well in the Crimea – out of their hospital in Great Ormond St, closed their hospital, turned the patients out into the street, one of whom died before she could reach home. . . . And all this to bring the ultramontanes, the "Sisters" of St-Vincent-de-Paul into the hospital.'[23]

It is clear that Manning's swift move towards hospital closure surprised and puzzled many observers. It was a startling turnaround from his previous goodwill towards the hospital and is more surprising given his well-documented concern for the London poor. Manning was the kind of bishop who would divert funds intended to build a new cathedral, to provide schools for the poor instead.[24] He was a man of ready sympathy. He detested the meanness of the workhouse system which implied, he said, that someone seeking help was 'a culprit or unworthy of help, and classes him with loafers, idlers and vagabonds'.[25]

Later he would be famous as the cardinal whose sympathetic mediation helped end a dock strike in 1889. What, then, was his motivation?

Manning's complaint about the divided governance of the hospital both concealed and hinted at the truth. In fact, the Knights of Malta were not involved in the management of the hospital. Bowyer recorded that 'the order, although contributing munificently to the Charity, has never interfered . . . in any way whatsoever with the management or administration of the Hospital'.[26] However, Manning had his eyes on a different issue of management. Bowyer claimed that he had obtained from Cardinal Wiseman an agreement granting the Sisters of Mercy a perpetual right to be the hospital community in residence. Bowyer told Manning that 'the Instrument of Canonical Institution rendered the Community irremovable by the Bishop, except for canonical offence, – & by regular legal process, with appeal to Rome'.[27] Manning could not accept this, because he intended to replace the Sisters of Mercy. He appealed to Rome, and on 11 December, Cardinal Barnabò, Prefect at the Propaganda Fide, issued a decree that Manning did indeed have the right to place whoever he wished in the convent.[28]

Manning wanted to remove the English Sisters of Mercy so that he could install the French Sisters of Charity. Nightingale wrote, 'My belief is that, from the very moment Dr M. became archbishop he determined to have the "Soeurs de la Charité".'[29] At first glance, this seems puzzling. The English Sisters of Mercy were completely faithful to the Catholic Church. But these were challenging times for the papacy. By September 1860 the nascent kingdom of Italy in its drive towards Italian unity had absorbed most of the Papal States, reducing the pope's dominion to Rome and its surroundings. Papal rule over its own state was called 'the temporal power'. Robert Gray in his biography of Manning says that the temporal power of the papacy attracted Manning's 'most fervent advocacy. . . . Sermons, articles and books poured out of Manning in defence of this view.'[30] Gray describes Manning as 'fanatical' on this issue, and it is true that Manning sometimes resorted to apocalyptic language. He said that removing the temporal power of the pope would presage the coming of the Antichrist and the last times.[31] He wrote to Gladstone, 'I believe the Temporal Power to be the nexus between the revelation of God's truth and law and the civil society of the world . . . it is the key of an order of politics, which keeps the Anti-Christ under the feet of truth and grace.'[32] Manning's belief that this temporal power was essential for the papacy was linked to his other great cause, the doctrine of papal infallibility.

In its newfound self-confidence, the English Catholic Church was adapting to a more flamboyant and affective style of worship. This ultramontane style was in contrast to the more reserved English traditions which had been necessary during the penal years. Manning sensed an English Catholic coolness towards ultramontanism and interpreted this as lukewarm support for the rights of the pope. Reluctance to accept Italianate devotions was interpreted as a sign of tacit resistance to papal claims.[33] In a much-quoted comment, Manning said that Newman had become

> the centre of those who hold low views about the Holy See, are anti-Roman, cold and silent, to say no more, about the Temporal Power, English, critical of Catholic devotions. . . . I see much danger of an English Catholicism, of which Newman is the highest type. It is the old Anglican, patristic, literary Oxford tone transplanted into the Church. It takes the line of deprecating exaggerations, foreign devotions, Ultramontanism . . . it will have the worldly on its side, and will deceive many.[34]

For Manning, enthusiasm about ultramontane forms of prayer and worship signified a correct attitude towards papal authority. It would have been in keeping with this policy for Manning to want the Hospital of St John and St Elizabeth to be part of this. A proudly ultramontane work of corporal mercy in central London would demonstrate the fervour of English Catholic loyalty to the papacy. If this interpretation is correct, then the worship in the chapel and the work on the wards would proclaim the same message.[35] This would have meant not only replacing the Sisters of Mercy but also taking control of the chapel from the Knights.

It is important to bear in mind here the material achievements of the growing number of nuns. The convents and schools they built were powerful expressions of the ultramontane outlook in brick and stone, needlework, glass, music and art. Convents founded in France were at the forefront of the rapid growth of religious life. Susan O'Brien shows that of 318 convents operating in England by 1887, 139 came from French or Walloon congregations, and these had a profound impact on the development of English religious life.[36] They had strong ties to the Continent and were in frequent communication with major religious superiors in France or Belgium. The artistic taste of these nuns reflected a Continental sensibility closer to Manning's expectations than the more restrained English style. O'Brien notes, 'They transferred something of the diversity and expertise which had developed out of a more confident, elaborate and large Catholic culture to the relatively small English Catholic subculture.'[37] The French Sisters of Charity could have run the hospital with a strong touch of Continental ultramontanism, which would have appealed to Manning.

Mother Clare Moore was baffled by Manning's conduct. She wrote to Bishop Grant, 'I have seen all the former letters & not one of them would make me feel justified in seeking to have the Community turned out of their convent.'[38] She told both Grant and the community at Great Ormond Street that there was nothing she could do except pray.[39] Moore would have been inhibited by the autonomy of Mercy convents, and by the fact that London north of the Thames was a different diocese. Manning had a tendency towards troubled relationships with religious orders. He waged a long struggle to prevent Jesuit expansion into education in his diocese,[40] even speaking in terms of waging war against them, and he similarly forbade the Religious of the Sacred Heart to open a school, on the grounds that they were too close to the Jesuits.[41] He suspected the Sisters of Nazareth at Hammersmith of insubordination.[42]

Other possible reasons for Manning's actions against the hospital may be discerned. Manning could have thought that the Sisters of Mercy were too close to Nightingale. He had met Amy Hutton, the superintendent of Koulali Hospital, and heard her defence of Bridgeman and her criticism of Nightingale.[43] Aware too of Nightingale's public esteem, he might have wondered if the nuns were too influenced by Nightingale's strong links with the establishment and by her liberalism in religion. He knew that Nightingale had turned away from Catholicism towards a more liberal understanding of Christian faith, and liberal Christianity was anathema to Manning. In earlier years Manning had accused Nightingale of eclecticism and intellectual dishonesty at a time when she was thinking of converting.[44] Her Unitarian connections would not have reassured him. Manning was not anti-intellectual: Newman was shocked when he learned that Manning was a member of London's Metaphysical Society, where free-ranging debate was encouraged and the Darwinian biologist Thomas Huxley sometimes twitted Manning.[45] But a Catholic bishop of the day would have taken it for granted that his Catholic people needed to be protected from radical ideas.

It should be noted, too, that earlier a strong bond of friendship had developed between Cardinal Wiseman and Gonzaga. In 1856 her letters to him begin, 'My Lord Cardinal'. By 1867 she was addressing him as 'My dearest Father' and signing herself 'Your most grateful & affectionate child'.[46] She nursed him during his final illness and at his deathbed, she snipped a lock of his hair as a keepsake. Moore said later that Wiseman had loved Gonzaga Barrie as if she were his own child.[47] Possibly Manning felt some jealousy. Her forthright character may also have been an issue. During the hospital controversy, a Protestant friend of her family wrote to them admiring 'her plain spoken honest words' addressed to Manning, but counselling that she should 'bend a little to the storm and meet the great churchmen with <u>smooth</u> instead of <u>sharp</u> words'.[48] Gonzaga Barrie was a woman of strong emotions whose face often betrayed her feelings.[49] The spontaneity that had won Wiseman's affections would have been less to the taste of the smooth-mannered Manning.

Barrie wrote directly to Manning about the hospital closure in February 1866. She told him that a chapter (i.e. a meeting of all the professed sisters) had instructed her to reply as superior to a letter from him. This letter, the sisters noted, 'contained accusations against the community'. The chapter minutes record that 'the Sisters unanimously demanded a Visitation'.[50] Under the Rule and Constitution of the Sisters of Mercy, a visitation meant that their bishop, or a priest appointed by him would come to the convent, interview each sister individually and examine the accounts. If there were any irregularities or abuses then he would address them.[51] The fact that the sisters now *demanded* a visitation indicates their confidence in their cause and their determination to vindicate themselves. Possibly they intended to use the individual interviews to make vigorous representations about the injustice of the closure. We do not know if their request was granted. We do know that Gonzaga Barrie wrote to him again on 4 April 1866. Her letter is remarkable in the way it combines the language of subservience with a determination not to be coerced:

> My Lord Archbishop
>
> Having assembled the Chapter according to our Holy Rule your Grace's letter was read to the Sisters they having each read it in privately yesterday, and they unanimously beg most humbly to declare their willingness to obey your commands and to engage in any work Your Grace appoints, as soon as it is made known to them, and the means of support as our Holy Rule requires. The Chapter again as they have already done assure Your Grace of their entire submission to you, and dependence on you as our only Superior except the Holy See, and of their readiness to do or undertake whatever you desire, and they wait for you to make known the place you command them to go, and the work you wish them to undertake with the means of support, and Your Grace may rest assured that they will not hesitate in executing your orders.[52]

In other words, he would have to provide for them if they moved. And so they stayed. The hospital was soon empty of patients, and to support themselves the nuns turned to needlework which they sold to shops.[53]

If Manning was indeed motivated by fear of Nightingale's influence on the Sisters of Mercy, then his concern would have been amplified by Nightingale's vigorous lobbying on behalf of the nuns. In August 1867 she wrote to Clare Moore, 'I have cried to all the authorities on earth and all the saints in heaven against Dr Manning.' She lobbied Lords Clarendon and Stanley, the previous and serving Foreign Secretaries. She wrote to Manning himself, but this produced, she said, 'a nasty letter (for which I never can forgive him) with insinuations against people'.[54] Nightingale also arranged for representations to be made in Rome. She sought a reliable Vatican intermediary for the nuns, as it was feared their letters were not getting through.[55]

The imbroglio brought Gonzaga Barrie to the point of reconsidering her vocation. Moore reported to Nightingale that Barrie was thinking of leaving for 'a holier life' which could imply entering a cloistered order or even leaving the religious life altogether.[56] The worry brought by the crisis contributed to a bout of pleurisy suffered by Clare Moore in the winter of 1867.[57] In August 1867 the nuns repeated their stance in another letter to Manning, this time from Stanislaus Jones, another Crimean War veteran who had been elected superior when Barrie stepped down. Stanislaus assured Manning that the sisters were 'all willing to go anywhere, or on any day, and to undertake any work that you may think fit to employ us in'. However, in that case, they expected him to honour the agreement with Wiseman that if they came to his diocese they would receive £200 a year, a house and the services of a chaplain.[58]

It took another year before Manning changed his mind. On 8 August 1868, a notice appeared in the *Tablet* announcing that the committee with the approval of Manning would re-open the hospital on 1 October.[59] Barrie left the hospital community and returned to Bermondsey, which suggests that Manning did indeed have some degree of animus towards her. But Manning also showed a largeness of spirit at this point. He sent a pastoral letter to be read in all churches of the diocese commending the hospital and its work. He said that until now the Sisters of Mercy

> have only nursed the sick, but henceforward they will have the further responsibility and burden of finding means for its support. We feel a full confidence that they will succeed. . . . We earnestly ask that those who used to contribute to this charity will renew their former subscriptions; and we gladly authorise the sisters to appeal, by letter or in person, to the generosity of the faithful throughout the diocese.

In a gesture of reconciliation, he went to the hospital chapel the following Tuesday evening where he officiated at Benediction and in a sermon commended the work of the hospital.[60]

In a sense, the outcome was a triumph for the nuns. They were bound to obey the bishop, but obedience had its limits. The sisters had the courage to stand their ground, fortified by a sense of the justice of their cause, and by the knowledge that 'Miss Nightingale' was determinedly on their side. The esprit de corps of the Crimean War had come to the fore once more.

In the following years, Nightingale not only kept in touch with Moore but also corresponded with Gonzaga Barrie and Stanislaus Jones.[61] The work of the Hospital of St John and St Elizabeth expanded, and in 1898, still under the management of the Sisters of Mercy it moved to a new and enlarged facility at St John's Wood, where it continues to this day. The Sisters of Mercy decided to withdraw from it in 1988.

Nightingale's ambivalent relationship with her family makes her friendships all the more significant. Her friendship with Mother Mary Clare Moore was forged in the theatre of war and lasted twenty years, from their first meeting in October 1854 to Moore's death in December 1874. It was a warm, mutually respectful relationship. In letters, each expressed concern for the health of the other. Nightingale sent gifts of food, including fresh produce from her family's gardens, to the Bermondsey convent, and 'splendid hampers' arrived at Christmas. In return, Moore sent books which amounted to an informal programme of reading on the history of Catholic spirituality. Thanks to the research of Mary C. Sullivan, we know that there are at least forty-seven letters extant from Nightingale to Moore, and ten from Moore to Nightingale.[62] Other letters were burned at Nightingale's request. The mid-1860s was a period of particularly intense correspondence between them, with twenty-three letters surviving for the period 1863–6. From 1863 onwards begins what Sullivan calls Nightingale's 'more explicit and intimate sharing with Clare on religious and spiritual topics'.[63] Nightingale was especially drawn to mystics who had faced misunderstanding, resistance and ridicule. She identified with them in her own experience of struggling for health care reform. Among her favourites was Catherine of Siena (1347–80), a Dominican tertiary deeply troubled by division and corruption in the church. Nightingale was also drawn to Teresa of Avila (1515–82) and John of the Cross (1542–91). In the course of their campaign to reform the Carmelite order, Teresa was suspected of heresy and John of the Cross was imprisoned by his confrères. Saints like these, caught up in the controversies of their days, spoke to Nightingale in her ongoing struggles for reform in the army and the establishment of proper nursing training.

Nightingale was confident that Moore would not seek to reel her in as a convert to Catholicism. Still, there is a hint of Moore's hope that immersion in classical writers of Western spirituality might bring Nightingale closer to the Catholic faith. In a letter written in 1862, Moore told Nightingale that although she was not formally a Catholic, her 'upright will & heart' made her the equivalent of one. Cryptically she added, 'I did not send you that life of St Teresa's faithful companion [St John of the Cross] only to give you pleasure.' The implication was that the books should enlarge Nightingale's understanding of the Catholic faith. Moore added tactfully that in loving and labouring for Christ, Nightingale was far in advance of her. Then in words that were obviously carefully phrased, Moore wrote: 'I have my advantages over you in the grace of the Sacraments & the direction of His holy Church. I think of you so much at Holy Communion & I wonder what is your faith there – but I am not asking nor do I wish you to tell me anything of yourself.'[64] The letter amounted to the discreet promotion of the advantages of Catholicism, tactfully balanced by the praise of Nightingale's Christian witness. It echoed what Moore had written six years previously when Nightingale visited the Bermondsey convent immediately on arrival in England from Crimea: 'It was a joyful yet a sad meeting, for [the sisters] felt that she . . . whose religious sentiment approached so nearly to their own, was not to enjoy with them the reward and happiness which they professed as members of the True Church. But her friendship continued, and still goes on undiminished.'[65] Moore admired and respected Nightingale's social witness, yet felt that her friend remained incomplete without the Catholic faith.

Both Florence Nightingale and Moore were impelled by their Christian principles. For Nightingale, there was an element of rugged individualism, strong character and the lonely soul accountable to God. Moore by contrast was nourished by the sacraments, had a strong sense of the importance of grace and was strengthened by community life. Nightingale's ability to question and challenge tenets of her faith made her more willing to challenge the status quo, and seek systemic solutions to the problems she saw. Moore's more corporate sense of belonging enabled her, and her sisters, to open up new avenues of service for women through the respectability of their disciplined life in the community, and through going, physically, to bring help to places where 'respectable' women were rarely seen. This shared vision of what women could do, and the comradeship of war, made possible a friendship that transcended denominational and theological differences.

After the Crimean War, the Sisters of Mercy grew rapidly in both England and Ireland. The polity of the Sisters of Mercy encouraged the leadership of new foundations to assume responsibility from an early stage. The sisters within each diocese constituted a self-governing congregation. Within this, there was further autonomy, each convent establishing its own novitiate and raising the necessary funds for its development. There was a recognizable Mercy tradition, but at the same time, this pattern allowed flexibility to adapt to different local requirements. O'Brien's remarks in general about the developing apostolic congregations could be said to apply to the Sisters of Mercy:

> As a group of women working together under the direction of women they were autonomous in many respects, but they were also part of a larger body in which institutional power and authority was vested in an all-male hierarchy. Catholic nuns became property-owners of significance, who mobilized the necessary finance and saw to the building of schools, colleges, orphanages, hospitals and hostels. Their situation promoted the development of personal and collective responsibility and, for some the possibility of exercising leadership, often at a relatively young age.[66]

The Sisters of Mercy usually enjoyed a close relationship with their bishop. The rule bound them to consult and generally obey their diocesan bishop until they were given more autonomy after being recognized as congregations of pontifical right in 1913.[67] Bishop Grant of Southwark was close to the sisters and greatly respected Clare Moore. Mary Sullivan says that 'their working relationship and mutual respect contributed steadily to the achievements of both'.[68] Sometimes, though, there could be friction between a community and its bishop. The clearest example would be the closure of the hospital cited earlier, but there were others. The Sisters of Mercy at Ormond Street dismissed a lay sister about whom they harboured grave doubts. In their chapter minutes, they recorded that she had been professed 'against the judgment of the community' at the behest of the Vicar General, Canon O'Neal.[69] The lay sister had promised him when she was still a novice that she would reform her ways but instead, she was disruptive and had to be sent away.

The rapid growth in both numbers and ministry of the Sisters of Mercy in England demonstrated their initiative and dynamism. From the Bermondsey convent alone, groups of sisters were sent out to help establish eighteen new convents between 1852 and 1900.[70] In the first twenty years of their existence in England, 304 Sisters of Mercy made their profession.[71] By 1931, a little under a century after the founding of their first convent in England in 1839, there were over 1,800 Sisters of Mercy in England and Wales operating from 104 convents.[72]

The eight Anglican sisters who had served under Nightingale returned to Britain at different times. Etheldreda Pillans, Elizabeth Wheeler and Clara

Sharpe came back in December 1854, followed by Emma Langston, Sarah Terrot and Harriet Erskine in April 1855. Bertha Turnbull and Margaret Goodman stayed for the duration of the campaign, leaving Castle Hospital near Balaclava right at the end of July 1856. Although the Anglican sisters had functioned as one group, they came from two communities, one centred at St Saviour's Osnaburgh St, near Regents Park in London, the other based at St Dunstan's Abbey in Plymouth, the latter being under the authority of the formidable Mother Priscilla Lydia Sellon. Sellon was in the process of uniting both communities under her leadership.

Emma Langston was superior of the community based at St Saviour's in London. On her return from Scutari, she found her convent in turmoil. Led by Etheldreda, the sisters had rejected Sellon's authority and banned her from the convent. There was some relief from the tension when Nightingale visited St Saviour's in July 1856. She greeted the nuns affectionately and praised their contribution to the war nursing, adding that they could expect a letter of thanks from the War Office. This letter never arrived.[73] Soon the crisis of leadership needed resolution. One of the sisters, Margaret Anna Cusack, loved Langston but noted that Langson was 'naturally timid and distrustful of herself, and somewhat wanting in the decision of character so necessary for successful government'.[74] This was the indecisiveness that hobbled Langston's leadership earlier when Nightingale put her in charge at Balaclava. There is good reason to believe that the problems at St Saviour's were as much structural as personal, and thus not to be laid at Emma Langston's door. Susan Mumm observes, 'The community contained the seeds of failure from the outset'.[75] She points out that other communities founded around this time began with strong female leadership, but the Park Village community had been the initiative of a committee of prominent Anglican men, with a rule compiled by Dr Pusey.[76]

The situation in London was made more serious by a financial crisis. The sisters at St Saviour's Osnaburgh Street were struggling to pay the mortgage for their 'medieval-looking convent, with its Gothic windows, gables and high-pitched roof' which had opened in 1852.[77] Langston's gentleness and hesitancy meant that effectively there was no choice but to merge the communities under Sellon's leadership, and on 28 October 1856, they joined together as the Society of the Holy Trinity. Langston departed to become a Catholic and was received into the church at the Ursuline convent at Moorfields in central London on 16 October 1856.[78] In 1858 she joined a small, recently formed community of Dominican nuns at Stroud in Gloucestershire, but by this point, she was around sixty. Her health could not cope with the demands of convent life, and she left before the end of the year.[79] Afterwards, she is said to have worked among the poor of the Spitalfields area, but little is known about her subsequent life.[80]

Her departure did not solve the problem of Sellon's leadership style. Allchin allowed that Sellon 'joined a somewhat masterful nature to her great gifts, and was not always a judicious Superior', adding that she was 'a person of very strong and positive character . . . people were either very much for or very much against her'.[81] Two of the Crimean returnees, Sarah Terrot and Margaret Goodman, struggled to adjust to Sellon's emphatic style. It must be remembered that Sellon was feeling her way forward in creating Anglican religious life. There was no tradition to draw upon, no template that she could consult as to how a superior was to lead her sisters. She could copy what she felt to be applicable from Catholic tradition, but essentially she drew from Catholic experience as an observer. While the sisters Sellon had sent to the Crimean War were away, life at St Dunstan's Abbey in Devonport had become more rigorous and austere. Margaret Anna Cusack was there throughout this period and later she wrote of Sellon:

> Had she been a Catholic she must have gone through a course of instruction and training *herself* before she would have been allowed to teach others. It was a case of the blind leading the blind. . . . She believed, or if she did not express her belief in words, she certainly expressed it in acts, that the Lady Abbess was a person to be exalted on a mighty pinnacle of honour . . . to be obeyed without the slightest consideration as to whether her commands were right or wrong; to rule without being in any way under rule.[82]

Cusack is a hostile witness here because at the time of writing she was militantly Roman Catholic and in a Catholic order. Sellon had to make decisions as a superior and was a strong personality. But those obeying her sometimes doubted whether she had the requisite wisdom, knowing that it was impossible for her to have had prior experience.

When Terrot and Goodman had been nursing at the Castle Hospital, Balaclava, they had formed a friendship with a group of nearby Piedmontese Sisters of Charity who were caring for the Italian sick and wounded. They were impressed by the good humour and cheerfulness of these sisters, 'their merry laugh could be heard ringing from hill to hill, as they took their evening walk'. The Anglican nuns wondered at the naturalness of it, knowing that Sellon discouraged such friendships in their own community.[83] But on return to Plymouth Devonport, they found that while they were away war nursing, 'strict conventual rules had been developed' which forbade the lively exchanges which they had become used to in Crimea.⁸⁴ Their difficulties of readjustment were of a kind often felt by returning veterans, who miss the camaraderie and excitement of war service. Both Terrot and Goodman decided to leave the community. Terrot left in late 1856 and with Nightingale's help, she found a position nursing at St Thomas's Hospital, London, later returning to help her ailing father in Edinburgh. Her caring work was all the more remarkable because she had returned from Scutari with impaired health as a result of the hardships there.⁸⁵

Goodman left in 1858 and wrote a memoir about her time in the East, *Experiences of an English Sister of Mercy*. It gave vivid pictures of Crimean War nursing but was critical of religious life. The life of a sister, she said, far from cultivating selflessness, was more likely to lead to a narrowing of the sympathies.⁸⁶ Worse criticism was to come, for the following year she wrote another, far more critical book, *Sisterhoods in the Church of England*. In this she said:

> Since it is possible for a young girl to be kept secretly, in strict seclusion, in a convent professedly connected with the Church of England, not only against her own inclinations, but against the wishes of her parents and friends, and even in despite of their efforts to remove or even communicate with her, it is superfluous to add that this fact is one of grave importance, and demands the consideration of the Legislature.⁸⁷

This allegation effectively supported the claims made in some of the more lurid novels about convent life, as described earlier in Chapter 4. Despite the good name, the sisters had won for their war nursing, and wider acceptance of their vocation, suspicions and hostility still lingered in English society. Itinerant lecturers filled halls where, as Mangion puts it, audiences heard stories of 'depraved nuns, tormented nuns, trapped nuns and escaped nuns'.⁸⁸ Goodman intended her remarks to be damaging, and her criticisms played into the hands of those asking parliament to legislate regular inspection of convents. There was more in the same vein in her book, but often a kernel of truth was presented with exaggerations.⁸⁹ Goodman described Sellon as demanding excessive obedience, acting as if she were 'quasi-divine', and she alleged that sisters were left trembling in fear by Dr Pusey, the abbey's spiritual adviser. Sisters were under pressure to leave their property to the order, and a sister who had fasted injudiciously had starved to death.⁹⁰

Florence Nightingale was appalled by these two books. She considered Goodman to have been 'dishonourable', and her conduct as 'treachery' in its abuse of trust. 'The difficulty in both Margaret Goodman's books is not to find what is false but to find what is true', she wrote.⁹¹ She said that Goodman and her reviewers had missed the main point, which was that nursing communities were useful according to the extent of their co-operation with the secular authorities.

Bertha Turnbull, like Goodman, had served the duration of the war. The war had developed her own gifts of leadership. Mother Lydia Sellon was asked to send sisters as missionaries to Hawaii, and Turnbull led a group there to establish a new convent. On Sellon's death in November 1876, Turnbull was elected superior. She had the difficult task not only of succeeding the founder but also of leading the nuns through another financial crisis, which she handled with aplomb. When Turnbull died in September 1890, Nightingale wrote to the community, 'How great the loss of Mother Bertha, as you say, to "many" – and to me. . . . She was a kind of hero. . . . I loved her indeed.'[92] As for Sarah Terrot, like Nightingale, she lived into the new century. In old age, her mind often wandered back to her days of nursing at Scutari, and she would speak of events there as if they had just happened. She died peacefully in 1902, 'by all accounts seeming to think she was back in her room at the Barrack Hospital'.[93]

9

'It was no time to save oneself'

The sisters, English and Irish, Catholic and Anglican, were only part of the story. Nightingale's achievements would have been impossible without the contribution of all the nurses. Throughout this book, the hired nurses have been a presence in absence. When they do appear in Crimean War history, it is usually to mention their alcohol consumption or allegations of immorality. This creates a lopsided impression. Unfortunately, the nurses have left little testimony. There is a first-person account by a Welsh nurse, Betsy Cadwaladyr, also known as Elizabeth Davis, who went out to the war zone with Mary Stanley's party and returned in November 1855. It is difficult to know how much of her book is reliable, especially as the text comes to us through a contemporary interviewer.[1] A careful assessment of her travels using shipping records has concluded that the book is 'a hybrid of truth, half-truth, exaggeration, embellishment, fabrication and omission'.[2] Parts of what she says about her time at Balaclava can be corroborated by other sources.

Issues of social class were never far away. The nuns shared some of the negative attitudes of the upper classes towards the paid nurses. In July 1855, Gonzaga Barrie described a new group of nurses as 'such low creatures that it is quite unpleasant to be in any way mixed up with them. The men have no respect for them and flirt and make low jokes with them.'[3] Clare Moore, usually generous in judgement, wrote that the nuns were uncomfortable mixing with nurses who 'although always respectful to the Sisters, were persons of doubtful character and almost daily intoxicated'.[4] Drunkenness was cited as the cause for dismissal in twelve of the forty-one nurses sent home by Nightingale up to the end of 1855, with another two dismissed for 'improper conduct'.[5] Of the nurses who came out with Mary Stanley and worked at Koulali Hospital, eleven out of twenty-one were dismissed for misconduct or drunkenness.[6]

There had been no shortage of applicants for Crimean positions as paid nurses. The wages offered were more than they could normally earn in Britain, and there was the attraction of adventure.[7] Many of the nurses were recently widowed, which indicates poverty as a motivation for taking up nursing at Scutari. When the first party was assembling at Euston Square in London prior to departure, Margaret Goodman read the strain and necessity on the faces of the nurses:

> The friends of the poor nurses took leave of them as those whom they were never to see again. Many of these nurses were widows, with large families, whom they found it a severe struggle to support by their labour in England. They were too well acquainted with disease not to understand the risk they ran from contagion; but they were under the impression that if their children were left orphans, the ladies of England would make them their charge.[8]

The risk of death was real. In 1855 two nurses died at Scutari. The first was Elizabeth Drake, a St John's House nurse who died of fever in August 1855. Helmstadter's researches in the St John's House papers show how pathetically little Drake possessed. Even her dresses belonged to St John's House. Drake bequeathed a bottle of scent, a pair of slippers, a flower jar, a glass box, three cups and a necklace. Her wages were to go to her widowed sister.[9]

The resort to alcohol might have been a way for the nurses to cope with the stress of their work, which was both physically and emotionally demanding. In today's terms, we might think of them as suffering from PTSD. The effects of stress on the nurses were noticed one day by Mary Seacole as she sat in the kitchen of the Barrack Hospital at Scutari, waiting to meet Nightingale. 'Nurses passed in and out with noiseless tread and subdued manner. I thought many of them had that strange expression of the eyes which those who have gazed long on scenes of woe or horror rarely lose.'[10] It was different for the nuns, who could draw upon their shared spiritual resources to fortify them in times of difficulty. As religious sisters, they were used to an ordered, disciplined life in the community, which they maintained as far as possible in the wartime setting. They could rely on one another's support under pressure. There was strength and companionship too in shared prayer and recreation. Their way of life must have given them a resilience that was not easily available to the nurses. Paid nurses worked like the nuns under great pressure, and endured the same harrowing scenes, especially during the first winter, and many contributed over and above the call of duty. Elizabeth Davis (or Cadwalladr) was hired as a cook but helped where she could. She remembered accompanying Jane Shaw Stewart through thick snow in the early hours of the morning to attend to sick men in the outlying hospital huts at Balaclava.[11] She said that she never got to bed before midnight, and even after taking her turn watching the sick all night, she resumed her duties in the morning: 'It was no time to save oneself when so many were suffering.'[12]

Despite attempts to keep nurses and soldiers separate socially, relationships developed nevertheless. One day, six nurses came as a group to tell Nightingale that they planned to marry, their betrothed sergeants and corporals in tow.[13] Perceptions of propriety differed according to the social class of the women. Nightingale tried to insist that nurses going out for a walk should always be accompanied by a lady, to prevent assignations with soldiers.[14] But Amy Hutton, the lady superintendent of Koulali Hospital, was courted by Scott Robertson, a senior purveyor, without censure. They were engaged before she returned to England.[15] Because of her status as a lady, Hutton would never have been subject to the controls that Nightingale regarded as essential for the working-class nurses. By late 1855 there was evidently some unease among the authorities about working-class nurses behaving in a way above their station in life. A circular outlining their terms and conditions included a clause which stated: 'It having been found that some of the Nurses have believed they were to be on an equality with the Ladies or Sisters, it is necessary that they should understand that they will remain in exactly the same relative position as that in which they were in England.'[16]

As indicated earlier, sometimes the nuns could reflect the judgements of the better-off towards the working-class nurses. One of the clearest examples came on the voyage out of the Irish sisters, when Bridgeman professed that she had been shocked to find that they were expected to travel second class on the ship, along with the other nurses. She protested about 'the evil consequences of being thrown thus into domestic contact with this class of people'.[17] Mary Peckham Magray, following the work of Catriona Clear and others, has argued that Irish sisters in the nineteenth century mostly came from the better-off farming and town middle classes, especially from the south and east of Ireland. Moreover, these nuns are said to have reflected the expectations and aspirations of their class and to have inculcated them in the girls they taught.[18] In fact, 'convent life as a new and highly respectable option was only for women of the right class or the right attitude'.[19] Many English Catholic communities recruited actively in Ireland, and drew from the same pool of bourgeois farming families.[20]

Yet despite elements of snobbery, when it came to their hands-on work, the nuns could transcend class expectations. Part of their success as nurses was their freedom from the usual stratification of the day. They won the trust, affection and respect of the men they nursed partly because they did not fit easily into any particular social class. In the mid-nineteenth century, it was axiomatic that ladies did not undertake manual work, and the main complaint against Anglican sisterhoods was that these upper-class women did the work normally assigned to servants.[21] As they battled rats, dressed wounds, emptied pails and deloused patients, the nuns, both Catholic and Anglican, were hardly living up to the stereotype of ladylike work. They mixed on a daily basis with all sorts and conditions of men and won their respect for the care they offered, not for what they were socially. Because they were recognized as consecrated women, Nightingale trusted them in a way that she did not trust the other nurses. There was even an element of quiet social subversion in the way the nuns could ignore the class expectations of their day to affirm the humanity of the soldier patients. Often they saw beyond the allegedly brute soldier to the person within. The Anglican sisters especially recorded many vignettes of the dignity, courage and comradely compassion of the patients. Sometimes they questioned the war as a grotesque waste of lives. Remembering the daily procession of bodies to Scutari graveyard, Terrot wrote, 'What a lavish waste of life was there! What accumulated wrecks of hopes and joys, all sacrificed, and for what? Such thoughts would come as we looked out daily.'[22] The question of what the war had achieved would continue to be asked long after the peace treaty had been signed.

10

Conclusion

What did it all achieve? In the Treaty of Paris ratified on 27 April 1856, Moldovia and Wallachia were given autonomy, the Danube was recognized as an open commercial waterway and the Black Sea was neutralized. Neither Russia nor Turkey could build arsenals on its coasts. The signatories agreed to respect the independence and territorial integrity of the Ottoman Empire. With regard to the Christian population, the treaty affirmed a *firman*, or declaration issued by the Sultan just before the treaty conference opened, which guaranteed the privileges and immunities of Christians and other non-Muslims. The signatories agreed they would not use these rights to interfere.[1] These treaty concessions were wrought at great cost. Just under 98,000 British soldiers and sailors served in the conflict, of whom 22,100 died in the campaign. Many of these deaths had been preventable: 4.4 per cent of the men who went out to the war had been killed in action or died of wounds; four times as many, 18 per cent, had died of disease, many of them while they were in hospital care. The French had lost 96,600 men, 31 per cent of their effective strength.[2] In Britain, the sense of victory was muted by disappointment that the British had not managed to match the achievements of the French at Sevastopol, and there was shame at the deaths that had accrued from the mistakes and inadequacies of the army and the government.[3] The Crimean War also left Russia with sensitivities about Crimea and Sevastopol, sensitivities that continue to affect international relations in the present day.

Acclaim in Britain for the achievements of Crimean War nursing should have gone to Nightingale's whole team, but in reality, Nightingale's name and reputation towered over everyone else. In Anne Summers' assessment, 'Florence Nightingale has monopolized the public imagination, and blotted out most of the history of Crimean War nursing ever since.'[4] This imbalance was noted at the time by Frances Duberly, an officer's wife who had accompanied her husband to the Crimea. In March 1856 she wrote to a correspondent, 'Miss N. has had her full share of praises. The nurses who had all the drudgery and hard work & especially the Catholic Sisters of Mercy have not had anything approaching to their share.'[5] In a rare admission late in life, Nightingale acknowledged the situation: 'I often think, or rather do not like to think, how all the people . . . who were with me in the Crimea must feel how unjust it is all that all the "testimonial" went to me.'[6] The adulation of Nightingale can be placed in a wider context of social change. By the middle of the century, economic growth had added greatly to the power and numbers of the middle class. The privileges of the aristocracy, and especially its assumption of leadership, were increasingly challenged by the middle class in calls for modernization. The perceived failures of military and civil leadership encouraged this growing assertiveness and confidence. The reforming zeal of Florence Nightingale fitted neatly into the middle class's emphasis on professionalism, industry and merit.[7] As Trudi Tate notes, 'The Crimean War gave new impetus to the struggle between the middle and upper classes.'[8]

The *Times* had blamed early debacles on the army's system of drawing officers from the aristocracy, with its propensity to promote one another and cover up for one another: 'We are hampered, not by the inexorable conditions of war, bad as they may be, but by the silken bonds of class, clique and kin.'[9] Nightingale's work during the war, and her subsequent campaign for nursing professionalization, were grist to this mill. As she became a household name, the nurses, nuns and ladies who had worked with her faded into the background of the public consciousness. Trudi Tate believes there was an ambivalence in this elevation of Nightingale. The middle class wanted innovation and progress, but it also worried that undermining the aristocracy would remove inspirational figures, and thus weaken British society.[10] If this analysis is correct, then Nightingale fitted this moment perfectly, for she was both icon and iconoclastic, a heroic figure who also challenged the status quo.

Some of this is reflected in what might metaphorically be called an actual icon, the famous painting *The Mission of Mercy: Florence Nightingale Receiving the Wounded at Scutari* (1857) painted by Jerry Barrett in 1858 and one of the best-known depictions of Scutari. Nightingale is at the centre, bathed in light from above. Near her, half-hidden in chiaroscuro, is Mother Mary Clare Moore, distinctive in her wimple and habit of the Sisters of Mercy. The other two dozen or so figures posed on either side of Nightingale are mostly those who worked with her, in particular those who, like her, had to work against the grain of the army system. Matthew Paul Lalumia comments that in *The Mission of Mercy* mid-Victorian viewers encountered 'a new definition of heroism' suitable to their age, in the painter's selection of hospital staff and 'enterprising individuals who set right the errors of government and the army'.[11] Thousands of prints of this picture were sold, despite a steep price of three to ten guineas.[12]

Over the years the significance of Nightingale's Crimean War has sometimes been scrutinized and found wanting.[13] One of the more recent critics is Michael Hinton who believes that the importance of nursing in the Crimean War has been exaggerated. Hinton's argument can be summarized as follows. The army's health problems were not strictly medical but came from factors such as food, transport, crowding together of soldiers and a filthy environment.[14] Medical officers lacked the power to order the necessary improvements.[15] From early 1855, as the army made these changes, better health care of troops in the Crimea led to better outcomes in the Bosphorus hospitals, because fewer gravely ill personnel were being shipped over the Black Sea. Also, the establishment of regimental hospitals allowed medical treatment closer to the place and time of need.[16] Hinton provides statistics to show that outcomes in hospitals in Turkey were indeed shadowing those in Crimea.[17] One example would be the dramatic drop in deaths in transit across the Black Sea. From mid-November 1854 to mid-February 1855, 11.2 per cent of the soldier patients died on board; from mid-February to mid-September 1855, the death rate was 0.4 per cent.[18] He also says that while the physical appearance of the general hospitals could have been improved, 'any upgrading was cosmetic rather than essential'.[19]

However, against this, it can be said that the effects of better nursing went far beyond immediate bedside aid. Nightingale and her team had a galvanizing effect. They caught a rising wave of public concern and gave it further impetus. At the beginning of 1855, the *Times* quoted an editorial in the *Civil Service Gazette* saying that probably 'that splendid spinster, Miss Nightingale' had more ability to organize hospitals than generals and civilians 'accustomed to the routine ideas and careless work of a military organization'.[20] Queen Victoria wrote to Sidney Herbert, asking him to forward her the reports he received from Nightingale.[21] The clergyman and philanthropist Sydney Godolphin Osborne kept up a drumbeat of pressure, via letters to newspapers and evidence to the Roebuck Committee. He visited Scutari at the end of 1854 and in his book *Scutari and Its Hospitals* said that he found the officials there in denial about the terrible state of the hospitals and resentful of non-military 'interference'.[22] He praised Nightingale for cutting through the bureaucracy and indifference, often mentioning a triad of Nightingale, sisters and nurses.

A situation where a hospital could be more deadly for a soldier than a battlefield had aroused widespread public anger in Britain. The public was emotionally involved in this war as never before through newspaper reports, photographs, panoramas and other representations.[23] The sending of Nightingale and her nurses captured the public mood, and in doing so helped to channel the pressure for change in the army. The nurses were an essential part of this equation. Nightingale could not have captured the public imagination on her own, because the nurses represented the possibility of change on a systemic level rather than the campaign of one individual. They represented the community's own desire to care. Women as army nurses, in the form of nuns and other nurses, meant that 50 per cent of the population previously disregarded was now represented at the heart of the war, putting their skills and capabilities to use for the good of the nation.

Hinton's analysis sidesteps the question of how the necessary improvements were made to happen. We may doubt if they would have happened without sustained public pressure. Three of the most significant changes came from private initiatives. Alexis Soyer revolutionized army catering, Nightingale and her team raised the standards of bedside treatment, and Samuel Peto built the Balaclava Railway in a matter of weeks at cost price. In fact, Peto made it a prior condition that the army had no control over any aspect of the project.[24] Regarding the improved state of Balaclava, Frances Duberly wrote in her journal, 'That it was effected through the agency of the Press, there can be no doubt.'[25] The government and the army had to be pushed into improvements, and Nightingale played a key role in this through the publicity attending her nursing enterprise, as well as the pressure she brought to bear on Sidney Herbert and others. The general hospital improvements she achieved were more than cosmetic. She and her nuns, along with the other nurses, made an indelible impression. An officer whose sergeant was seriously injured at Alma later received a letter from the man saying that for seven days at Scutari he and other patients were never visited by a doctor, whereas 'Miss Nightingale & her attendant angels he speaks most enthusiastically of. They were everywhere amongst the sick, doing more good than any doctors, & as he somewhat naively observed, "there was no sort of delicacy about them, Sir".'[26]

The domination of Nightingale in subsequent accounts of Crimean War nursing continued to rankle in Ireland, where it was felt that Britain had overlooked the contribution of Bridgeman and her sisters. Bolster wrote that the 'Nightingale Legend' had exaggerated Nightingale's contribution while simultaneously depreciating the work of the Irish Sisters of Mercy.[27] Similarly, Mary Ellen Doona believed that the story of the Irish Sisters of Mercy had long been unspoken, whereas 'the myth of Florence Nightingale' obscured the reality of Crimean War nursing.[28] Sometimes the overshadowing of the Irish sisters is presented as evidence of deeper prejudice. A recent Foucauldian and postcolonialist approach has argued that British structural prejudice is responsible for undervaluing the work of the Irish nuns: 'The British Establishment, both then and now, largely ignores them because ... they are the ultimate "outsiders" for either a protestant-dominated past or a secularising modern multi-racial present – Catholic, nuns and Irish.'[29] All that can be safely said about such an assertion is that the issue has become inflected with the historic tensions of the Irish–British relationship. At least the Irish nuns had the consolation of recognition in Ireland, not least the gratitude of the soldiers. By contrast, the wider public in England was largely unaware of the role of the English nuns led by Clare Moore, which was ironic, given that it was the cry in England for 'Sisters of Charity' which precipitated the sending out of the first party.

Two associated lines of criticism, in particular, have been levelled against Nightingale. It is said that her achievements and abilities in nursing have been exaggerated. Second, it is alleged that Nightingale learned a great deal from the Irish nuns who brought with them their own distinctive system of nursing, a debt which she never acknowledged.

The suggestion that Nightingale's abilities and achievements were overrated is not new. Immediately after the war, Bridgeman said that Nightingale was incapable of organizing systematic nursing: 'The want of system [at Scutari], and the misconduct of the paid nurses made her and their presence be regarded as worse than useless.'[30] More recently Mary Ellen Doona has doubted Nightingale's capacities, saying that although Nightingale went out in 1854 as a hospital nurse, 'She was not, of course. . . . She knew a lot *about* nursing, but had little – almost no – experience *in* nursing.'[31] But Nightingale had nursed at hospitals in Germany and in Paris, and in the Middlesex Hospital in London during the cholera epidemic. While at Kaiserswerth she had observed the amputation of a leg and care of the stump.[32] Her superintendence of the nursing home for elderly ladies in Harley Street also involved nursing. None of her nursing experience in these places had been for prolonged periods, but it was backed up by continual study and reflection on best practices.

Bridgeman was sceptical of Nightingale's capabilities after what she observed of her at Scutari, but this had been an emergency situation. For six months from October 1854 to March 1855, there had been relentless pressure on the staff at

Scutari hospitals, who had to improvise time and again. The strain is indicated by the swift arrival and departure of three medical superintendents at Scutari in January 1855, two of them pleading a collapse in their health.[33] The hospitals at Koulali and Balaclava where the Irish sisters nursed so successfully were considerably smaller than the hospitals at Scutari, and at Balaclava, the Sisters of Mercy were in sole charge of the nursing. These situations made for tighter control and greater oversight compared with the maelstrom at Scutari. Far from lacking experience or system, Nightingale's powers of nursing and management can be seen in her subsequent years of campaigning for professional nursing and for healthcare reform. She had a particular ability to join the bigger strategic picture with detailed knowledge of working hours, wages, hygiene and many other matters relating to the daily reality of nursing. She was also a pioneer in the collection and analysis of hospital statistics.

The claim that Nightingale learned from the Irish nuns was made by Evelyn Bolster. In particular, she claimed that Nightingale's popular *Notes on Nursing* depended significantly on what she had learned from Bridgeman's system, without Nightingale ever acknowledging her source.[34] To this accusation, Lynn McDonald has replied that Bolster 'gave no evidence in support of this inference, and none is evident'.[35] Bolster does refer to Bridgeman's description of Nightingale taking notes during the handover of the Balaclava Hospital.[36] But in almost any walk of life, it would seem common sense to take notes on assuming a new responsibility. If Nightingale had not done so she could have been accused later of being lackadaisical or indifferent.

The claim that Nightingale learned from the Irish sisters has been made more recently by Therese Meehan, who held that the Sisters of Mercy had their own distinct method of skilled nursing. She called this method careful nursing.[37] The phrase occurs in a letter from Mother Vincent Whitty to the War Office in 1854, in which she wrote, 'Attendance on the sick is, as you are aware, part of our Institute, and sad experience of the poor has convinced us that, even with the advantage of medical aid, many valuable lives are lost for want of careful nursing.'[38] Meehan believes that this model characterized the nursing practice of the Irish Sisters of Mercy throughout the Crimean War. Lynn McDonald's critique of this claim is wide-ranging. She notes inter alia that Meehan relies on linguistic analysis of documents without employing 'any objective, computer-based analysis programme'. Moreover, as described in Chapter 5, statistics do not support a claim that Koulali was a model hospital.

It is true that Bridgeman repeatedly emphasized how much the Mercy system of nursing of her sisters differed from that of Nightingale.[39] But what was this system? The closest we get to a description of it can be found in a letter from Bridgeman to Hall, in which Bridgeman says it should be remembered that under her Sisters of Mercy

> all the extras, food, as well as stimulants, pass, not through the orderlies' hands but through those of the Sisters to the patients; that the food is prepared under the *constant* direction of the Sisters; that we have had much night watching by the express desire of the Medical Officers, who require the constant attendance of the Sisters for those patients who need constant doses of medicine or stimulants.[40]

This suggests little that was distinctive, except for night nursing, which Nightingale had forbidden to the nurses at Scutari for fear of immorality. Night nursing allowed any sudden deterioration in a patient to be reported, and in cases of fever, spoon-feeding needed to continue at frequent intervals day and night. The Anglican sisters had already been undertaking night watch at Scutari, so it is difficult to see Bridgeman's system as unique. Bridgeman also criticized Nightingale for insisting that nothing be administered to the patients at Scutari without medical authorization.[41] Nightingale's concern had always been to obey the medical officers in such a way that no criticism could be made against her and her nurses. But the system of everything having to be signed for began to be relaxed anyway in February 1855.[42] Ironically, reinstating the rigour of the requisitions was one of the ways that Bridgeman's ally Sir John Hall tried to frustrate Nightingale after Bridgeman's departure from Crimea.

Carol Helmstadter offers a careful comparison of the nursing practices of Nightingale and Bridgeman. It does not support the idea that Nightingale learned her trade from Bridgeman. Moreover, Helmstadter points out that Nightingale's holistic approach was more aware of the wider context that could affect health outcomes. Nightingale asked the government to provide proper surgical equipment and microscopes; she organized recreational activities for soldiers; she took upon herself purveying duties during the supplies crisis in the first months of the war. Helmstadter finds Nightingale's hospitals as well run as those of Bridgeman. Bridgeman lacked flexibility because she 'could not take a transnational view . . . she genuinely believed she could not provide a good nursing service until she had replicated the conditions under which she worked in Ireland'.[43]

It might be asked why Bridgeman and her sisters were so adamant about leaving Balaclava Hospital as soon as possible. The swiftness of their departure was certainly not in the best interests of the patients. A memorandum circulating in the War Office after their departure favoured the Irish sisters, but a notation on it, possibly by Panmure, said that it did not express his own mind. The writer added, 'These ladies as nurses had no sufft. grounds for resigning – they all agreed originally to place themselves under Miss N's Superintendence.'[44] So why did Bridgeman act as she did? There was, of course, the ongoing antipathy between herself and Nightingale. But something more seems to be at work here. Bridgeman's horror – the word is not too strong – about being under a laywoman and a Protestant is striking. This unease about lay supervision was shared more widely in the Catholic Church. Even before they left Ireland when Archbishop Paul Cullen heard that the Sisters of Mercy were to be under Florence Nightingale. He wrote:

> I hope this is not true, as it would be unseemly and perhaps very inconvenient to have nuns under such jurisdiction. The Pope thinks that such a thing ought not to be agreed to (. . .)
>
> I dare say there will be great difficulties and dangers to be encountered in a Protestant camp, if it be true that Miss Nightingale is such a Protestant. I am persuaded that great experience and prudence would be required to prevent the evils which might spring up under such trying circumstances.[45]

Yet his English colleague Bishop Grant had seen no problem in consigning the English Sisters of Mercy to Nightingale's oversight. The Irish and English approaches differed radically. The Irish Sisters of Mercy sought to establish a sphere of autonomy where their nursing would not be answerable to secular authority, except for their day-to-day dealings with the medical officers. This resistance to lay appraisal and oversight suggests a movement towards an autonomous sphere of authority for healthcare controlled by the church. If so, in the long run, this development would turn out to be unwise. The different national backgrounds may have influenced these different approaches. The Irish sisters came from a church that was increasingly identified with the character of Ireland and the Irish people, a power in the land to the extent that the UK government subsidized the training of its priests in the national seminary at Maynooth until 1868. The English sisters, on the other hand, came from a church that had long been a minority, suspected as something alien to the national character, and whose members were used to keeping their heads down.

This assertiveness of the Irish nuns reflected more than their sense of being part of a powerful national church. Irish writers in the nineteenth century struggled to find a voice in which they could articulate the story of their own people. The trauma of the famine and the homogenizing influence of British culture made this especially difficult.[46] The Crimean War accounts by the Irish Sisters of Mercy were performative utterances, which not only described a given reality but also contributed to a sense of national identity. Bridgeman and her sisters had answered the call of the imperial government but wanted at the same time to demonstrate the distinctiveness of their offering as Irish Catholic nuns. Their contestation of the narrative amounted to a refusal to be subsumed into a Whiggish story of progress, in which religion was marginal and Ireland represented backwardness. By asserting the professionalism of their nursing, the importance of their faith and their links with Ireland, they offered a different perspective. Their narrative was part of the multifaceted process in which nineteenth-century Ireland found its voice.

Earlier chapters stressed the sense of Irish communality among chaplains, soldiers and nuns, an identity defined partly in contradistinction to English class and cultural assumptions. This was typified in Bridgeman's comment that Nightingale 'had ever played the part of an insidious, dangerous enemy' assisted by 'English infatuation and bigotry'.[47] This camaraderie gave the Irish strength in solidarity, a solidarity that was especially valuable in the life and death struggle against frostbite, disease, poor nutrition and Russian attacks. However, the solidarity tended to become a closed circle. Irish chaplains championed Bridgeman and her sisters, to the extent of twice denying the sacraments to Moore's Sisters of Mercy because of their support for Nightingale. An English chaplain, Fr John Bagshawe, defended the English sisters, writing to Grant that the Irish chaplains were 'the most detestable set of snobs'.[48] Snobbery went the other way too, with Nightingale's dismissive and deprecating attitudes towards the Irish in general, including allegations that they lied, and insinuations about cleanliness. These insults arose from her resentment that the Irish sisters had evaded her control. Moreover, just as the Irish nuns were prone to see her as personifying English bigotry, so was Nightingale prone to see them as representing an aggressive and aggrandizing Catholicism.

The Anglican contingent under Nightingale had always been small in numbers. Of the eight who were sent out in October 1854, three returned before the end of the year. Three more, including the highly capable Sarah Terrot, served from October 1854 to April 1855. The remaining two, Bertha Turnbull and Margaret Goodman stayed to the end. Overall the Anglican sisters made a modest contribution but made it under particularly challenging circumstances. The Catholic Sisters of Mercy went out with episcopal blessing, knowing that they represented their church. The Anglican sisters were a new and fragile development in the Church of England and regarded with considerable suspicion by the authorities. Church leaders not only feared that these women might be evangelizing for Rome, but also that they might be prone to spiritual excesses such as fasting. This meant that the Anglican nuns had no avenue of validation beyond the witness of their lives.

Despite the modesty of their contribution, the war nursing of these sisters demonstrated the seriousness of purpose of those who entered the Anglican religious life. It also showed how nursing could be combined with community life, with the implicit message that others could follow their initiative. For example, the All Saints Sisters, founded in London in 1851 began nursing at University College Hospital in central London in 1860, with such success that the management committee there invited them to expand their commitment.[49] The growth of Anglican religious orders was helped by developments within Anglican spirituality. Initially, Anglican religious orders drew upon the older High Church and more recent Tractarian traditions, which sought to recover and enhance an implicit catholicity in the faith and practice of the Church of England. In the late nineteenth and early twentieth centuries, a more adventurous Anglo-Catholic party emerged, which did not hesitate to raid Roman Catholicism for usages that would benefit religious orders.

Nightingale and the Anglican nuns also helped to create a more positive appreciation of single women in society. Of course, this was the achievement of the Catholic sisters as well, but Anglican communities offered many reassuring tokens of Englishness. The liturgy in their chapels would include morning and evening prayer from the Book of Common Prayer, and the chaplains attending to them came from the Church of England. As Michael Hill puts it, 'It was largely as a result of the work done by individuals like Florence Nightingale and by the Anglican sisterhoods that female celibacy became defined as a role which might be consciously chosen, and thus it lost some of its negative valuation.'[50] Catholic nuns had long shown this as a positive role, but now this could now develop within Anglicanism in a reassuring English way.

A survey of religious communities in the Church of England published in 1918 concluded that until Anglican sisters went to the Crimean War, there had been 'fanatic animosity' against them, but their Crimean War service meant that they were no longer seen as 'dreaming enthusiasts and Jesuit agents'. The tide of public opinion had turned and 'the value of the training and discipline and devotion of religious Communities of women was now realized'.[51] Yet the sisterhoods remained in an ambivalent position in the Church of England. Nothing in Church of England canon law regulated sisterhoods, meaning that 'they existed in a legal limbo'.⁵² Sellon sent her sisters out to the Crimean War on her own initiative. While this lack of official recognition had its drawbacks, it did give her and later superiors considerable freedom of manoeuvre. Although individual bishops might provide oversight, the Church of England did not devise specific canon law for Anglican religious until 2019.⁵³

The sisters, both Catholic and Anglican, had rendered sterling service at Scutari and in Crimea. They had helped keep the Scutari hospitals going, first through the crisis of the Inkerman aftermath, and then later during the terrible winter of 1855, when services were stretched to breaking point. The Irish nuns under Bridgeman were the backbone of Koulali Hospital and later, Balaclava General. At the Castle and Land Transport Corps hospitals, nuns had again strengthened the nursing in times of difficulty. The work of both the nuns and the paid nurses had shown the vital contribution that women could make in what had been a male sphere, and the better quality of care that could be offered in the future through professional nursing. The nuns were distinctive in the reliability, discipline and consistency of the nursing they offered.

The high publicity that attended Nightingale and the Crimean War drew attention to the achievements of the religious sisters. The early feminist writer Anna Brownell Jameson thought that Nightingale's team represented a breakthrough for women: 'It will be the true, the lasting glory of Florence Nightingale and her band of devoted assistants, that they have broken through . . . prejudices religious, social, professional; and established a precedent which will indeed "multiply the good to all time".'⁵⁴ Yet ironically Nightingale herself did not see the nursing of the nuns as an unmitigated good. After the Crimean War, she was at best ambivalent about the use of nuns in hospital nursing, tending towards a faute de mieux attitude on this issue. She feared that they had dual loyalties, to both the hospital and their own order, which did not fit into the attitude of obedience that she expected of nurses under her system. The memory of her clash with Bridgeman made Nightingale wary about the future employment of religious sisters in army nursing. We can chart Nightingale's changing mind on this issue. In May 1856, she had allowed that English nuns might be useful: 'Give me *Nurses*, with a very small admixture of *experienced* ladies, & a larger one of *English* Nuns for the Army Hospitals.'⁵⁵ By 1858 her attitude had hardened and she was advising the British military that as few nuns as possible should be employed as nurses, and ideally none at all.⁵⁶ In Carol Helmstadter's assessment, 'the religious sisterhoods provided topflight nursing services'.⁵⁷ They had indeed been the reliable corps of her nursing contingent, but beyond her deeply felt friendship with Clare Moore, Nightingale struggled to acknowledge the value of their contribution.

A similar distortion affected Francis Bridgeman's perceptions of Nightingale. Realizing that Moore's nuns were friendly to Nightingale she despised them for living in poverty and sharing the hardship of Scutari. She recycled a myth about Nightingale wining and dining luxuriously at Scutari, and put it about that far from admiring Nightingale the soldiers actually disliked her. No good, it seemed, could ever come from Nightingale's leadership. Referring to nurses as 'trained instruments' Nightingale wrote near the end of 1855: 'It is obvious that the experiment of sending Nurses to the East has been eminently successful – & that the supplying of trained instruments to the hands of the Medical Officers has saved much valuable life and remedied many deficiencies.'[58] Bridgeman, with her dislike of Nightingale and her judgement that English nurses were common and low, demurred: 'Everyone else who has observed or considered this subject in the East has come to very opposite conclusion, i.e. the experiment may be said to be a total failure.'[59] Ethnic and personal tensions bedevilled the Nightingale–Bridgeman relationship to the end. It needs, however, to be borne in mind that the army medical system forced both of them to work through structures organized and controlled by men, in which they were the first women to claim a working place. Power had been given to Nightingale but it had also been taken away. In her letter of appointment, Sidney Herbert had written, 'Every thing related to the distribution of the Nurses, the hours of their attendance, the allotment to particular duties, is placed in your hands, subject of course to the sanction and approval of the Chief Medical Officer.'[60] The conditional aspect of her power was made even clearer in a letter from him published in the *Morning Post* the next day: 'She [Nightingale] will act in the strictest subordination to the chief medical officer of the hospital.'[61]

In charting the Nightingale–Bridgeman relationship we should see their tension and frustrations as partly the by-product of being caught up in male-dominated structures that inhibited their capabilities. Their different approaches to overcoming this limitation contributed to the tension between them. Nightingale became increasingly confrontational and challenging towards the army establishment. Bridgeman's approach was more collaborative and emollient. Florence Nightingale, Francis Bridgeman, Clare Moore and the nuns who nursed with them managed nonetheless to achieve an agency that had its own authority, an authority deriving from their face-to-face contact with their soldier patients.

The French–Lithuanian philosopher Emmanuel Levinas has challenged postmodern thought through his emphasis on the face as a source of truth, transcendence and obligation. He was deeply sceptical of metaphysical accounts of human nature based on universalizing categories, which he believed erased the uniqueness of each person.[62] This simple summary cannot convey the power of Levinas's challenge to traditional epistemology, but it is a reminder of the importance of the face-to-face encounter that runs through so much human awareness and on which so much of our knowledge depends. The nuns had looked at the face of suffering in the faces of countless individuals. There is a traditional cultural understanding of close quarters caring as particularly the responsibility of women. This association of women and caring could confine women to domesticity, but in the Crimean War nursing, it enabled an expansion of women's agency in the public sphere. Public opinion demanded that female nurses be sent out, but the army did not want women in its hospitals. The resulting demonstration of the abilities and strength of women caught the public imagination. As consecrated women, the nursing nuns were at the centre of this development. Along with the other nurses they offered a personal involvement in caring which also commanded respect. They had been there, and they had seen suffering etched on many a face, and they had responded to it. They had the authority of face-to-face experience.

Belated national recognition eventually came to the nuns who had nursed in the Crimean War. In July 1897 Queen Victoria awarded the Royal Red Cross to the four surviving English Sisters of Mercy. This decoration was instituted by Queen Victoria for women 'who showed special devotion while nursing the sick and wounded of the Army and Navy'.[63] By royal command, they went to Windsor Castle for their award: Helen Ellis, aged eighty-one; Stanislaus Jones, seventy-four; De Chantal Hudden, seventy-one; and Anastasia Kelly, sixty-nine. A royal carriage took them from Windsor station to the castle, where after lunch they were received by the Queen who gave each of the sisters her medal.[64] The only surviving Anglican sister, Sarah Terrot was similarly honoured, travelling from Edinburgh to Balmoral to receive her medal in October.[65] It was belatedly realized that one of the Irish sisters was also alive, and in February 1898 the Royal Red Cross was awarded to Aloysius Doyle. At seventy-six, she felt too infirm to travel to London, and the medal was sent to her in the convent at Gort.[66] This was not quite the final public recognition of the service of the Sisters of Mercy. In 1913 Stanislaus Jones died, the last survivor of the Crimean sisters, and as a mark of respect she was borne to her graveside by a bearer party from the Royal Army

Medical Corps.[67] The strong, dependable Gonzaga Barrie had died in 1873, aged only forty-seven, having contracted typhus while visiting the poor.

Much of the nursing in the Crimean War involved conflict. Nightingale struggled to achieve the respect and co-operation of the medical officers. Everyone, it seems, had to wrestle with the Commissariat to obtain sufficient supplies. In the winter months, there was an unremitting struggle against the elements, and in the background, constantly, there was the war itself. The story is also one of personal conflict. The antagonism between Florence Nightingale and Francis Bridgeman derived from proud and strong personalities, ethnic sensitivities and religious prejudice. Each insisted on the righteousness of their cause. Bridgeman and Nightingale set out with high ideals that had to be tempered in the crucible of war. Somehow they could not find a way to affirm the generosity, dedication and spirit of sacrifice of the other. This frozen relationship may have impeded their work, but did not prevent it. The nursing nuns in the Crimean offered an example of how, even with clashing personalities, a greater cause could prosper, a vocation be fulfilled and a way opened for future generations of women.

Notes

A note on names and terminology

1 Caitriona Clear, *Nuns in Nineteenth-Century Ireland* (Dublin: Gill and Macmillan, 1987), 78.

Introduction

1 Norman Rich, *Why the Crimean War? A Cautionary Tale* (Hanover: University Press of New England, 1885), 137.
2 Ibid., 138.
3 Michael Hinton, *Victory over Disease: Resolving the Medical Crisis in the Crimean War, 1854–1856* (Warwick: Helion, 2019), 38.
4 David Fitzgerald, 'Confidential Report on the Nursing System', in *'I Have Done My Duty': Florence Nightingale in the Crimean War, 1854–56*, ed. Sue Goldie (Manchester: Manchester University Press, 1987), 301.
5 'The Sick and Wounded Fund', *The Times*, 19 March 1855, 10.
6 Charles Bryce, *England and France before Sebastopol, Looked at from a Medical Point of View* (London: John Churchill, 1857), 70.
7 John Henry Newman, 'Reflections on the First Lecture on the Present Position of Catholics', in *A Chronology of Faith: English Catholic History since the Reformation*, quoted in Peter Kirkpatrick (Bath: Downside Abbey Press, 2011), 92.
8 Paul Huddie, *The Crimean War and Irish Society* (Liverpool: Liverpool University Press, 2015), 198.
9 Evelyn Bolster, *The Sisters of Mercy in the Crimean War* (Cork: Mercier Press, 1964).
10 Maria Luddy, ed., *The Crimean Journals of the Sisters of Mercy* (Dublin: Four Courts Press, 2004).
11 Mary C. Sullivan, ed., *The Friendship of Florence Nightingale and Mary Clare Moore* (Philadelphia: University of Pennsylvania Press, 1999).
12 Margaret Goodman, *Experiences of an English Sister of Mercy* (London: Smith, Elder, 1862); Sarah Anne Terrot, *Nurse Sarah Anne: With Florence Nightingale at Scutari*, ed. Robert Richardson (London: John Murray, 1977).
13 See https://historyofwomenreligious.org/.
14 There is a good bibliography on the above website. See for instance Carmen Mangion, *Contested Identities: Catholic Women Religious in Nineteenth-Century*

England and Wales (Manchester: Manchester University Press, 2008); Maria Luddy, *Women and Philanthropy in Nineteenth-Century Ireland* (Cambridge: Cambridge University Press, 1995); Susan Mumm, *Stolen Daughters, Virgin Mothers: Anglican Sisterhoods in Victorian Britain* (Leicester: Leicester University Press, 1999). See also the research articles of Susan O'Brien.

15 Carol Helmstadter, *Beyond Nightingale: Nursing on the Crimean War Battlefields* (Manchester: Manchester University Press, 2020).
16 Matthew Paul Lalumia, *Realism and Politics in Victorian Art of the Crimean War* (Ann Arbor: UMI Research Press, 1984), 115. On the role of photography, see Chapter 6.
17 Trudi Tate, *A Short History of the Crimean War* (London: I.B. Tauris, 2019), 141.
18 Christopher Hibbert, *The Illustrated London News Social History of Victorian Britain* (London: Angus & Robertson, 1976), 13.
19 Lalumia, *Realism and Politics in Victorian Art of the Crimean War*, 54.

Chapter 1

1 For details of their arrival, see *Annals of the Convent of Our Lady of Mercy*, vol. 1, 225–7 (Unpublished: Bermondsey Archives, henceforth *Annals*); Goodman, *Experiences*, 67–70.
2 'A Member of the Order of Mercy' [Mary Austin Carroll] *Leaves from the Annals of the Sisters of Mercy*, vol. 2 (New York: Catholic Publication Society, 1885), 132. Subsequently cited as *Leaves*.
3 Terrot, *Nurse Sarah Anne*, 141.
4 Thomas Jay Williams, *Priscilla Lydia Sellon: The Restorer after Three Centuries of the Religious Life in the English Church* (London: SPCK, 1965), 64.
5 Helmstadter, *Beyond Nightingale*, 31.
6 John Shepherd, *The Crimean Doctors: A History of the British Medical Services in the Crimean War*, vol. 1 (Liverpool: Liverpool University Press, 1991), 172. In the text Shepherd dates this letter as 10 November 1854, but the associated footnote, 202 n41, says 5 October.
7 *Annals*, 227–8.
8 Mark Bostridge, *Florence Nightingale: The Woman and Her Legend* (London: Viking, 2008), 223–4; Gillian Gill, *The Nightingales: The Extraordinary Upbringing and Curious Life of Miss Florence Nightingale* (New York: Ballantine Books, 2004), 216–17.
9 Bostridge, *Nightingale*, 224.
10 Terrot, *Nurse Sarah Anne*, 83.
11 Shepherd, *Crimean Doctors*, vol. 1, 174–5.

12 Cecil Woodham-Smith, *Florence Nightingale 1820–1910* (London: Reprint Society/Constable, 1952), 114–15.
13 Goodman, *Experiences*, 115–16.
14 Captain Wilson, quoted by Orlando Figes, *Crimea: The Last Crusade* (London: Penguin, 2011), 53.
15 Shepherd, *Crimean Doctors*, vol. 1, 234.
16 *Report upon the State of the Hospitals of the British Army in the Crimea and Scutari* (London: HMSO, 1855) (hereafter *Hospitals Commission*), 322.
17 Letter 1 to Priscilla Lydia Sellon, nd [but November 1854], APA 28.8.
18 Terrot, *Nurse Sarah Anne*, 88–9.
19 Barrie, letter to her sister Julia Boodle, 13 November 1854, BA 400/2/11/1.
20 I am grateful to Stewart Emmens of the Science Museum, London, for emailed quotations from the history of medicine which encourage this interpretation.
21 *Annals*, 230.
22 Ibid., 222.
23 Letter to Julia Boodle, 13 November 1854, BA 400/2/11/1.
24 Goodman, *Experiences*, 102. One of the criticisms levelled against Nightingale was immodesty, because she attended surgical operations where men were naked. See Shepherd, *Crimean Doctors*, vol. 1, 281–2.
25 I am grateful to Professor Saul David for information about the impact of these weapons.
26 *Henry Clifford VC: His Letters and Sketches from the Crimea* (London: Michael Joseph, 1956), 191.
27 Letter to William Bowman, 14 November 1854, *CW* 14, 63.
28 Notes and letters from C. H. and Selina Bracebridge, 9 November 1854, *CW* 14, 60–1, emphasis in original.
29 Goodman, *Experiences*, 103.
30 Letter to William Bowman, 14 November 1854, *CW* 14, 62.
31 Terrot, *Nurse Sarah Anne*, 93.
32 Ibid., 84.
33 Ibid., 85.
34 Goodman, *Experiences*, 157.
35 Terrot, *Nurse Sarah Anne*, 126.
36 Goodman, *Experiences*, 133–4.
37 Woodham-Smith, *Nightingale*, 139; Goodman, *Experiences*, 129–30.
38 Letter 1 to Priscilla Lydia Sellon, nd [1854], APA 28.8.
39 *Annals*, 228–9.
40 Nightingale, letter to William Bowman, 14 November 1854, *CW* 14, 63.
41 Terrot, *Nurse Sarah Anne*, 89–90.
42 Ibid., 85–6.
43 Letter 2 to Priscilla Lydia Sellon, nd [1854], APA 28.8.

44　Ibid., 86–7.
45　'The Military Hospitals at Scutari', *The Times*, 8 December 1854, 8.
46　'Letters from the Crimea', *The Times*, 8 December 1854, 8.
47　Hospitals Commission, 330–1.
48　Thomas Jay Williams and Allan Walter Campbell, *The Park Village Sisterhood* (London: SPCK, 1965), 56–7, 101.
49　Letter to Priscilla Lydia Sellon, 5 December 1855, *CW* 14, 74.
50　Quoted in John Cook, *The Life of Florence Nightingale*, vol. 2 (London: Macmillan, 1914), 369.
51　Terrot, *Nurse Sarah Anne*, 69.
52　*Annals*, 231.
53　Letter from Sister Marie des Neiges to Manning, 22 December 1854, typescript and translation, AAW, Manning Papers, Crimean War folder.
54　Letter to Herbert, 25 December 1854, *CW* 14, 98.
55　Terrot, *Nurse Sarah Anne*, 128.
56　Ibid., 128–9.
57　Nightingale, 'Notes on the Health of the British Army', *CW* 14, 749.
58　Terrot, *Nurse Sarah Anne*, 127.
59　Letter to Sidney Herbert, 8 January 1855, *CW* 14, 107.
60　*Annals*, 247–8.
61　Goodman, *Experiences*, 120–1.
62　Terrot, *Nurse Sarah Anne*, 129.
63　'A Precedent for Protestants', *The Times*, 19 December 1854, 5.
64　Manning's and Grant's comments are in *Annals*, 237–9.
65　Letter to Herbert, 25 December 1854, *CW* 14, 94.

Chapter 2

1　Candan Badem, *The Ottoman Crimean War (1853–1856)* (Leiden: Brill, 2010), 58–9.
2　Ibid., 62–3.
3　Jack Fairey, *The Great Powers and Orthodox Christendom: The Crisis Over the Eastern Church in the Era of the Crimean War* (Basingstoke: Palgrave Macmillan, 2015), 63.
4　Sotiros Roussos, 'The Greek Orthodox Community of Jerusalem in International Politics: International Solutions for Jerusalem and the Greek Orthodox Community in the Nineteenth and Twentieth Centuries', in *Jerusalem: Its Sanctity and Centrality to Judaism, Christianity and Islam*, ed. Lee Levine (New York: Continuum, 1999), 486.
5　Figes, *Crimea*, 3–4.
6　Roussos, 'The Greek Orthodox Community of Jerusalem', 484.
7　Quoted in Fairey, *The Great Powers and Orthodox Christendom*, 141.

8 Ibid., 98.
9 Stefanie Markovits, *The Crimean War in the British Imagination* (Cambridge: Cambridge University Press, 2009), 21 and 223 n.34.
10 'Arrival of the Wounded in the Bosphorus', *The Times*, 9 October 1854, 8.
11 'The Crimea', *The Times*, 12 October 1854, 7.
12 'Every Man of Common Modesty', *The Times*, 12 October 1854, 6.
13 'Turkey', *The Times*, 13 October 1854, 8. Writers frequently confused the Sisters of Mercy and the Sisters of Charity.
14 'A Sufferer in the Present War', Letters, *The Times*, 14 October 1854, 7.
15 Lord Nelson quoted in Williams, *Sellon*, 134. The *Guardian* newspaper cited here was a Church of England weekly. This Lord Nelson was a nephew of the famous admiral.
16 *The Times*, 18 October 1854, 6.
17 Clarence Gallagher, 'The Church and Institutes of Consecrated Life', *The Way* 50, no. Supplement (1984): 7–8. *Quamvis Iusto* was a response to the need to clarify the status of the order founded by Mary Ward in 1609.
18 James E. Kelly, *English Convents in Catholic Europe, c.1600–1800* (Cambridge: Cambridge University Press, 2020), 1.
19 Tonya J. Moutray, *Refugee Nuns, the French Revolution, and British Literature and Culture* (Abingdon: Routledge, 2016), 40.
20 Susan O'Brien, 'The Nun in Nineteenth-Century England', *Past and Present* 121 (November 1988): 111.
21 Ibid., 119.
22 Liza Picard, *Victorian London: The Life of a City, 1840–1870* (London: Weidenfeld and Nicolson, 2006), 5.
23 H. E. Malden, ed., *A History of the County of Surrey*, vol. 4 (London: Constable, 1912,) 17–24.
24 Quoted in Michael Hill, *The Religious Order: A Study of Virtuoso Religion and its Legitimation in the Nineteenth-Century Church of England* (London: Heinemann, 1973), 182.
25 Isaiah Berlin, *The Crooked Timber of Humanity: Chapters in the History of Ideas* (London: Pimlico, 2013), 96.
26 Susan Mumm, '"A Peril to the Bench of Bishops": Sisterhoods and Episcopal Authority in the Church of England, 1845–1908', *Journal of Ecclesiastical History* 59, no. 1 (2008): 64–5.
27 Letter Sidney Herbert to Nightingale, 15 October 1854, in *'I Have Done my Duty'*, ed. Sue Goldie, 23 and 24.
28 *Annals*, 210–11.
29 Gill, *Nightingales*, 318.
30 *Annals*, 218–19. The memorandum of agreement with the government is on pages 220–1.
31 Williams, *Sellon*, 134–6.

32 Goodman, *Experiences*, 57–8.
33 Terrot, *Nurse Sarah Anne*, 66.
34 Goodman, *Experiences*, 58–9.
35 Ibid., 60–1.
36 Helmstadter, *Beyond Nightingale*, 32.
37 Bostridge, *Nightingale*, 97.
38 Ibid., 47.
39 Ibid., 99.
40 Richard Temple Godman, *The Fields of War: A Young Cavalryman's Crimea Campaign*, ed. Philip Warner (London: John Murray, 1977), 106–7.
41 For the history of this community, see Peter Anson, *The Call of the Cloister: Religious Communities . . . in the Anglican Communion*, revised edn (London: SPCK, 1964), 280–5, and JoAnn Widerquist, '"Dearest Friend": The Correspondence of Colleagues Florence Nightingale and Mary Jones', *Nursing History Review* 1, no. 1 (1993): 25–42.
42 Bostridge, *Nightingale*, 95.
43 Anne Summers, 'Pride and Prejudice: Ladies and Nurses in the Crimean War', in *Patriotism: The Making and Unmaking of British National Identity: Vol. 2, Minorities and Outsiders*, ed. Raphael Samuel (London: Routledge, 1989), 63.
44 Letter from Manning to the Irish Sisters, 1 December 1854, quoted in Aloysius Doyle, 'Memories of the Crimea' in *The Crimean Journals of the Sisters of Mercy 1854–56*, ed. Maria Luddy (Dublin: Four Courts Press, 2004), 46. Henceforth cited as Doyle/Luddy.
45 Francis Bridgeman, 'An Account of the Mission of the Sisters of Mercy in the Military Hospitals of the East', in *The Crimean Journals of the Sisters of Mercy 1854–56*, ed. Maria Luddy, 125. Henceforth cited as Bridgeman/Luddy.
46 Ibid., 126.
47 Ibid., 127.
48 McDonald, editorial note in *CW* 14, 76.
49 *Leaves*, 144.
50 'The Sick and Wounded', *The Times*, 26 October 1854, 10.
51 'Nurses for the Sick and Wounded', *The Times*, 27 October 1854, 6.
52 Doyle/Luddy, 8–9. Kingstown is now Dún Laoghaire.
53 Nurses for the Sick and Wounded', *The Times*, 30 November 1854, 6.
54 Letter to Sidney Herbert, 15 December 1854, *CW* 14, 83.
55 Letter to Sidney Herbert, 25 December 1854, *CW* 14, 96–7, emphasis in original.
56 Letter to Grant 7 December 1854, AAS C40.12.
57 Bridgeman/Luddy, 128.
58 Mary C. Sullivan, *Catherine McAuley and the Tradition of Mercy* (Dublin: Four Courts Press, 2000), 312.
59 'Diary of Sister M. Joseph Croke', in *The Crimean Journals of the Sisters of Mercy 1854–56*, ed. Maria Luddy, 71. Henceforth cited as Croke/Luddy.
60 *Annals*, 231.

61 Letter to Herbert, 25 December 1854, *CW* 14, 97.
62 *Annals*, 231–2.
63 Doyle/Luddy, 11.
64 Letter, Ronan to Cullen, 22 January 1855, quoted in Luddy, *Crimean Journals* Introduction, xvii. Mothers superior of that era were often referred to as 'Mrs'.
65 Letter to Herbert 4 January 1855, *CW* 14, 104.
66 Letter to Sidney Herbert, 25 December 1854, CW 14, 97–8.
67 Bolster, *Sisters of Mercy*, 97.
68 Mary Sullivan, *The Path of Mercy: The Life of Catherine McAuley* (Dublin: Four Courts Press, 2012), 181.
69 Ibid., 213–16, quoting from 213 and 215.

Chapter 3

1 'Summary of Operations in the Crimea', *Manchester Guardian*, 3 December 1854, 6.
2 J. B. Conacher, *Britain and the Crimea 1855-56: Problems of War and Peace* (London: Macmillan 1987), 83–8.
3 Figes, *Crimea*, 288–9.
4 Nightingale, 'Notes on the Health of the British Army', *CW* 14, 577.
5 Hospitals Commission, 37.
6 Nightingale to Sidney Herbert, 4 January 1855, *CW* 14, 103.
7 Nathaniel Steevens, *The Crimean Campaign with the Connaught Rangers, 1854-55-56* (London: Griffith and Farran, 1878), 163.
8 Saul David, *Victoria's Wars* (London: Penguin, 2012), 250.
9 *The Times*, editorial, 1 January 1855, 6.
10 David, *Victoria's Wars*, 251–2.
11 George Bell, *Soldier's Glory: Being, 'Rough Notes of an Old Soldier'* (Tunbridge Wells: Spellmount, 1991), 255.
12 Ibid., 265.
13 Shepherd, *Crimean Doctors*, vol. 1, 297 and 324.
14 Hospitals Commission, 20 and 22.
15 Hospitals Commission, 327. Wells was injured not in battle but in an industrial accident when 10 tons of ammunition collapsed on soldiers moving it.
16 Bell, *Soldier's Glory*, 267.
17 'Letters from the Crimea', *The Times*, 3 January 1855, 7.
18 On overcrowding, see Hospitals Commission, 30.
19 Goodman, *Experiences*, 174.
20 Terrot, *Nurse Sarah Anne*, 116–17.
21 Ibid., 158.

22 Goodman, *Experiences*, 157.
23 Doyle/Luddy, 20.
24 Hinton, *Victory over Disease*, 196.
25 Quoted in David, *Victoria's Wars*, 252–3.
26 Terrot, *Nurse Sarah Anne*, 120.
27 *Leaves*, 171.
28 Letter to Master Atkins, 9 February 1855, *CW* 14, 138.
29 Goodman, *Experiences*, 90.
30 Doyle/Luddy, 21.
31 Undated fragment of letter, HMA GB1856/0/200/11/47.
32 Goodman, *Experiences*, 158–9.
33 Terrot, *Nurse Sarah Anne*, 117.
34 Goodman, *Experiences*, 185.
35 Ibid., 109.
36 Ibid., 133.
37 Terrot, *Nurse Sarah Anne*, 95, 120.
38 Testimony of Drs McGrigor and McIlree to Hospitals Commission, 306, 307.
39 Hospitals Commission, 32.
40 *Leaves*, 172.
41 Helmstadter, *Beyond Nightingale*, 49–50.
42 Ibid., 65–70.
43 *Annals*, 248.
44 Nightingale, 'Notes on the Health of the British Army', *CW* 14, 619.
45 Hospitals Commission, 41.
46 'Rules and Regulations for Nurses Attached to the Military Hospitals in the East', NA WO 43/963, f 241.
47 Letter to Mary Clare Moore, 20 January 1864, in Sullivan ed., *Friendship*, 116.
48 *Annals*, 249.
49 Terrot, *Nurse Sarah Anne*, 91–2.
50 *Annals*, 249–51.
51 Terrot, *Nurse Sarah Anne*, 159.
52 Letter to Mother Eldress Catherine Chambers, 28 February 1855, APA 28.4.
53 Terrot, *Nurse Sarah Anne*, 160.
54 Letter, Goodman to Chambers, 14 February 1855, APA 28.4.
55 Letter to Sidney Herbert, 26 March 1855, *CW* 14, 174.
56 Letter to Priscilla Lydia Sellon, *CW* 14, 160.
57 Terrot, *Nurse Sarah Anne*, 162.
58 Edwin Wrench, 'The Lessons of the Crimean War', *British Medical Journal* 2, no. 2 (1899): 206.
59 Letter, to Nightingale family, 22 April 1855, *CW* 14, 180.
60 Letter to Chambers, 28 February 1855, APA 28.4.

61 Letter to Chambers, nd, APA 28.4.
62 Terrot, *Nurse Sarah Anne*, 118.
63 Letter to Priscilla Lydia Sellon, nd [1854], APA 28.8.
64 *Annals*, 252–3 and 270.
65 Ibid., 254–5.
66 Letter, William Ronan SJ to his superior in Dublin. Quoted in David Murphy, *Ireland and the Crimean War* (Dublin: Four Courts Press, 2002), 134.
67 Goodman, *Experiences*, 182–3.
68 Terrot, *Nurse Sarah Anne*, 130–1.
69 Ibid., 101.
70 Ibid., 125.
71 Letter to Julia Boodle, 29 October 1855, BA 400/2/Crimea/11/13.
72 *Annals*, 230.
73 Terrot, *Nurse Sarah Anne*, 112.
74 Figes, *Crimea*, 178.
75 Brian Griffin, 'Irish Identity and the Crimean War', in *War: Identities in Conflict 1300–2000*, ed. Bertrand Taithe and Tim Thornton (Stroud: Sutton, 1998), 114–15.
76 Ibid., 119.
77 Quoted in Woodham-Smith, 120.
78 Goodman, *Experiences*, 197.
79 Frances Taylor, *Eastern Hospitals and Eastern Nurses: The Narrative of Twelve Months' Experience in the Hospitals of Koulali and Scutari* (1857), vol. 1 (Uckfield: Naval and Military Press Reprint, 2009), 42–3.
80 Croke/Luddy, 74. In fact, Christians in Ottoman domains numbered twelve to thirteen million.
81 Letter to her sister Parthenope, 31 May 1851, *CW* 7, 418.
82 'We Have Not Gone Through a Generation of War', *The Times*, 9 October 1854, 6.
83 Figes, *Crimea*, 162–3.
84 Letter probably to Parthenope Nightingale, 2 June 1856, *CW* 14, 411.
85 Conacher, *Britain and the Crimea*, 19–21. The other two were Gladstone and Sir James Graham.
86 Sanitary Commission, 13 and 18.
87 Shepherd, *Crimean Doctors*, vol. 2, 400; 403–4.
88 Ibid., 518.
89 Bridgeman/Luddy, 138.
90 Taylor, *Eastern Hospitals*, vol. 1, 55.

Chapter 4

1 Hansard, House of Commons, 28 February 1854, vol. 131 col. 54.

2 Mangion, *Contested Identities*, 37. There were an estimated 10,000 women religious in these convents.
3 W. J. Battersby, 'The Educational Work of the Religious Orders of Women', in *The English Catholics 1850–1950*, ed. George Beck (London: Burns Oates, 1950), 340.
4 Herbert Thurston S. J. quoted in Walter Arnstein, *Protestant versus Catholic in Mid-Victorian England: Mr Newdegate and the Nuns* (Columbia: University of Missouri Press, 1982), 62.
5 Kathryn Gleadle, *British Women in the Nineteenth Century* (Basingstoke: Palgrave, 2001), 51, 53.
6 Ibid., 89, 176–8.
7 Sarah Stickney Ellis, *The Women of England*, quoted in Mumm, 'A Peril to the Bench of Bishops', 64. Ellis's book was published in 1839 and by 1850 was in its tenth edition.
8 Quoted in O'Brien, '*Terra Incognita*: The Nun in Nineteenth-Century England', *Past and Present* 121 (1988): 138.
9 Gleadle, *British Women in the Nineteenth Century*, 15, 20.
10 Luddy, *Women and Philanthropy*, 13.
11 Sullivan, *Path of Mercy*, 145.
12 Barbara Walsh, *Roman Catholic Nuns in England and Wales 1800–1937: A Social History* (Dublin: Irish Academic Press, 2002), 154.
13 Susan O'Brien, 'Lay Sisters and Good Mothers: Working-class Women in English Convents, 1840–1910', in *Studies in Church History, Vol. 27, Women in the Church*, ed. W. J. Sheils (Oxford: Blackwell, 1990), 454.
14 Ibid., 455.
15 O'Brien, '*Terra Incognita*', 138.
16 Mumm, *Stolen Daughters, Virgin Mothers*, 36.
17 Anna Jameson, *Sisters of Charity Catholic and Protestant at Home and Abroad* (London: Longman, 1855), 1.
18 Ibid., 8–10.
19 Ibid., 13.
20 Ibid., 83.
21 Ibid., 86–7.
22 Ibid., 92.
23 Ibid., 94.
24 Ibid., 105.
25 'Suggestions for Thought', *CW* 11, 570, 575.
26 Ibid., 548.
27 Ibid., 571.
28 Ibid., 584.
29 Ibid., 570.

30 Letter to Manning, 30 June 1852, *CW* 3, 248.
31 See for example in *CW* 11, 358, 363, 381, 410.
32 'Suggestions for Thought', *CW* 11, 516.
33 Letter to Benjamin Jowett, July 1862, *CW* 11, 42.
34 See for example the struggles of Elizabeth Prout, founder of the Sisters of the Cross and Passion: Gloria McAdam, 'Willing Women and the Rise of Convents in Nineteenth-Century England', *Women's History Review* 8, no. 3 (1999): 424–6.
35 O'Brien, '*Terra Incognita*', 136.
36 Mangion, *Contested Identities*, 87.
37 Anne Stott, 'Women and Religion', in *Women's History: Britain, 1700–1850*, ed. Hannah Barker and Elaine Chalus (London: Routledge, 2005), 117.
38 Mumm, *Stolen Daughters, Virgin Mothers*, 14–15.
39 Ibid., 208–9.
40 Mangion, *Contested Identities*, 48.
41 Mary Heimann, 'Devotional Stereotypes in English Catholicism 1850–1914', in *Catholicism in Britain and France since 1789*, ed. Frank Tallett and Nicholas Atkin (London: Hambledon Press, 1999), 22–3.
42 Owen Chadwick, *The Victorian Church*, Part 1, 3rd edn (London: Adam & Charles Black, 1971), 363–9.
43 Philip Hughes, 'The English Catholics in 1850', in ed. Beck, 45.
44 Linda Colley, *Britons: Forging the Nation 1707–1837* (London: BCA/Yale, 1992), 18.
45 Edward Norman, *The English Catholic Church in the Nineteenth Century* (Oxford: Clarendon Press, 1984), 201.
46 Sullivan, *Path of Mercy*, 268.
47 Susan Griffin, *Anti-Catholicism and Nineteenth-Century Fiction* (Cambridge: Cambridge University Press, 2004), 114–15. See also 121–2.
48 There is a useful discussion of its etymology in the Wikipedia article 'Muscular Christianity': https://en.wikipedia.org/wiki/Muscular_Christianity.
49 Miriam Burstein, *Narrating Women's History in Britain 1770–1902* (Aldershot: Ashgate, 2004), 130–1.
50 Ibid., 138–9.
51 Griffin, *Anti-Catholicism*, 35.
52 Quoted in ibid., 140, 145.
53 Letter from Kate Innes, quoted by Bridgeman/Luddy, 161.
54 Quoted in G. I. T. Machin, *Politics and the Churches in Great Britain 1832 to 1868* (Oxford: Oxford University Press, 1977), 217.
55 Hansard, House of Commons, 25 March 1851, vol. 115, column 568.
56 Machin, *Politics and the Churches*, 264.
57 Hansard, House of Commons 28 February 1854, vol. 131, column 53.
58 Ibid., columns 54, 64–5.

59 Ibid., column 58.
60 John Ball, MP for Carlow, ibid., column 86.
61 Robert Potter, MP for Limerick, ibid., columns 91–2.
62 Ibid., columns 112–14.
63 Anthony Trollope, *The Warden* (London: Penguin, 1986), 62.
64 Arnstein, *Protestant versus Catholic*, 67–8.
65 Ibid., 63 and Chapter 9, *passim*.
66 *Annals*, 257–8.
67 Quoted in *Leaves*, 135.

Chapter 5

1 *Leaves*, 131, 140.
2 Taylor, *Eastern Hospitals*, vol. 1, 292.
3 Ibid., 101–3.
4 Ibid., 260.
5 Shepherd, *Crimean Doctors*, vol. 2, 351.
6 Bridgeman/Luddy, 142.
7 Sanitary Commission Report, 24, 38.
8 Bridgeman/Luddy, 142.
9 Letter to Sidney Herbert, 22 February 1855, CW 14, 149.
10 Doyle/Luddy, 23–4.
11 Taylor, *Eastern Hospitals*, vol. 1, 120.
12 Letter to family, 4 March 1855, CW 14, 157.
13 Letter to Hawes, 2 April 1855, NA, WO 43/963, f 205.
14 Doyle/Luddy, 47.
15 Bridgeman/Luddy, 157 n.60.
16 Taylor, *Eastern Hospitals*, vol. 1, 145.
17 Shepherd, *Crimean Doctors*, vol. 2, 472.
18 Letter to Elizabeth Hersey, 5 July 1855, CW 14, 196.
19 Letter to Bridgeman, 15 July 1855, CW 14, 199; also letter to the Bracebridges, 7 August 1855, CW 14, 208; Bridgeman/Luddy, 170–4.
20 *The Times*, 15 January 1855, 4.
21 Terrot, *Nurse Sarah Anne*, 139.
22 Letter to Nightingale, 20 October 1854, NA, WO 43/963 f 252.
23 Letter to Sidney Herbert, 24 October, 1854, NA, WO/963 f 253, emphasis added.
24 Letter to Sidney Herbert, 15 February 1855, CW 14, 142.
25 Letter to Sabin, 27 April 1855, NA WO 43/963 ff 262–3.

26 Correspondence April–May 1855, MCA CR/1/4. This correspondence is reprinted in Bolster, *Sisters of Mercy*, 307–9.
27 Bridgeman/Luddy, 146, 150.
28 Letter to Paulet, 27 April 1855, NA WO 43/963 ff 272–3.
29 Bridgeman/Luddy, 163–5.
30 Letter to Ronan, 13 May 1855, MCA CR/1/5. This letter is also in Bridgeman/Luddy, 165–7.
31 Bridgeman/Luddy, 166–7.
32 Doyle/Luddy, 28. These words were omitted when her memoir was published in 1897.
33 Bridgeman/Luddy. She takes care to add that the fifty or so who converted at Koulali did so by going to Fr Ronan's room, without telling the sisters, saying that the soldiers did not want to get the sisters into difficulty.
34 Bridgeman/Luddy, 154 n.56.
35 Doyle/Luddy. The italicized words were omitted from the published version.
36 Doyle/Luddy, 28.
37 Doyle/Luddy, 25.
38 Bridgeman/Luddy, 177.
39 Figes, *Crimea*, 364–72; Julian Spilsbury, *The Thin Red Line: An Eyewitness History of the Crimean War* (London: Cassell, 2005), 279–90. A Naval Brigade was part of the British attacking force.
40 Clifford, *Henry Clifford VC*, 236–7. As quoted, he oscillates between calling them Sisters of Charity and Sisters of Mercy.
41 Helmstadter, *Beyond Nightingale*, 255–66.
42 John Shelton Curtiss, 'Russian Sisters of Mercy in the Crimea, 1854–1855', *Slavic Review* 25, no. 1 (1966): 89.
43 Ibid., 93.
44 Godman, *Fields of War*, 180.
45 Lady [Emilia] Hornby, *Constantinople during the Crimean War* (London: Richard Bentley, 1863), 35–6.
46 Conacher, *Britain and the Crimea*, 140, 169–73.
47 Doyle/Luddy, 25.
48 Taylor, *Eastern Hospitals*, vol. 1, 262.
49 Bridgeman/Luddy, 131 and 153.
50 Lynn McDonald, 'Florence Nightingale, Statistics and the Crimean War', *Journal of the Royal Statistical Society Series A* 177, no. 3 (2014): 577–8. The Scutari figure covers both Barrack and General Hospitals there.
51 Ibid., 580.
52 Ibid.
53 'Turkey', *The Times*, 9 March 1855, 11.
54 Taylor, *Eastern Hospitals*, vol. 1, Chapter 11 *passim*, quoting from 251.

55 Letter probably to Sidney Herbert, 5 November 1855, *CW* 14, 257.
56 Ibid., 258.
57 Bryce, *England and France before Sebastopol*, 69.
58 Ibid., 70.
59 Quoted in Cook, vol. 1, 156.
60 'Subsidiary Notes as to the Introduction of Female Nursing into Military Hospitals in Peace and in War', *CW* 15, 28.
61 Bridgeman/Luddy, 145.
62 Letter to John Henry Lefroy, 11 January 1856, *CW* 14, 307, emphasis in original.
63 Spilsbury, *Thin Red Line*, 103. For a helpful context to Hall's comment, and some defence of him, see Hinton, *Victory over Disease*, 294–5.
64 Letter to Sidney Herbert, 3 April 1856, *CW* 14, 370.
65 Helmstadter, *Beyond Nightingale*, 89–90, 108–9. Bostridge's account, *Nightingale* 286, is not entirely accurate.
66 Bostridge, *Nightingale*, 287.
67 Letter to Mai Smith, 19 October 1855, *CW* 14, 245.
68 Letter to Frances Nightingale, 24 October 1855, *CW* 14, 251.
69 Letter to Bridgeman, 25 December 1855, *CW* 14, 92.
70 Letter to Lefroy, 11 January 1856, *CW* 14, 306.
71 Bridgeman/Luddy, 193.

Chapter 6

1 Sanitary Commission Report, 87–9.
2 Letter to Lord Grey, 5 July 1857, *CW* 14, 519.
3 Figes, *Crimea*, 409.
4 Luddy/Bridgeman, 211.
5 *Leaves*, 188.
6 Doyle/Luddy, 30.
7 'The Balaclava Hospitals', *Illustrated London News*, 17 November 1855, 594.
8 Bolster, *Sisters of Mercy*, 264–5.
9 Luddy/Bridgeman, 200–2.
10 Croke/Luddy, 79 and 84.
11 Doyle/Luddy, 33.
12 Croke/Luddy, 83.
13 Bridgeman/Luddy, 197.
14 Annotation by Hawes on Nightingale's letter of 7 January 1856. NA WO 43/963, notionally f 224, but folio pagination is erratic at this point.
15 *Annals*, 266.

16 Ibid., 270–1.
17 Helen Rappaport, *No Place for Ladies: The Untold Story of Women in the Crimean War* (London: Aurum, 2007), 189.
18 Croke/Luddy, 99–100.
19 Shepherd, *Crimean Doctors*, vol. 2, 574–7.
20 Croke/Luddy, 100–1; Doyle/Luddy, 39. Contrary to Croke, Doyle says that Butler experienced no agony.
21 Doyle/Luddy, 32.
22 Ibid., 38; Croke/Luddy, 101.
23 Clifford, *Henry Clifford VC*, 108.
24 Bridgeman/Luddy, 199, emphasis in original.
25 David Fitzgerald, 'Confidential Report on the Nursing System, since its Introduction to the Crimea on the 23rd January 1855', NA WO 43/963, ff 299–300.
26 Letter to Lefroy, 11 January 1856, *CW* 14, 304 and 311.
27 Letters to Sam Smith, 16 March 1856, *CW* 14, 356, where Nightingale refers to Fitzgerald as a Catholic.
28 Letter to Sam Smith, 6 March 1856, *CW* 14, 351.
29 Letter to Sam Smith, 16 March 1856, *CW* 14, 358, emphasis in original.
30 Letter to Herbert, 4 January 1855, *CW* 14, 104.
31 Bridgeman/Luddy, 224.
32 Ibid., 228.
33 Ibid., 230.
34 Ibid., 233.
35 Ibid., 232.
36 Hinton, *Victory over Disease*, 11.
37 Bridgeman/Luddy, 239.
38 Goldie, *I Have Done My Duty*, editorial comment, 243.
39 Fitzgerald letter to Bridgeman, 28 August 1856, MCA, CR/1/13.
40 See for example extract quoted from letter of 11 April 1856 in Goldie, *I Have Done My Duty*, 239.
41 Letter to unnamed recipient, 12 April 1856, *CW* 14, 380.
42 Letter to Sam Smith, 17 April 1856, *CW* 14, 384.
43 See for instance undated the letter to an unnamed recipient in which Nightingale queries an order of '8 bottles of brandy in 24 hours, beside port wine' by the sisters, adding 'it *does not go into the wards*'. *CW* 14, 255, emphasis in original.
44 Letter to Sidney Herbert, 16 March 1856, *CW* 14, 358.
45 Letter to John Henry Lefroy, 5 April 1856, *CW* 14, 376.
46 Croke/Luddy, 80.
47 *Annals*, 292.
48 Ibid., 293.
49 Letter to Moore, 8 April 1856, *CW* 14, 377.

50 *Annals*, 281.
51 Letter to Moore, 15 April 1856, *CW* 14, 381.
52 *Annals*, 283.
53 Duffy, *Ireland and the Crimean War*, 140.
54 Ibid., 282. Emphasis in original.
55 The reference to being a 'disgrace' is in a letter from Nightingale to Sidney Herbert of 3 April 1856 in Goldie, *I Have Done My Duty*, 246; the relevant paragraph does not appear in the same letter in *CW* 14, 370.
56 Letter to Bridgeman, 21 April 1856, MCA CR/1/13.
57 Letter to Bridgeman, 28 April 1856, MCA CR/1/13.
58 Letter to Stanislaus Jones, 3 April 1856, HMA GB/1856/0/200/11/46.
59 Goodman, *Experiences*, 209.
60 Letter to Lefroy, 11 January 1856, *CW* 14, 306.
61 Goodman, *Experiences*, 213–16.
62 Hornby, *Constantinople during the Crimean War*, 306–7.
63 Letter to Moore, 10 April 1856, *CW* 14, 378
64 *Annals*, 297.
65 Sullivan, *Friendship*, 72.
66 Letter to Moore, 29 April 1856, *CW* 14, 396–7.
67 Hornby, *Constantinople during the Crimean War*, 263–4.
68 'The British Army', *The Times*, 9 April 1856, 10.
69 *Annals*, 304.
70 Goodman, *Experiences*, 233.
71 Williams, *Sellon*, 172.
72 Undated notes, 1856, *CW* 14, 437.
73 Letter, probably to Parthenope Nightingale, 2 June 1856 *CW* 14, 410.
74 Letter to Moore, 7 July 1856, Sullivan, *Friendship*, 77.
75 Notes, in *CW* 14, 435–6.
76 Quoted in Williams, *Sellon*, 173.

Chapter 7

1 Bolster, *Sisters of Mercy*, 276–7.
2 *Southern Reporter and Cork Commercial Courier*, 27 May 1856, 2.
3 Murphy, *Ireland and the Crimean War*, 206–12.
4 See: https://victoriancommons.wordpress.com/2018/02/22/mp-of-the-month-andrew-carew-odwyer-1800-1877/
5 *Dublin Evening Post*, 23 October 1856, 4.

6 Mary Seacole, *Wonderful Adventures of Mrs Seacole in Many Lands* (London: Penguin, 2005), 82.
7 'The Sisters of Mercy and Miss Nightingale', *Carlow Post*, 17 May 1856, 2, emphasis in original.
8 'Miss Nightingale and the Sisters of Charity and Mercy', *Freeman's Journal*, 14 November 1856, 3.
9 *The Tablet*, 3 May 1856, 284.
10 Luddy, ed., 'Editorial Notes', xxvii.
11 Bridgeman/Luddy, 230.
12 Bridgeman/Luddy, 145, quoting 1 Corinthians 1:27. By 'fail her' Bridgeman means 'defeat her'.
13 Roy Foster, *Modern Ireland 1600–1972* (London: Allen Lane, 1988), 342.
14 Emmet Larkin, *The Historical Dimensions of Irish Catholicism* (Washington: Catholic University of America Press, 1997), 82.
15 Catherine Flanagan, *The Great Famine in Kinsale* (Dublin: Four Courts Press, 2018), 36. I am grateful to Vincent Clarke for drawing my attention to this reference.
16 Ibid., 41.
17 Ibid., 58–9.
18 Ibid., 65.
19 Bolster, *Sisters of Mercy*, 97.
20 *Dictionary of Irish Biography* (accessed online) 'Joanna Bridgeman (Sister Mary Francis)'.
21 Quoted in Clear, *Nuns in Nineteenth-Century Ireland*, 131–2.
22 Bostridge, *Nightingale*, 316.
23 Ibid., 309–10.
24 'Answers to Written Questions', Question 39, *CW* 14, 930. This was question 10,020 in the Royal Commission report.
25 'Answers to Written Questions', Question 41, *CW* 14, 931. Question 10,022 in the Royal Commission Report.
26 L. P. Curtis, *Anglo-Saxons and Celts: A Study of Anti-Irish Prejudice in Victorian Ireland* (Bridgeport: University of Bridgeport, 1968), 4, 27, 68–9, 72.
27 Copy of Bridgeman to Huish, 3 March 1858, MCA CR/1/13. The original letter by Huish is lost.
28 Hall to Herbert, 20 March 1858, in Bolster, *Sisters of Mercy*, 312–13.
29 Bridgeman's letter is dated 15 April 1858, in Bolster, *Sisters of Mercy*, 263–8. The supporting statement by Dr Murray is on page 261.
30 Letter to 'Sir', from Whitfield, 25 March 1858, MCA CR/1/13, part of the papers assembled by Hall and shared with Bridgeman.
31 Bolster, *Sisters of Mercy*, 268.
32 Letter to William Bowman, 14 November 1854, *CW* 14, 65.

33 Helmstadter, *Beyond Nightingale*, 68.
34 Letter to Sam Smith, 17 April 1856, *CW* 14, 384.
35 Helmstadter, *Beyond Nightingale*, 123.
36 Bolster, *Sisters of Mercy*, 263.
37 See, for instance Declan Kiberd, *Inventing Ireland: The Literature of the Modern Nation* (London: Vintage, 1995), or Seamus Deane, *Strange Country: Modernity and Nationhood in Irish Writing since 1790* (Oxford: Oxford University Press, 1997).
38 Doyle/Luddy, 10.
39 Croke/Luddy, 113.
40 Bridgeman/Luddy, 145.
41 Paul Huddie, 'The Crimean War, 1854–56: Ireland's Happiest Nineteenth-Century War', in *Happiness in Nineteenth-Century Ireland*, ed. Mary Hatfield (Liverpool: Liverpool University Press, 2021), 35–52.
42 Quoted in Ibid., 41.
43 Quoted in Ibid., 42.
44 Quoted in Brian Griffin, 'Ireland and the Crimean War', *Irish Sword* 22, no. 87 (2000): 303.
45 Murphy, *Ireland and the Crimean War*, 220. At least twenty cannons were given to town councils and corporations.
46 William Davis, *The Diary of an Offaly Schoolboy 1858–59*, ed. Sandra Robinson (Tullamore: Esker Press, 2010), 19. I am grateful to Maria Luddy for this reference.
47 Griffin, 'Irish Identity and the Crimean War', 117.
48 Sean Connolly, *Religion and Society in Nineteenth-Century Ireland* (Dundalk: Economic and Social History Society of Ireland/Dundalgan Press, 1985), 3.
49 Philip O'Flaherty, *Sketches of the War: Being a Second Series of Letters* (Edinburgh: Shepherd and Elliot, 1855), 29, 40–1. Later in life he was an Anglican missionary in Uganda.
50 Huddie, *Crimean War and Irish Society*, 192. This modifies his earlier view that support came from 'purely domestic, Irish considerations rather than because of intense loyalty to Britain or her empire' ('Irish Identity and the Crimean War', 117).
51 Kevin Kenny, 'The Irish in the Empire', in *Ireland and the British Empire*, ed. Kevin Kenny (Oxford: Oxford University Press, 2004), 90–122.
52 *Leaves*, 211–12.
53 Larkin, *Historical Dimensions of Irish Catholicism*, 82.
54 Matthew Campbell, 'Victorian Ireland, 1830–1880: A Transitional State' in *Irish Literature in Transition*, ed. Matthew Campbell (Cambridge: Cambridge University Press, 2020), 12.
55 Larkin, *Historical Dimensions of Irish Catholicism*, 77–8.
56 Ibid., 83.

57 Thomas McGrath, 'The Tridentine Evolution of Modern Irish Catholicism: A Re-examination of the "Devotional Revolution" Thesis', in *Irish Church History Today*, ed. Réamonn Ó Muiri (Monaghan: Ardagh Diocesan Historical Society, 1990), 84–109.
58 Oliver P. Rafferty, S. J., *Violence, Politics and Catholicism in Ireland* (Dublin: Four Courts Press, 2016), 110–11.
59 Luddy, *Women and Philanthropy in Nineteenth-Century Ireland*, 46.
60 Mary Peckham Magray, *The Transforming Power of the Nuns: Women, Religion and Cultural Change in Ireland 1750–1900* (New York: Oxford University Press, 1998), 11.
61 Bridgeman/Luddy, 233.
62 Colin Barr, *Ireland's Empire: The Roman Catholic Church in the English-Speaking World, 1829–1914* (Cambridge: Cambridge University Press, 2020), 56.
63 Bridgeman/Luddy, 128.
64 See Bostridge, *Nightingale*, 269.
65 *Leaves*, 141–2.
66 *Hampshire Telegraph*, 10 May 1856, 4; *Portsmouth Times and Naval Gazette*, 10 May 1856, 8.
67 Bolster, *Sisters of Mercy*, 272.
68 Sister Joseph Croke, 'Journal of Her Experiences During the Crimean War', MCA CR/1/2. Possibly several versions of the Croke journal were in circulation and Bolster was quoting a typed variant that had the story. I am grateful to Marianne Cosgrove for this suggestion.
69 Bridgeman/Luddy, 221.
70 Bostridge, *Nightingale*, 279. See also 260, for letters from Scutari by soldiers praising her.
71 Bridgeman/Luddy, 242.
72 Bolster, *Sisters of Mercy*, 267–8, quoting a letter to Hall. Emphasis in original.
73 'Subsidiary Notes', *CW* 15, 34–5.
74 Quoted in Lynn McDonald, *Florence Nightingale: A Reference Guide to Her Life and Works* (Lanham: Rowman & Littlefield, 2020), 94.
75 Bridgeman/Luddy, 246.
76 Ibid., 245–6.
77 Bolster, *Sisters of Mercy*, 296. I have been unable to establish Bridgeman's date of birth.
78 Clear, *Nuns in Nineteenth-Century Ireland*, 166.
79 Magray, *Transforming Power of the Nuns*, 129. Magray adds that the generation of leadership that followed was more compliant.
80 Advertisement, *Dublin Evening Post*, 5 July 1856, 2; and daily throughout July in the *Freeman's Journal*.
81 *The Tablet*, 19 July 1856, 8.

82. Ciara Breathnach, '... It Would Be Preposterous to Bring a Protestant Here', in *Healthcare in Ireland and Britain 1850–1970: Voluntary, Regional and Comparative Perspectives*, ed. Donnacha Seán Lucey and Virginia Crossman (London: University of London Press, 2014), 161–2; Luddy, *Women and Philanthropy*, 49–50.
83. Gerard Fealy, *A History of Apprenticeship Nurse Training in Ireland* (London: Routledge, 2006), 33.
84. See https://sistersofmercy.org/civil-war-sisters-healing-the-wounds-of-the-nation/
85. Luddy, *Crimean Journals*, Introduction, xvii.
86. Bolster, *Sisters of Mercy*, 268, 290. Sister Paula Rice of Cork died on 1 June 1857, and Sister Clare Lalor of Charleville on 29 December 1858 (information kindly supplied by Marianne Cosgrave).

Chapter 8

1. Letter to Stanislaus Jones, 12 June 1856, Wellcome Institute MS 9104/2.
2. Letter to Grant, 30 June 1856, AAS H54.2. A postulant is an inquirer living with the community with a view to becoming a novice.
3. *The Tablet*, 15 February 1856, 105.
4. *The Tablet*, 19 July 1856, 456.
5. Louis Marteau, *An Historical Tradition: Hospital of St John and St Elizabeth*, 14.
6. *The Tablet*, 7 March 1857, 160.
7. 'Notes on the History of St John & St Elizabeth Hospital', f1, HMA GB1856/0/300/2/1/5.
8. Quoted in *Leaves*, 219.
9. Hospital [Annual] Report 1864, published January 1865, 1–2. HMA GB1856/0/300/2/5/1.
10. *Hospital of St John & St Elizabeth: A History in Photographs*, 8.
11. Oxford Dictionary of National Biography (online), 'Bowyer, Sir George, Seventh Baronet'.
12. John Martin Robinson, 'The Hospital of St John and St Elizabeth' (typescript), 3, HMA GB/1856/0/200/15/6.
13. Copy of Memorandum by Sir George Bowyer 'With a View to Re-opening the Hospital', 19 March 1867, f2, HMA GB1856/0/400/4/19.
14. The clearest account of these events is in *The Tablet* of 7 April 1866, 211–12, which includes the committee minutes.
15. *The Tablet*, 24 February 1866, 123.
16. *The Tablet*, 7 April 1866, 211–12. See also Bowyer's comments on page 219.
17. *The Times*, 10 April 1866, 9.
18. *The Tablet*, 19 May 1866, 314.
19. Oxford Dictionary of National Biography (online), 'Maskell, William'.
20. *The Tablet*, 24 February 1866, 123.

21 Letter to Grant, 10 November 1865, BA IOLM/BER/400/2/333.
22 Letter to Sam Smith, possibly November 1865, *CW* 3, 272.
23 Letter to Mary Jones, 7 November 1866, *CW* 3, 273.
24 Vincent Alan McClelland, *Cardinal Manning: His Public Life and Influence* (London: Oxford University Press, 1962), 32.
25 Quoted in Robert Gray, *Cardinal Manning: A Biography* (London: Weidenfeld and Nicolson, 1985), 302.
26 Memorandum, 19 March 1867, f1, HMA GB1856/0/400/4/19.
27 Copy of letter, Bowyer to Manning, 19 March 1865, HMA GB1856/300/2/1/7, emphasis in the original.
28 Decretum S. Congnis. de Propaganda Fide, HMA GB1856/0/300/2/1/12.
29 Letter, Nightingale to Clare Moore, 5 August 1867, *CW* 3, 296.
30 Gray, *Cardinal Manning*, 175.
31 Jeffrey von Arx, 'Manning's Ultramontanism and the Catholic Church in British Politics', *Recusant History* 19, no. 3 (1989): 335.
32 Quoted in Shane Leslie, *Henry Edward Manning: His Life and Labours* (Westport: Greenwood Press, 1970), 190.
33 Gray, *Cardinal Manning*, 212.
34 Letter to Mgr Talbot, 25 February 1866, quoted in Purcell, *Life of Cardinal Manning, Archbishop of Westminster*, vol. 2 (London: Macmillan, 1895), 323.
35 It should be stressed however that ultramontanism was more than a top down development. The spirit of religious intensity and interiority that was characteristic of nineteenth-century England helped create an analogous devotion in English Catholicism. See Mary Heimann, *Catholic Devotion in Victorian England* (Oxford: Clarendon Press, 1995), 30–7, 147–50.
36 Susan O'Brien, 'French Nuns in Nineteenth-Century England', *Past and Present* 154 (1997): 156.
37 Ibid., 158.
38 Letter to Grant, 21 April 1856, AAS H54.2.
39 Letter to Grant, 29 April 1856, AAS H54.2.
40 McClelland, *Cardinal Manning*, 53–7. According to McClelland, Manning feared that the Jesuits would educate the sons of the wealthy instead of a broader social cohort, and would not include a proper education in science.
41 Michael J. Walsh, *The Westminster Cardinals: The Past and the Future* (London: Continuum, 2008), 47.
42 Purcell, *Life of Cardinal Manning*, 404.
43 Bridgeman/Luddy, 215.
44 Letters, Nightingale to Manning, 15 and 22 July 1852, *CW* 3, 253 and 255.
45 Leslie, *Henry Edward Manning*, 320–4. See also McClelland, *Cardinal Manning*, 49–51.
46 See for example letters 28 November 1856 AAW WI/1/4/84, and 27 February 1862, AAW WI/1/4/143.

47 Moore quoted in *Leaves*, 242.
48 Letter, Alfred Green to Julia Boodle [Barrie's sister] 20 May 1866, from a copy in collection of Mary Sullivan. Emphasis in the original.
49 Letter, Moore to Bishop Grant, 14 March 1857, AAS H54.2.
50 Chapter decision, 17 February 1866, Acts of the Elections and Capitular Assemblies of the Convent of the Sisters of Mercy, Bloomsbury, HMA GB1856/0/200/13/11.
51 Mary C. Sullivan, *Catherine McAuley and the Tradition of Mercy* (Dublin: Four Courts Press, 2000), 317–18.
52 Chapter decision and letter to Manning, Acts of the Elections and Capitular Assemblies, of the Convent of the Sisters of Mercy, Bloomsbury, HMA GB1856/0/200/13/11.
53 'Hospital of St John and St Elizabeth: Foundation and Progress under the Care of the Sisters of Mercy', manuscript, no pagination, no date, GB1856/0/300/2/1/25.
54 Letter to Moore, 5 August 1867, *CW* 3, 294–5.
55 Letter to Emily Verney, *CW* 3, 275 where the date is given as 19 March 1871, so presumably Nightingale was writing in retrospect. Mary Sullivan has suggested in an email to the present writer that Lady Mary Herbert, Sidney Herbert's widow, by now a Catholic, may have made representations in Rome at Nightingale's request.
56 Letter to Moore, 3 May 1867, *CW* 3, 294.
57 Sullivan, *Friendship*, 146, 156–7.
58 Letter to Manning of 19 August 1867, Acts of the Elections and Capitular Assemblies of the Convent of the Sisters of Mercy, Bloomsbury, HMA GB1856/0/200/13/11.
59 'Catholic Intelligence', *The Tablet*, 8 August 1868, 500.
60 'Hospital of St John and St Elizabeth', *The Tablet*, 12 December 1868, 201, which includes the text of the pastoral letter.
61 For correspondence with Gonzaga Barrie and Stanislaus Jones, see *CW* 8, 1014–21.
62 Sullivan, *Friendship*, 12.
63 Sullivan, *Friendship*, 48.
64 Letter to Nightingale, 28 December 1862, Sullivan, *Friendship*, 106.
65 *Annals*, 309.
66 O'Brien, 'Terra Incognita', 116.
67 Sullivan, *Catherine McAuley*, 317.
68 Ibid., 80.
69 Acts of the Elections and Capitular Assemblies of the Convent of the Sisters of Mercy, Bloomsbury, HMA GB1856/0/200/13/11, 30 August 1865.
70 *Trees of Mercy* (Wickford, Essex: Sisters of Mercy of Great Britain, 1993), 10.
71 Mangion, *Contested Identities*, 45.
72 Walsh, *Roman Catholic Nuns in England and Wales*, 65. Over the course of the nineteenth century one-third of recruits came from Ireland (Mangion, ibid., 191).

73 Williams, *Sellon*, 175.
74 Margaret Anna Cusack, *Five Years in a Protestant Sisterhood and Ten Years in a Catholic Convent* (London: Longmans, 1869), 62. Cusack see-sawed between Catholic and Protestant identities, and her witness is always to be treated with an element of caution. She was later known as 'The Nun of Kenmare'.
75 Mumm, *Stolen Daughters, Virgin Mothers*, 6.
76 Anson, *Call of the Cloister*, 226–9.
77 Williams, *Sellon*, 82; Anson, *Call of the Cloister*, 240.
78 Manning, Letter to Clare Moore, 17 October 1856, HMA GB1856/0/300/2/1/2.
79 Anselm Nye, *A Peculiar Kind of Mission: The English Dominican Sisters 1845–2010* (Leominster: Gracewing, 2011), 63.
80 Anson, *Call of the Cloister*, 241.
81 A. M. Allchin, *The Silent Rebellion: Anglican Religious Communities, 1845–1900* (London: SCM, 1958), 127–8.
82 Cusack, *Five Years in a Protestant Sisterhood*, 103. Emphasis in original.
83 Goodman, *Experiences*, 221–2.
84 Ibid., 234.
85 Robert Richardson, foreword to Terrot, *Nurse Sarah Anne*, 7.
86 Goodman, *Experiences*, 7.
87 Margaret Goodman, *Sisterhoods in the Church of England* (London: Smith Elder, 1863), vii.
88 Mangion, *Contested Identities*, 24.
89 Williams, *Sellon*, 205–15.
90 Goodman, *Sisterhoods*, 11–13, 24.
91 Letter to Hilary Bonham Carter, 18 January 1863, *CW* 3, 448.
92 Quoted in Williams, *Sellon*, 390.
93 Terrot, *Nurse Sarah Anne*, 169.

Chapter 9

1 There are several editions. Her recollections were first published in two volumes in 1857 edited by Jane Williams, *Autobiography of Elizabeth Davis* (London: Hurst and Blackett). Quoted here is Elizabeth Davis, *Betsy Cadwaladyr: An Autobiography of Elizabeth Davis* (Dinas Powys, Wales: Honno Classics, 1987).
2 Gruffydd Jones, 'The Incredible Adventures of Betsi Cadwaladr: "Welsh Florence Nightingale" or "Munchausen in Petticoats"? An Evaluation of The Autobiography of Elizabeth Davis as a Historical Source', unpublished B.A. dissertation, Open University, 2019, 30. Accessed online: http://oro.open.ac.uk/62652/3/JONES_A329_RVOR.pdf.

3. Letter, 18 July 1855, BA 400/2/Crimea/11/11.
4. *Annals*, 251.
5. Figures compiled from 'List of Nurses and Sisters Who Have Ceased to be Employed', *CW* 14, 290.
6. Helen Rappoport, *No Place for Ladies: The Untold Story of Women in the Crimean War*, 170.
7. Figes, *Crimea*, 208.
8. Goodman, *Experiences*, 61.
9. Helmstadter, *Beyond Nightingale*, 70.
10. Seacole, *Wonderful Adventures of Mrs Seacole*, 81–2.
11. Davis, *Betsy Cadwaladyr*, 202.
12. Ibid., 210.
13. Alicia Blackwood, *A Narrative of Personal Experiences and Impressions During a Residence on the Bosphorus throughout the Crimean War* (London: Hatchard, 1881), 232.
14. Helmstadter *Beyond Nightingale*, 74.
15. Bridgeman/Luddy, 238.
16. NA WO 43/963 f242.
17. Bridgeman/Luddy, 125.
18. Magray, *Transforming Power of Nuns*, 33–6, 88–9, 106.
19. Ibid., 44.
20. Walsh, *Roman Catholic Nuns in England and Wales*, 154.
21. Mumm, *Stolen Daughters, Virgin Mothers*, 199–200.
22. Terrot, *Nurse Sarah Anne*, 136.

Chapter 10

1. Rich, *Why the Crimean War?*, 189–95.
2. Hinton, *Victory over Disease*, 38.
3. Figes, *Crimea*, 467.
4. Anne Summers, *Angels and Citizens: British Women as Military Nurses, 1854–1914* (London: Routledge, 1988), 47.
5. Quoted in Editor's Introduction to Frances Duberly, *Mrs Duberly's War: Journals and Letters from the Crimea, 1854–6*, ed. Christine Kelly (Oxford: Oxford University Press, 2007), xxvi. The correspondent is not named. Her diary was originally published in 1855.
6. Letter to Mai Smith, 30 July 1888, *CW* 8, 1021.
7. Figes, 469.
8. Tate, *A Short History of the Crimean War*, 66.
9. Editorial, *The Times*, 1 January 1855, 6.

10 Tate, *A Short History of the Crimean War*, 67–8.
11 Lalumia, *Realism and Politics in Victorian Art of the Crimean War*, 90.
12 Figes, *Crimea*, 477.
13 See for example Hugh Small, *Florence Nightingale: Avenging Angel* (London: Constable, 1998).
14 Hinton, *Victory over Disease*, 320.
15 Ibid., 29–30, 280.
16 Ibid., 253, 290, 321.
17 Ibid., 247–54.
18 Ibid., 158, 163, using a weighted average of the figures on page 158. I thank Professor Dan Graham of Imperial College for assistance with this.
19 Hinton, *Victory over Disease*, 76.
20 'The Military Chiefs of Departments', *The Times*, 4 January 1855, 9.
21 'Autograph Letter of the Queen', *The Times*, 5 January 1855, 6.
22 Sydney Godolphin Osborne, *Scutari and Its Hospitals* (London: Dickinson Brothers, 1855), 25.
23 Tate, *A Short History of the Crimean War*, 117.
24 Ibid., 91.
25 Duberly, *Mrs Duberly's War*, 249. She wrote this in September 1855 after a visit to Balaclava.
26 George Frederick Dallas, *Eyewitness in the Crimea: The Crimean War Letters of Lieutenant Colonel George Frederick Dallas*, ed. Michael Mawson (London: Greenhill Books, 2001), 59.
27 Bolster, *Sisters of Mercy*, 301.
28 Mary Ellen Doona, 'Sister Mary Joseph Croke: Another Voice from the Crimean War, 1854–1856', *Nursing History Review* 3, no. 1 (1995): 37–8.
29 John Wells and Michael Bergin, 'British Icons and Catholic Perfidy – Anglo-Saxon Historiography and the Battle for Crimean War Nursing', *Nursing Inquiry* 23, no. 1 (2016): 43, 49.
30 Bridgeman/Luddy, 143.
31 Mary Ellen Doona, 'Isabella Croke: A Nurse for the Catholic Cause during the Crimean War', in *Gender Perspectives in 19th Century Ireland*, ed. Margaret Kelleher and James H. Murphy (Dublin: Irish Academic Press, 1997), 151. Emphasis in original.
32 Bostridge, *Nightingale*, 157.
33 Shepherd, *Crimean Doctors*, vol. 2, 352.
34 Bolster, *Sisters of Mercy*, 252.
35 Lynn McDonald, 'Florence Nightingale and Irish Nursing', *Journal of Clinical Nursing* 23 (2014): 2427.
36 Bolter, *Sisters of Mercy*, 250.
37 Therese Meehan, 'Careful Nursing: A Model for Contemporary Nursing Practice', *Journal of Advanced Nursing* 44, no. 1 (2003): 99–107.

38 Quoted in Therese Meehan, 'The Careful Nursing Philosophy and Professional Practice Model', *Journal of Clinical Nursing* 21 (2012): 2909.
39 See for example Bridgeman/Luddy, 143, 145, 153, 228.
40 21 March 1856, Bolster, *Sisters of Mercy*, 310. Similar description in Bridgeman/Luddy, 219.
41 Bridgeman/Luddy, 146.
42 For relaxation of requisitions see Shepherd, *Crimean Doctors*, vol. 2, 356, 363.
43 Helmstadter, *Beyond Nightingale*, 127. For fuller comparison of the two, see 120–8.
44 Memorandum, NA WO 43/263, f 355, 25 April 1856.
45 Undated letter to unknown recipient, Bolster, *Sisters of Mercy*, 307.
46 Deane, *Strange Country*, 56.
47 Bridgeman/Luddy, 145.
48 Thomas Morrissey, S. J., *William Ronan SJ 1825–1907: War Chaplain, Missioner, Founder of Mungret College* (Dublin: Messenger Publications, 2002), 32.
49 Anson, *Call of the Cloister*, 321.
50 Hill, *Religious Order*, 274.
51 Allan Cameron, *The Religious Communities of the Church of England* (London: Faith Press, 1918), 18–19.
52 Mumm, 'A Peril to the Bench of Bishops', 74.
53 See https://www.theguardian.com/world/2019/jul/04/c-of-e-to-recognise-religious-communities-for-first-time-in-centuries. Both men and women religious were, however, given representation in General Synod from its inception in 1970.
54 Jameson, *Sisters of Charity*, 105.
55 Quoted in Helmstadter, *Beyond Nightingale*, 83, emphasis in original.
56 'Subsidiary Notes as to the Introduction of Female Nursing into Military Hospitals in Peace and in War', CW 15, 34.
57 Helmstadter, *Beyond Nightingale*, 303. The full quotation is: 'The religious sisters provided topflight nursing services, but in a secularizing world they would later find it difficult to recruit enough women to provide services on the scale they did in the Crimean War.'
58 Quoted in Helmstadter, *Beyond Nightingale*, 94.
59 Bridgeman/Luddy, 220, emphasis in original.
60 Letter of Appointment, Sidney Herbert to Florence Nightingale, 20 October 1854, NA WO 43/263 f 251.
61 Quoted in Goldie, *I Have Done my Duty*, 29.
62 See for example Emmanuel Levinas, *Totality and Infinity* (The Hague: Nijhoff, 1979).
63 https://discovery.nationalarchives.gov.uk/details/r/C14352.
64 *The Tablet*, 10 July 1897, 14.
65 Terrot, *Nurse Sarah Anne*, 165.
66 Bolster, *Sisters of Mercy*, 299–300.
67 *Trees of Mercy*, 24.

Bibliography

Primary sources: Archival

Sisters of Mercy Archives (Institute of Our Lady of Mercy), Bermondsey
Sisters of Mercy (Union of Sisters of Mercy in Great Britain) Handsworth, Birmingham
Mercy Congregational Archives, Dublin
Archives of the Archdiocese of Westminster
Archives of the Archdiocese of Southwark
Ascot Priory Papers, Pusey House, Oxford
National Archives, Kew
Wellcome Institute, London

Primary sources: Published

'Memories of the Crimea' by Sister M. Aloysius Doyle; 'Diary' by Sister M. Joseph Croke; and 'An Account of the Mission of the Sisters of Mercy in the East – beginning in December 1854 ending in May 1856' by Mother Francis Bridgeman in Luddy, Maria, ed. *The Crimean Journals of the Sisters of Mercy 1854-6*. Dublin: Four Courts Press, 2004.
Nightingale, Florence. *Collected Works:* published by Wilfrid Laurier University Press, Waterloo, Ontario. Except Volume 4, all volumes are edited by Lynn McDonald
Vol. 2, *Spiritual Journey: Biblical Annotations, Sermons and Journal Notes* (2001)
Vol. 3, *Theology: Essays, Letters and Journal Notes* (2002)
Vol. 4, *Mysticism and Eastern Religions*, Gérard Vallée, ed. (2003)
Vol. 8, *Women, Medicine, Midwifery and Prostitution* (2005)
Vol. 11, *Suggestions for Thought* (2008)
Vol. 13, *Extending Nursing* (2009)
Vol. 14, *The Crimean War* (2010)
Vol. 15, *Wars and the War Office* (2011)
Bell, George. *Soldier's Glory: Being, 'Rough Notes of an Old Soldier'*. Tunbridge Wells: Spellmount, 1991.
Blackwood, Alicia. *A Narrative of Personal Experiences and Impressions During a Residence on the Bosphorus Throughout the Crimean War*. London: Hatchard, 1881.
Bryce, Charles. *England and France before Sebastopol, Looked at from a Medical Point of View*. London: John Churchill, 1857.

Carroll, Mary Austin. *['A Member of the Order of Mercy']. Leaves from the Annals of the Sisters of Mercy*, vol. 2. New York: Catholic Publication Society, 1885.
Clifford, Henry. *Henry Clifford VC: His Letters and Sketches from the Crimea*. London: Michael Joseph, 1956.
Cusack, Margaret Anna. *Five Years in a Protestant Sisterhood and Ten Years in a Catholic Convent*. London: Longmans, 1869.
Dallas, George Frederick. *Eyewitness in the Crimea: The Crimean War Letters of Lieutenant Colonel George Frederick Dallas*, edited by Michael Mawson. London: Greenhill Books, 2001.
Davis, Elizabeth. *Betsy Cadwaladyr: An Autobiography of Elizabeth Davis*. Dinas Powys, Wales: Honno Classics, 1987.
Davis, William. *The Diary of an Offaly Schoolboy 1858–59*, edited by Sandra Robinson. Tullamore: Esker Press, 2010.
Duberly, Frances. *Mrs Duberly's War: Journal and Letters from the Crimea, 1854–56*, edited by Christine Kelly. Oxford: Oxford University Press, 2007 (1855).
Godman, Richard Temple. *The Fields of War: A Young Cavalryman's Crimea Campaign*, edited by Philip Warner. London: John Murray, 1977.
Goodman, Margaret. *Experiences of an English Sister of Mercy*. London: Smith Elder, 1862.
Goodman, Margaret. *Sisterhoods in the Church of England, with Notices of Some Charitable Sisterhoods in the Romish Church*. London: Smith Elder, 1863.
Hornby, Lady [Emilia]. *Constantinople during the Crimean War*. London: Richard Bentley, 1863.
O'Flaherty, Philip. *Sketches of the War: Being a Second Series of Letters*. Edinburgh: Shepherd and Elliot, 1855.
Osborne, Sydney Godolphin. *Scutari and Its Hospitals*. London: Dickinson Brothers, 1855.
Seacole, Mary. *Wonderful Adventures of Mrs Seacole in Many Lands*. London: Penguin, 2005.
Steevens, Nathaniel. *The Crimean Campaign with the Connaught Rangers, 1854-55-56*. London: Griffith and Farran, 1878.
Taylor, Frances. *Eastern Hospitals and English Nurses: The Narrative of Twelve Months' Experience in the Hospitals of Koulali and Scutari*, 2 vols, 1857. Uckfield: Naval & Military Press reprint, 2009.
Terrot, Sarah Anne. *Nurse Sarah Anne: With Florence Nightingale at Scutari*, edited by Robert Richardson. London: John Murray, 1977.

Official government publications

Catholic Relief Act, 1829 (10 Geo. 4 c. 7)
Hansard Parliamentary Debates in the House of Commons
Report on the State of British Hospitals of the British Army in the Crimea and Scutari. London: HMSO, 1855

Report to the Right Hon. Lord Panmure, G. C. B., &c., Minister at War, of the proceedings of the Sanitary Commission dispatched to the Seat of War in the East, 1855-56. London: HMSO, 1857

Report of the Commissioners Appointed to Inquire into the Regulations Affecting the Sanitary Condition of the Army, the Organization of Military Hospitals, and the Treatment of the Sick and Wounded. London: HMSO, 1858

Reference online

Dictionary of Irish Biography
Oxford Dictionary of National Biography

Periodicals, newspapers

The Times; The Manchester Guardian; The Tablet; Local newspapers, Ireland and Hampshire

General sources

Allchin, A. M. *The Silent Rebellion: Anglican Religious Communities, 1845–1900.* London: SCM, 1958.

Anson, Peter. *The Call of the Cloister: Religious Communities . . . in the Anglican Communion*, revised edn. London: SPCK, 1964.

Arnstein, Walter. *Protestant versus Catholic in Mid-Victorian England: Mr Newdegate and the Nuns.* Columbia: University of Missouri Press, 1982.

Arx, Jeffrey von. 'Manning's Ultramontanism and the Catholic Church in British Politics'. *Recusant History* 19, no. 3 (1989): 332–47.

Badem, Candan. *The Ottoman Crimean War (1853–1856).* Leiden: Brill, 2010.

Barr, Colin. *Ireland's Empire: The Roman Catholic Church in the English-Speaking World, 1829–1914.* Cambridge: Cambridge University Press, 2020.

Battersby, William Joseph 'The Educational Work of the Religious Orders of Women'. In *The English Catholics 1850–1950*, edited by George Beck, 337–64. London: Burns Oates, 1950.

Berlin, Isaiah. *The Crooked Timber of Humanity: Chapters in the History of Ideas.* London: Pimlico, 2013.

Bolster, Evelyn. *The Sisters of Mercy in the Crimean War.* Cork: Mercier Press, 1964.

Bostridge, Mark. *Florence Nightingale: The Woman and her Legend.* London: Viking, 2008.

Breathnach, Ciara. '. . . It Would be Preposterous to Bring a Protestant Here: Religion, Provincial Politics and District Nurses in Ireland, 1890–1914'. In *Healthcare in*

Ireland and Britain 1850–1970: Voluntary, Regional and Comparative Perspectives, edited by Donnacha Seán Lucey and Virginia Crossman, 161–80. London: University of London Press, 2014.

Burstein, Miriam. *Narrating Women's History in Britain 1770–1902*. Aldershot: Ashgate, 2004.

Cameron, Allan. *The Religious Communities of the Church of England*. London: Faith Press, 1918.

Campbell, Matthew. 'Victorian Ireland, 1830–1880: A Transitional State'. In *Irish Literature in Transition*, edited by Matthew Campbell, 3–21. Cambridge: Cambridge University Press, 2020.

Clear, Caitriona. *Nuns in Nineteenth-Century Ireland*. Dublin: Gill and Macmillan, 1987.

Clifton, Michael. 'Bishop Thomas Grant as Government Negotiator'. *Recusant History* 25, no. 2 (2000): 304–11.

Colley, Linda. *Britons: Forging the Nation 1707–1837*. London: BCA/Yale, 1992.

Conacher, J. B. *Britain and the Crimea, 1855–56: Problems of War and Peace*. London: Macmillan, 1987.

Connolly, Sean. *Religion and Society in Nineteenth-Century Ireland*. Dundalk: Dundalgan Press, 1985.

Connolly, S.J. 'Cardinal Cullen's other Capital: Belfast and the "Devotional Revolution"'. In *Cardinal Paul Cullen and his World*, edited by Dáire Keogh and Albert McDonnell, 289–307. Dublin: Four Courts Press, 2011.

Cook, John. *The Life of Florence Nightingale*, 2 vols. London: Macmillan, 1914.

Corish, Patrick. *The Irish Catholic Experience: A Historical Survey*. Dublin: Gill & Macmillan, 1986.

Curtis, L. P. *Anglo-Saxons and Celts: A Study of Anti-Irish Prejudice in Victorian Ireland*. Bridgeport: University of Bridgeport, 1968.

Curtiss, John Shelton. 'Russian Sisters of Mercy in the Crimea, 1854–1855'. *Slavic Review* 25, no. 1 (1966): 84–100.

Daly, Mary E. 'Historians and the Famine: A Beleaguered Species'. *Irish Historical Studies* 30, no. 120 (1997): 591–601.

David, Saul. *Victoria's Wars*. London: Penguin, 2007.

Deane, Seamus. *Strange Country: Modernity and Nationhood in Irish Writing Since 1790*. Oxford: Oxford University Press, 1997.

Doona, Mary Ellen. 'Sister Mary Joseph Croke: Another Voice from the Crimean War, 1854–1856'. *Nursing History Review* 3, no. 1 (1995): 3–41.

Doona, Mary Ellen. 'Isabella Croke: A Nurse for the Catholic Cause During the Crimean War'. In *Gender Perspectives in Nineteenth-Century Ireland: Public and Private Systems*, edited by Margaret Kellegher and J. H. Murphy, 148–56. Dublin: Irish Academic Press, 1997.

Dorsey, Barbara. *Florence Nightingale: Mystic, Visionary, Healer*. Springhouse: Springhouse Corporation, 2000.

Fairey, Jack. *The Great Powers and Orthodox Christendom: The Crisis Over the Eastern Church in the Era of the Crimean War*. Basingstoke: Palgrave Macmillan, 2015.

Fealy, Gerard. *A History of Apprenticeship Nurse Training in Ireland*. London: Routledge, 2006.
Figes, Orlando. *Crimea: The Last Crusade*. London: Penguin, 2011.
Flanagan, Catherine. *The Great Famine in Kinsale*. Dublin: Four Courts Press, 2018.
Foster, Roy. *Modern Ireland 1600–1972*. London: Allen Lane, 1988.
Gallagher, Clarence. 'The Church and Institutes of Consecrated Life'. *The Way* 50, Supplement (1984): 1–15.
Gill, Gillian. *The Nightingales: The Extraordinary Upbringing and Curious Life of Miss Florence Nightingale*. New York: Ballantine Books, 2004.
Gleadle, Kathryn. *British Women in the Nineteenth Century*. Basingstoke: Palgrave, 2001.
Goldie, Sue, ed. *"I Have Done My Duty": Florence Nightingale in the Crimean War 1854–56*. Manchester: Manchester University Press, 1987.
Gray, Robert. *Cardinal Manning: A Biography*. London: Weidenfeld and Nicolson, 1985.
Griffin, Brian. 'Irish Identity and the Crimean War'. In *War: Identities in Conflict 1300–2000*, edited by Bertrand Taithe and Tim Thornton, 113–24. Stroud: Sutton, 1998.
Griffin, Brian. 'Ireland and the Crimean War'. *Irish Sword* 22, no. 87 (2000): 281–312.
Griffin, Susan. *Anti-Catholicism and Nineteenth-Century Fiction*. Cambridge: Cambridge University Press, 2004.
Heimann, Mary. *Catholic Devotion in Victorian England*. Oxford: Clarendon Press, 1995.
Heimann, Mary. 'Devotional Stereotypes in English Catholicism 1850–1914'. In *Catholicism in Britain and France since 1789*, edited by Frank Tallett and Nicholas Atkin, 13–25. London: Hambledon Press, 1999.
Helmstadter, Carol. *Beyond Nightingale: Nursing on the Crimean War Battlefields*. Manchester: Manchester University Press, 2020.
Hibbert, Christopher. *The Illustrated London News Social History of Victorian Britain*. London: Angus & Robertson, 1976.
Hill, Michael. *The Religious Order: A Study of Virtuoso Religion and its Legitimation in the Nineteenth-Century Church of England*. London: Heinemann, 1973.
Hinton, Michael. *Victory Over Disease: Resolving the Medical Crisis in the Crimean War, 1854–1856*. Warwick: Helion, 2019.
Holmes, J. Derek. *More Roman than Rome: English Catholicism in the Nineteenth Century*. London: Burns & Oates, 1978.
Hospital of St John & St Elizabeth: A History in Photographs.
Huddie, Paul. *The Crimean War and Irish Society*. Liverpool: Liverpool University Press, 2015.
Huddie, Paul. 'The Crimean War, 1854–56: Ireland's Happiest Nineteenth-Century War'. In *Happiness in Nineteenth-Century Ireland*, edited by Mary Hatfield, 35–52. Liverpool: Liverpool University Press, 2021.
Hughes, Philip. 'The English Catholics in 1850'. In *The English Catholics 1850–1950*, edited by George Beck, 42–85. London: Burns Oates, 1950.

Jackson, Alvin. *Ireland 1798–1998*. Oxford: Blackwell, 1999.
Jameson, Anna Brownell. *Sisters of Charity Catholic and Protestant at Home and Abroad*. London: Longman, 1855.
Jones, Gruffydd. 'The Incredible Adventures of Betsi Cadwaladr: "Welsh Florence Nightingale" or "Munchausen in Petticoats"? An evaluation of The Autobiography of Elizabeth Davis as a historical source'. B.A. dissertation, Open University, 2019. https://oro.open.ac.uk/62652/3/JONES_A329_RVOR.pdf
Kelly, James E. *English Convents in Catholic Europe, c.1600–1800*. Cambridge: Cambridge University Press, 2020.
Kenny, Kevin. 'The Irish in the Empire'. In *Ireland and the British Empire*, edited by Kevin Kenny, 90–122. Oxford: Oxford University Press, 2004.
Kiberd, Declan. *Inventing Ireland: The Literature of the Modern Nation*. London: Vintage, 1995.
Kirkpatrick, Peter. *A Chronology of Faith: English Catholic History Since the Reformation*. Bath: Downside Abbey Press, 2011.
Lalumia, Matthew Paul. *Realism and Politics in Victorian Art of the Crimean War*. Ann Arbor: UMI Research Press, 1984.
Larkin, Emmet. *The Historical Dimensions of Irish Catholicism*. Washington: Catholic University of America Press, 1997.
Leslie, Shane. 'Forgotten Passages in the Life of Florence Nightingale'. *Dublin Review* 323, October (1917): 179–98.
Leslie, Shane. *Henry Edward Manning: His Life and Labours*. Westport: Greenwood Press, 1970.
Levinas, Emmanuel. *Totality and Infinity*. The Hague: Nijhoff, 1979.
Luddy, Maria. *Women and Philanthropy in Nineteenth-Century Ireland*. Cambridge: Cambridge University Press, 1995.
Machin, G. I. T. *Politics and the Churches in Great Britain 1832 to 1868*. Oxford: Oxford University Press, 1977.
Magray, Mary Peckham. *The Transforming Power of the Nuns: Women, Religion and Cultural Change in Ireland 1750–1900*. New York: Oxford University Press, 1998.
Malden, Henry Elliot, ed., *A History of the County of Surrey* (Victoria County Histories) vol. 4. London: Constable, 1912.
Mangion, Carmen. *Contested Identities: Women Religious in Nineteenth-Century England and Wales*. Manchester: Manchester University Press, 2008.
Markovits, Stefanie. *The Crimean War in the British Imagination*. Cambridge: Cambridge University Press, 2009.
Marteau, Louis. *An Historical Tradition: Hospital of St John and St Elizabeth*.
McAdam, Gloria. 'Willing Women and the Rise of Convents in Nineteenth-Century England'. *Women's History Review* 8, no. 3 (1999): 411–41.
McClelland, Vincent Alan. *Cardinal Manning: His Public Life and Influence*. London: Oxford University Press, 1962.

McDonald, Lynn. 'Mythologizing and De-Mythologizing'. In *Notes on Nightingale: The Influence and Legacy of a Nursing Icon*, edited by Siobhan Nelson and Anne Marie Rafferty, 91–114. Ithaca: Cornell University Press, 2010.
McDonald, Lynn. 'Florence Nightingale and Irish Nursing'. *Journal of Clinical Nursing* 23 (2014): 2424–33.
McDonald, Lynn. 'Florence Nightingale, Statistics and the Crimean War'. *Journal of the Royal Statistical Society. Series A* 177, no. 3 (2014): 569–86.
McDonald, Lynn. *Florence Nightingale: A Reference Guide to Her Life and Works*. Lanham: Rowman & Littlefield, 2020.
McGrath, Thomas. 'The Tridentine Evolution of Modern Irish Catholicism: A Re-examination of the "Devotional Revolution" Thesis'. In *Irish Church History Today*, edited by Réamonn Ó Muiri, 84–109. Monaghan: Ardagh Diocesan Historical Society, 1990.
Meehan, Therese. 'Careful Nursing: A Model for Contemporary Nursing Practice'. *Journal of Advanced Nursing* 44, no. 1 (2003): 99–107.
Meehan, Therese. 'The Careful Nursing Philosophy and Professional Practice Model'. *Journal of Clinical Nursing* 21 (2012): 2905–16.
Morrissey, Thomas. *William Ronan SJ 1825–1907: War Chaplain, Missioner, Founder of Mungret College*. Dublin: Messenger Publications, 2002.
Moutray, Tonya J. *Refugee Nuns, the French Revolution, and British Literature and Culture*. Abingdon: Routledge, 2016.
Mumm, Susan. *Stolen Daughters, Virgin Mothers: Anglican Sisterhoods in Victorian Britain*. Leicester: Leicester University Press, 1999.
Mumm, Susan. '"A Peril to the Bench of Bishops": Sisterhoods and Episcopal Authority in the Church of England, 1845–1908'. *Journal of Ecclesiastical History* 59, no. 1 (2008): 62–78.
Murphy, David. *Ireland and the Crimean War*. Dublin: Four Courts Press, 2002.
Norman, Edward. *The English Catholic Church in the Nineteenth Century*. Oxford: Clarendon Press, 1984.
Nye, Anselm. *A Peculiar Kind of Mission: The English Dominican Sisters 1845–2010*. Leominster: Gracewing, 2011.
O'Brien, Susan. '*Terra Incognita*: The Nun in Nineteenth-Century England'. *Past and Present* 121 (1988): 110–40.
O'Brien, Susan. 'Lay-Sisters and Good Mothers: Working-class Women in English Convents, 1840–1910'. In *Women in the Church: Studies in Church History*, vol. 27, edited by W. J. Sheils, 453–65. Oxford: Blackwells, 1990.
O'Brien, Susan. 'Making Catholic Spaces: Women, Decor, and Devotion in the English Catholic Church, 1840–1900'. In *The Church and the Arts: Studies in Church History*, vol. 28, edited by Diana Wood, 449–64. Oxford: Blackwells, 1992.
O'Brien, Susan. 'French Nuns in Nineteenth-Century England'. *Past and Present* 154 (1997): 142–80.

Picard, Lisa. *Victorian London: The Life of a City, 1840–1870*. London: Weidenfeld and Nicolson, 2006.
Purcell, Edmund. *Life of Cardinal Manning, Archbishop of Westminster*, vol. 2. London: Macmillan, 1895.
Rafferty, Oliver. *Violence, Politics and Catholicism in Ireland*. Dublin: Four Courts Press, 2016.
Rappoport, Helen. *No Places for Ladies: The Untold Story of Women in the Crimean War*. London: Aurum, 2007.
Reed, John Shelton. *Glorious Battle: The Cultural Politics of Victorian Anglo-Catholicism*. London: Tufton Books, 1996.
Rich, Norman. *Why the Crimean War? A Cautionary Tale*. Hanover: University Press of New England, 1885.
Roussos, Sotiros. 'The Greek Orthodox Community of Jerusalem in International Politics: International Solutions for Jerusalem and the Greek Orthodox community in the Nineteenth and Twentieth Centuries'. In *Jerusalem: Its Sanctity and Centrality to Judaism, Christianity and Islam*, edited by Lee Levine, 482–93. New York: Continuum, 1999.
Shepherd, John. *The Crimean Doctors: A History of the British Medical Services in the Crimean War*, 2 vols. Liverpool: Liverpool University Press, 1991.
Showalter, Elaine. 'Florence Nightingale's Feminist Complaint: Women, Religion and *Suggestions for Thought*'. *Journal of Women in Culture and Society* 6, no. 3 (1981): 395–412.
Small, Hugh. *Florence Nightingale: Avenging Angel*. London: Constable, 1998.
Spilsbury, Julian. *The Thin Red Line: An Eyewitness History of the Crimean War*. London: Cassell, 2005.
Stott, Anne. 'Women and Religion'. In *Women's History: Britain, 1700–1850*, edited by Hannah Barker and Elaine Chalus, 100–23. London: Routledge 2005.
Sullivan, Mary C. *The Friendship of Florence Nightingale and Mary Clare Moore*. Philadelphia: University of Pennsylvania Press, 1999.
Sullivan, Mary C. *Catherine McAuley and the Tradition of Mercy*. Dublin: Four Courts Press, 2000.
Sullivan, Mary C. *The Path of Mercy: The Life of Catherine McAuley*. Dublin: Four Courts Press, 2012.
Sullivan, Mary C. 'The Value of Archives'. *The Journal of the Mercy Association in Scripture and Theology*, 27, no. 2 (2021): 45–51.
Summers, Anne. *Angels and Citizens: British Women as Military Nurses, 1854–1914*. London: Routledge, 1988.
Summers, Anne. 'Pride and Prejudice: Ladies and Nurses in the Crimean War'. In *Patriotism: The Making and Unmaking of British National Identity: vol. 2, Minorities and Outsiders*, edited by Raphael Samuel, 57–78. London: Routledge, 1989.
Tate, Trudi. *A Short History of the Crimean War*. London: I. B. Tauris, 2019.

Trees of Mercy. [no author stated] Wickford, Essex: Sisters of Mercy of Great Britain, 1993.
Trollope, Anthony. *The Warden*. London: Penguin, 1986/1855.
Walsh, Barbara. *Roman Catholic Nuns in England and Wales 1800–1937: A Social History*. Dublin: Irish Academic Press, 2002.
Walsh, Michael J. *The Westminster Cardinals: The Past and the Future*. London: Continuum/Burns and Oates 2008.
Watson, William Boog. 'An Edinburgh Surgeon of the Crimean War – Patrick Heron Watson (1832–1907)'. *Medical History* 10 (1966): 166–76.
Wells, John and Bergin, Michael. 'British Icons and Catholic Perfidy – Anglo-Saxon Historiography and the Battle for Crimean War Nursing'. *Nursing Inquiry* 23, no. 1 (2016): 42–51.
Widerquist, JoAnn. 'The Spirituality of Florence Nightingale'. *Nursing Research* 41, no. 1 (1992): 49–55.
Widerquist, JoAnn. '"Dearest Friend": The Correspondence of Colleagues Florence Nightingale and Mary Jones'. *Nursing History Review* 1, no. 1 (1993): 25–42.
Williams, Thomas J. *Priscilla Lydia Sellon: The Restorer after Three Centuries of the Religious Life in the English Church*, revised edn. London: SPCK, 1965.
Williams, Thomas Jay and Campbell, Allan. *The Park Village Sisterhood*. London: SPCK, 1965.
Woodham-Smith, Cecil. *Florence Nightingale 1820–1910*. London: Reprint Society/Constable, 1952.
Wrench, Edward. 'The Lessons of the Crimean War'. *British Medical Journal* 2, no. 2 (1899): 205–8.

Index

alcohol, as medicine 44–5
amputations 10–11
Anglican sisters
   at Castle Hospital 106–7
   complain about conditions 14
   and female celibacy 158
   growth and expansion of
      communities 26–7
   leadership crisis after war 141–2
   life after Crimean War 140–4
   nursing combined with religious
      vocation 158
   praised by Nightingale 110
   recruited by Priscilla Lydia
      Sellon 28–30
   three sent back 17–18
   war service validates 158–9
   on waste of war 148
   without official recognition 110, 157–8

Balaclava, general hospital
   Described 94
   dispute about state of hospital at
      handover 102, 115–17
   leadership vacuum 1855 93–4
   statistics 101
Balaclava, town 93
Barrack Hospital, Scutari
   description of 8
   overcrowding 41
Barrett, Jerry and *The Mission of Mercy*
      painting 150–1
Barrie, Gonzaga
   amputations, care of 10–11
   assists German patients 96–7
   character of 6, 136
   death 161
   first superior Hospital of St
      Elizabeth 130
   friendship with Wiseman 135–6
   letter to Presbyterian widow 19–20
   vocational crisis 137

Bermondsey, convent 64
Bermondsey, poverty in 25–6, 129
Bolster, Evelyn 36–7, 122, 152–4
Bowyer, Sir George
   defended by pamphleteer William
      Maskell 132
   donation to Hospital of St
      Elizabeth 130–1
Bridgeman, Francis
   corresponds with Hall to refute
      Nightingale 116–18
   given charge upper hospital,
      Koulali 72–3
   nationalist connections 114–15
   negotiates move to Balaclava 89–91
   personality 33, 125
   rejected by Nightingale 33
   says Nightingale is a failure 160
   shuns publicity 123–4
   and social class 32
   on spiritual consolations for Irish
      soldiers 77–8
   withdraws her sisters from
      Balaclava 101–2
   writes her Account as
      corrective 113–14
   zeal of 34
Bryce, Andrew (Dr) 88–9
Butler, Elizabeth, death and funeral
      of 98–9

Cadwalladr, Betty, *see* Davis, Elizabeth
Careful Nursing 154–5
Chambers, Thomas 57
Chenery, Thomas 23
cholera 41–2, 95–7
Clarendon, Lord 22, 137
Clifford, Henry 80
confession, sacrament of, and Sisters of
      Mercy, *see* sacramental abuse
Convent of the Faithful Virgin, *see*
      Norwood Sisters

Convents, *see also* religious life
   growth in numbers of 57
   parliamentary campaign to regulate 65, 67–9
   and paternal control 65
Crimean War
   hospitals in Crimea and improved outcomes 74
   nursing worked through male structures 160
   private enterprise brings improvements 152
   public pressure on government 15, 23–4, 151–2
   as religious struggle 51
   reportage in new mass media 3–4, 23
Cullen, Paul
   and devotional revolution 120
   Irish sisters not given due recognition 113
   war had raised esteem of Catholics 118
Cusack, Margaret Anna 141–2

Davis, Elizabeth 94, 145–6
devotional revolution 120–1
dissociation as coping mechanism 48–9
Duberly, Mrs Frances 149, 152
Dublin banquet 111–12
dysentery 41–2, 45–6, 73, 87–8, 107

evangelical influence 62–3

Faithful Virgin, Sisters of the, *see* Norwood Sisters
famine, Irish 114, 120
Fitzgerald, David
   character 102
   obstructionism 102, 103
food, shortage of
   at Balaclava 40, 47
   at Scutari 14
France, as protector of Latin Christians 22
frostbite 40, 42–3, 73

Goodman, Margaret
   books written by her and condemned by Nightingale 143–4
   faith tested 48
   praised by Nightingale 110
   struggles to adjust after war 142–3
Grant, Thomas (Bishop)
   recruits Sisters of Mercy, Bermondsey 27–8
   work of sisters silences anti-Catholicism 69

Hall, (Sir) John
   alleges Balaclava deteriorates under Nightingale 102
   censured by War Office 100–1
   denies crisis at Scutari hospitals 7
   discourages use of anaesthesia 90
   refused appointment as director-general 115
   seeks to refute Nightingale evidence to Royal Commission 116–18
Hawes, Benjamin 96
Herbert, Mary, wife of Sidney, friend of Nightingale 31, 184 n.55
Herbert, Sidney
   asks Nightingale to lead Scutari nurses 27
   friendship with Nightingale 7–8
   gives and limits Nightingale's power 160
   instructions to nuns 29
   Nightingale contacts regarding supplies 19
   Nightingale's anger with 34
   proselytizing, warns against 75–6
Hinton, Michael 151–2
Hornby, Emilia 80, 107
Hospital of St Elizabeth (later, Hospital of St John and St Elizabeth)
   expansion and new chapel 130–1
   founded at request of Wiseman 129–30
   links with Knights of Malta and new name 130–1
   moves to new home 138
   newspapers publicize struggle for control 131–2
   sisters insist on their rights 136
Huish, Henry 116
Hutton, Amy 74, 88, 147

Illustrated London News 4, 94
Inkerman
    battle of 8–9
    treatment of wounded 10–12
Ireland
    admiration of sisters on
        departure 33
    Irish identity and Crimean
        War 118–19, 157
    proportion of soldiers from 51–2
    proud of their soldiers 118–19

Jameson, Anna Brownell 59–60

Kingsley, Charles 64–5
Koulali Hospital
    description 71–2
    'model hospital' compared with
        Scutari 86
    patients starved at 86–9
    Stanley lobbies for 55
    superintendent Amy Hutton 74

Land Transport Corps Hospital 103–5
Langston, Mother Emma, Anglican nun
    character 6
    in charge at Balaclava 46–7
    leader, Anglican nuns 29
    resigns leadership and leaves 141
    sent back to England 47–8
Larkin, Emmet 120

Malakoff, attack on 79–80
Manning, Henry
    advice for departing Sisters of
        Mercy 32
    attempts to take control of hospital
        from Sisters of Mercy 131–8
    difficulties with Bridgeman 34
    on temporal power of the pope
        133–4
    and ultramontanism 133–5
McCauley, Catherine 37
Mercy, Sisters of, from England
    come to aid of Nightingale at
        Balaclava 103–5
    daily timetable at Scutari 43
    growth in England after war 139
    loyalty to Nightingale 104
    praised by Nightingale 109–10
    privacy, lack of 49
    Ronan criticizes 36, 49–50
    trusted by soldiers 49
Mercy, Sisters of, from Ireland
    accused of proselytizing 76–9
    at Balaclava General Hospital 93–5
    Balaclava Hospital and their
        departure 155–6
    conversions of British soldiers 78–9
    criticized by Nightingale 103
    and devotional revolution 121
    England as enemy 78, 113
    fear of supervision by
        Protestants 156
    funerals of sisters and Irish
        solidarity 95, 98
    nuns overlooked in historical
        record 3, 152–3
    'overshadowed' by Nightingale 112
    pastoral ministry, confidence
        in 79–80
    praised in Fitzgerald report 99,
        121–3
    silence as patients starved 87–9
    their distinctive narrative 156–7
    turned away at Scutari 33–4
    unreliable historiography 121–3
Moore, Clare
    character 6
    criticized by priests for co-operation
        with Nightingale 36, 105–6
    encourages Nightingale to consider
        Catholicism 140
    illness forces return to England
        107–8
    praised by Nightingale 108
    'worn out' after return 129

Newdegate, Charles 68–9
Nightingale, Florence:
    accuses nuns of proselytising 75–6
    anger at Bridgeman arranging move to
        Balaclava 90–1
    anti-Irish slurs and falsehoods 100,
        103, 115–16
    asked by Herbert to go Scutari 27
    Bridgeman, compromise with at
        Scutari 34–5

criticizes restrictions on women 60-2
discipline, emphasis on 19
dismisses nurses 44, 48
dominates story of Crimean War
    nursing 149-50
fears religious imbalance 34
on female emotions 18-19
on Fitzgerald report 98-100
friendship with Clare Moore after
    war 138
interest in mysticism 138-9
Koulali Hospital, severs links
    with 73-4
middle class avatar 150
*Notes on the Health of the British
    Army* 18
nursing ability allegedly learned from
    Irish sisters 154-5
nursing ability questioned 71, 101,
    153-4
obstructed by medical staff 7
powers confirmed by War
    Office 100-1
rejects Stanley party 16-17
on religious sisters 61-2
sceptical about nuns as nurses 124,
    159-60
scorns Mary Stanley 73
Sidney Herbert 7-8, 34
Suggestions for Thought 60-1
supports Sisters of Mercy against
    Manning 132, 136-7
uses Royal Commission to criticize
    Bridgeman group 115-16
War Office opposition 96
Norwood Sisters
    arrival at Scutari 14
    priests condemn Nightingale
        treatment of 36
    sent back to UK 17-18
novels, anti-Catholic 64-6
nuns, *see* religious life; religious sisters
nurses
    and alcohol 31, 146
    applicants 31, 146
    night nursing 155
    poverty of 146
    professional training 30-1
    and social class 147

orderlies, unreliability of 13-14, 44, 91
Orthodoxy, Eastern
    attitude of nuns and Nightingale
        to 52-3
Ottoman empire
    Western commercial interests 21-22

Paulet, Lord William
    forbids nurses to talk of religion 77-8
peace treaty, celebration of 108-9
proselytizing, accusations of
    at General Hospital, Scutari 75-6
    at Koulali Hospital 76-9
Pugin, A. W. 64

Redan, attack on 79-80
religious life (under vows in community),
        see also Anglican religious
        communities
    attraction of 57-62
    definition of 24-5
    expansion in Britain 25-6, 57, 64
    lay sisters 59
    leadership opportunities within 140
    papal approval of 25
    and property 140
    and social class 59
    as un-English 64
    women allegedly lack judgement 66
religious sisters
    and Orthodox Christians 52-3
    public call for 24
    recruit from Irish middle class 147
    suspicion of 24
Roberts, Eliza 147
Ronan, William
    criticizes Mother Clare Moore 36
    refutes charge of proselytizing 75-6
Royal Red Cross awarded 161
Russian nuns 80

Sabin, John 75-6
sacraments, abuse of 36, 105-6
St John's House 31
St Saviour's Convent, Osnaburgh
    St 141-2
Sanitary Commission improvements 54,
    93

Seacole, Mary   112, 146
Sellon, Priscilla Lydia
    accused of alienating a daughter from her family   67–8
    authoritarian tendency   142–3
    instructions to sisters as they depart   29–30
    recruits Anglican nuns for Crimea   28–30
Smith, Andrew   101–2
soldiers
    burial of   13, 98
    improved conditions for   97–8
    recruited from Ireland   51–2
    and social class   51–2
    stoicism   43–4, 98
    Terrot praises   51
Sprey, Winifred, death of   95–6
Stanley, Mary
    becomes Catholic before return to England   73
    composition of her nursing party   32
    entrusted with Koulali Hospital   71–3
    Nightingale describes as 'insane'   73
    rejection by Nightingale   16–17
stuping   42
supplies crisis, and maladministration   39–40, 54

Taylor, Francis
    and Charles Bryce's experiment   87–8
    praises Sisters of Mercy, Koulali   74
Tebbutt, Miss   76
Terrot, Sarah Anne
    character of   6–7
    death of   144
    illness and return   46–7
    praises Catholic sisters but ambivalent   50
    respect for Nightingale   29
    Royal Red Cross   161
    soldiers 'Christlike'   51
    struggles to adjust after war   142–3
The Times
    influence of   23, 152
    on medical conditions at Scutari   23–4
transport of wounded soldiers
    across Black Sea   40–1
    after Inkerman   9
Trollope, Anthony   69
Turnbull, Bertha
    character   6
    praised by Nightingale   110, 144
    succeeds Sellon as superior   144
typhus, sisters ill with   46–7, 98, 151

ultramontanism   120–1, 133–5

Vermin infestation   45–6

Wheeler, Elizabeth
    extra food for patients   14–15
    letter to *Times* and dismissal   15–16, 18
Wiseman, Nicholas, Cardinal
    on lack of recognition for Sisters of Mercy   129
Wives of soldiers   8

www.ingramcontent.com/pod-product-compliance
Lightning Source LLC
Chambersburg PA
CBHW061828300426
44115CB00013B/2288